FASHION

A VISUAL HISTORY
from REGENCY & ROMANCE
to RETRO & REVOLUTION

FASHION

A VISUAL HISTORY
from REGENCY & ROMANCE
to RETRO & REVOLUTION

*A complete illustrated chronology of fashion
from the 1800s to the present day*

NJ Stevenson

ST. MARTIN'S GRIFFIN
NEW YORK

For my Mum and Dad

FASHION. Copyright © 2011 by The Ivy Press Limited.
All rights reserved. For information, address St. Martin's Press,
175 Fifth Avenue, New York, N.Y. 10010.

www.stmartins.com

Library of Congress Cataloging-in-Publication Data Available
Upon Request

ISBN 978-0-312-62445-3

First U.S. Edition: February 2012

10 9 8 7 6 5 4 3 2 1

This book was conceived, designed, and produced by

Ivy Press
210 High Street
Lewes
East Sussex BN7 2NS
United Kingdom

Creative Director: Peter Bridgewater
Publisher: Jason Hook
Editorial Director: Caroline Earle
Art Director: Michael Whitehead
Senior Project Editor: Stephanie Evans
Design: JC Lanaway
Picture Manager: Katie Greenwood
Assistant Editor: Jamie Pumfrey

Cover Design: James Watson.
Image credits: top Hulton Archive/Getty Images;
center Popperfoto/Getty Images; bottom François Guillot/
AFP/Getty Images

Image Reproduction: Ivy Reproductions
Printed and bound in China

Contents

Introduction

The words "new" and "fashion" go together —the mercurial nature of fashion means that it is always new. However, if we look through fashion history, we will see that the same shapes and colors come around, again and again. It is the interpretations by new designers, for new times, that make those shapes and colors fresh and alive once more. The chronology of fashion is not just a story of looking back, but also one of looking forward.

Over time, our perceptions of historical fashion styles become blurred. Impressions of the clothing of a particular period become tainted by second-hand memories and interpretations of costume designers for movies and television. We often use a style to describe a moment in time, pinpointing it to a decade. The miniskirt, for example, will never be far from an examination of the 1960s. Yet, it took almost half that decade for skirts to reach the height that we call "mini." Ideas that appear avant-garde and shocking at first gradually become assimilated into

People's choice of dress has been hallmarked by more than necessity for protection, comfort, and modesty. In the history of Western fashion, the introduction of certain iconic items—bowler hat or hobble skirt, corset or crinoline, mini or bikini—pinpoints a moment where clothing conveys a message of status, personality, and preference.

everyday dress, or perhaps rejected and forgotten, only to be revisited much later. *Fashion: A Visual History* is a story that follows the oscillations of style and reveals the tenuous process of its development. It is about the evolution of an industry that reflects and is influenced by changing times.

Evolution of fashion

Charting the development of the fashion system also shows how it became a part of popular culture. At the start of the 19th century, fashion was an elitist indication of status, not so very far from the sumptuary laws of the Middle Ages, when rank dictated the color and fabric that you could wear. The Emperor of France, Napoleon Bonaparte, was one of the greatest military achievers, while his wife, Josephine, became an early influential leader in fashion history. As the 20th century unfolded, fashion expanded to selectively pick influences from art, music, movies, and current affairs. The function of clothing is not just protection from

the elements: what we wear is a projection of our personalities (and our purses); our likes and dislikes; our knowledge; our values and aspirations.

When Charles Worth shaped haute couture into a definite industry in the 1860s, he gave kudos to the dressmaking trade by attempting to place fashion into the realm of fine art. Literally, haute couture means "high sewing," and the artisan's work that goes into the production of a couture gown justifies its price. By the mid-20th century, new markets brought ready-to-wear designer clothing into the fashion system. The art in this was creating styles that retained chic but could be mass-produced.

In the 21st century we are all familiar with the concept of fashion design, and it is applied to every tier of the fashion system. Designer ranges at shopping mall prices and affordable online copies of catwalk pieces are part of the instant shopping experience of 2011, where the season's trends are laid out for us in gossip magazines and fashion blogs. Even children's lines in retail stores are "on-trend."

Magazines and models

Celebrity has been linked with fashion since Hollywood first started turning its cameras. Now copies of the clothes of the stars can be bought with the click of a mouse. "Fast fashion" has been accused of having a homogenizing effect, to which the reaction was the growth of alternatives such as craft-based activities, embellishing and restyling old clothes. Despite a recession, 2010 also brought reports of an upturn in the turnover of haute-couture revenue as new clients sought the reassuring value of the ultimate status symbol. So how did we get to the point where fashion has pervaded the public consciousness?

The fashion magazine is the tried-and-tested means of communication that is integral to the chronology of fashion. From *La Belle Assemblée*, which displayed fashion plates to the gentry of the Regency period, to the 21st-century *EverManifesto*, which only distributes its free print copies at fashion shows or when it has something valid about sustainable fashion to say, the magazine has remained a touchstone between the designers and the public.

The magazine must convey ideas of fashion to its readership but also, via its editors, stylists, models, and photographers, has to contextualize these ideas within the zeitgeist of the times. For a *Vogue* reader, picking up the latest issue with a sumptuous photo story detailing the latest shape of skirt increases the desirability of that skirt. Looking at the same issue in hindsight—the style of the photographer, the use of color, the makeup, the figure of the model—contributes to our understanding of social history.

The market is now huge, as fashion magazines aimed at different demographics all include style pages. Fashion is channeled into advertising, music, and movies. Market saturation led to the presentation of the magazine as a luxury item in the 1990s, with the conceptual magazine *Visionaire* being launched at $295 an issue. Now, with online versions of most magazines, the printed copy is a relative luxury.

Flicking back through fashion magazines, the changing content charts the journey of fashion. The staged studio-portrait style of the photography of Edward Steichen and Baron de Meyer at the turn of the 20th century has progressed into the editorial and advertising pictures of the 21st century that highlight the artistic merit of fashion.

A constant dialogue between art and commerce has been partly responsible for shaping fashion through the years. The fashion photographer can imbue an item of clothing with emotion, timeliness, and iconic status in a single image. By the 1980s, the stylist was part of the process, not only translating the fashion onto the page but also creating looks, pulled together from a myriad of references, which contribute to the cultural significance of fashion.

As soon as fashion becomes established, it changes. Its adolescent fickleness is a constant. It lives on the new, and so the accepted must be rejected. This applies to another component of the fashion image: the model. In the 1950s the hauteur of Britain's first

supermodel, Barbara Goalen; in the 1970s Twiggy's fringed eyes looking as surprised as anyone else to find herself on the cover of a magazine; and Kate Moss's youthful smile dismissing supermodel pizzazz in the 1990s—all caught the mood of their times.

Seeing fashion chronology as an aid to social history, it is interesting that the next push in style is for the industry to become socially aware. Ethical issues and sustainability have developed from seeming faddish in the 1990s to imperative by the 2010s as our future becomes a subject endlessly discussed.

Fashion has weathered wars and financial crises. It has fluctuated between the conceptual and the functional. It is a pendulum, swinging back to reinterpret the past and forward to imagine the future. In the 21st century, fashion is not only interwoven with technology, it has also been given a new validity. The fashion galleries of museums are now popular attractions in themselves, as fashion is used to engage us in its story and to unravel a moment in history. That is the charge of this book.

1800–
1837

Regency &
Romantic

Introduction

In fashion terms, the 19th century began before the year 1800. The 1790s saw a huge change that had repercussions not least in dress, but also heralded major social, economic, and political shifts.

After the Revolution in France, no one wanted to appear as aristocracy, and fashion was directly dictated by politics. Social upheaval instigated a rejection of powdered periwigs, embroidery, and brocade and the panniers and corsets of the rococo court style and simpler styles of dress were adopted.

The neoclassical influence on dress that is resonant of early 18th-century fashion had its origins in the post-revolutionary tastes of the republicans, although contrary to the accusations of her detractors, it was Marie Antoinette herself who had first rebelled against the restrictive clothing of the *ancien régime* and privately preferred simple, comfortable dresses.

Artist Jacques-Louis David (1748–1845) was a supporter of Robespierre in the Revolution and subsequently a prominent member of the National Assembly. During this time, David was responsible for festivals to commemorate the deaths of revolutionaries who died fighting royalists. David, who painted in a neoclassicist style, designed republican costumes for these parades drawn from classical Greek images. After Robespierre was guillotined, David radically changed his allegiance. Under the Directoire, neoclassicism was associated with ideals of ancient Greek and Roman republican virtue, but Napoleon was drawn to the Empirical implications of such style and David later associated himself with Napoleon and Josephine Bonaparte, depicting the emperor in portraits as a classical hero. Napoleon did away with the egalitarian dress of the Revolution, which had been adopted in sympathy with the *Sans-culottes*—the poorly dressed proletariat—and reestablished court dress in a grand style.

The English effect

Anglomania was also evident in France during the period before the Terror, because English sartorial style was seen as a simpler alternative to French rococo court clothes. Some women adopted the

As empress, Josephine became extremely influential in fashion and surpassed Marie Antoinette in embracing the sartorial expectations of wife of the ruler of France, going so far as to buy herself the former queen's pearls.

In Regency England, court dress was more understated than its 18th-century equivalent, largely due to the sartorial interpretation of Beau Brummell, an army captain, whose influence tempered the extravagances of his friend, the Prince Regent.

robe à l'anglaise, a jacket inspired by a man's redingote and a dress with fitted bodice and skirt with a train over a horsehair underskirt instead of panniers. Post-Revolution, it was seen as patriotic to break with the past and dress less extravagantly. Young men adopted an exaggerated form of English tailoring, which became the established dress of the "incroyables," the French Dandies.

In England itself, women remained taken with Paris fashion, and by 1800 the Empire dress was as apparent in London as it was across the English Channel, even if the neoclassicist influence was less marked. Instead, a new influence—Eastern style—became popular, prompted by Napoleon's expedition to Egypt and by the importance of the East India Company to Britain.

During the war with France, London and Paris were cut off from each other and their fashions diverged markedly, with the waist dropping in English modes. In 1814, the first English visitors to Paris quickly reverted to the French *mode*— a higher bustline and slightly flared skirt—after English styles were severely mocked.

The prince regent, later King George IV of England, was unconcerned with the politics of the time and preferred to spend the coffers of the Crown on extravagance and luxury while the ordinary people suffered. The Industrial Revolution required cheap labor and conditions were poor. The plight of the workforce was championed by the Romantic movement, whose creative output made an impact on fashion, favoring gowns in historic style and wan complexions, while men wore their hair long and sported flowing neck scarves.

In any age there is a difference between fashion expressed by a few and the adaptation of styles for everyday wear. Describing the mannered world of Regency England, Jane Austen wrote of the caps, bonnets, parasols, and other accessories necessary to maintain female decorum. Times and demands change, however, and by 1837 the early Victorian age, as the British called it, was dawning. Dress once more became restrictive and rigid. Memories of the daring early 18th-century fashions were reduced to romantic depictions in book illustrations.

The Empire Dress 1790–1810

The origins of fashion

Although the high-waisted, straight-cut gown came to be known as the Empire dress, its origins lay in pre-revolutionary times as the T-shaped, white muslin chemise dress first favored by Marie Antoinette. Wearing the chemise as an alternative to the structured and restrictive court dress when relaxing with her children at their retreat, the Petit Trianon, in the grounds of Versailles, Marie Antoinette posed for a portrait. Her appearance caused a scandal when the picture was displayed in an exhibition in Paris. The lack of formality of the chemise, however, was far more in tune with the atmosphere of the new Republic and was widely adopted.

Dress and undress, 1807
Although the slim, high-waisted silhouette of the time was a natural state for the slight of figure, more voluptuous women still required foundation garments. A shift, known as a chemise, was worn next to the skin and preserved the delicate dress from repeated washings. Stays (a soft corset) could be worn over this, followed by a petticoat. These undergarments also protected the wearer's modesty under the diaphanous muslin.

The neoclassical influence, ca. 1800
This English dress demonstrates how the neoclassical style became diluted away from the political zeal of the Directoire in Paris and the court of Napoleon that followed it. Parisian dresses of this time were far more literal in their usage of Greco-Roman detailing and construction. English fashions tended to be less extreme, but employed the shape and cut of the Empire line.

"Fashion condemns us to many follies, the greatest of which is to make ourselves its slave."

NAPOLEON BONAPARTE

Rising waistline, 1790s

At the end of the 18th century, the waistline took a radical shift upward and came to settle under the bust in the recognizable empire or regency style. The 1794 dress (on the left) is an example of a *robe à l'anglaise,* a style that became popular with the wave of post-Revolution Anglomania. A roll of fabric padded out the skirt beneath a natural waistline. The 1798 (center) and 1799 (right) dresses show how the waist rose by the end of the decade, although the skirt remained relatively full.

ELEMENTS OF FASHION

- *Classical influences, Parisian fashions*
- *Indian muslin, French tulle and batiste*
- *high waistline, low, décolleté neckline*
- *chemisette and short, puffed sleeves*
- *pale skin*

The classical influence, ca. 1800

In lieu of a seam, the sleeves of this dress are held together with small clasps or buttons at intervals along the top of the arm, one of the construction techniques that was used in women's dress in ancient Greece and Rome. The narrow twin stripes adorning the hem mimic the decoration on a Roman tunic.

Low-cut bodice, ca. 1800

"Morning dress," which actually meant clothing worn at home during the day, was expected to cover both the arms and bust, an effect often achieved by layering different garments. It was accepted that evening wear displayed areas of exposed flesh, with extremely décolleté gowns that had short sleeves above the elbow. Some ladies of high fashion went so far as to (discreetly) reveal their nipples, giving satirists cause for comment.

CHRONOLOGICAL CATWALK
The Early 19th-Century Female

The influence of Josephine Bonaparte

A divorcee six years Napoleon's senior, who survived imprisonment during the Terror of the Revolution, Josephine was an independent woman who shared the wedding costs with her second husband. Josephine's beauty, her lavish tendencies, and natural style were implicit in establishing the ostentation of Napoleon's empire and reinstating Paris fashion.

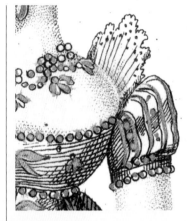

Jewelry

In 1805, Napoleon commissioned Etienne Nitot, who had opened the house of Chaumet on the Rue St. Honoré in Paris, to make the coronation jewels. Josephine understood the power of the statement piece and the reestablishment of court dress led to the introduction of designer jewelry in the 19th century. Tiffany, Cartier, Bulgari, and Fabergé subsequently opened in New York, London, Paris, and Moscow.

Empire line

Josephine's svelte figure suited the Empire line and her tailor, Leroy, made her dresses with a deep décolleté and short puffed sleeves to show her white skin. After Napoleon declared himself emperor in 1804, designers significantly utilized classical influences in decor, architecture, and costume to establish an imperial style. Josephine's gowns fell from the bust and flowed in imitation of the toga, held with fastenings of the most lavish materials.

Silhouette of grandeur

The chemise dress had risen to popularity with the post-revolutionary neoclassical styles adopted in France. Trains were also introduced to lend majesty to the style and also to increase the bulk of fabric used. Parures (matching sets of tiaras, necklaces, and earrings) were in vogue at court and elaborate feathered headdresses were matched to ball gowns.

White dress

The popularity of the white dress is accredited to Josephine's influence, following her husband's preference. White became the accepted color for evening gowns and the fashion transcended politics on both sides of the English Channel. The classical white dress was also habitually worn by Josephine's archrival, Madame Recamier, an outspoken opposer of the emperor. The Empire line is still alternatively known as the Recamier line.

Silk fabric

Josephine incorporated the honeybee, Napoleon's adopted symbol, across the white fabric of her dress. She also favored the fashion of wearing shawls, and as war with England made it difficult to import cashmere, factories in France were established to produce alternatives. Revenue was generated by imposing duties on English fabrics, while Josephine's tailor reestablished the use of French textiles, in particular reviving the Lyons silk industry with formal court dress.

Imperial style, ca. 1805

Josephine had been mistress to several high-ranking officials before capturing the heart of Napoleon, and as the new empress she appreciated the importance of presenting an image. She enjoyed perfecting her appearance, employing a lengthy beauty regime that involved hair stylists and cosmeticians, and made it her duty to amass an extensive wardrobe trimmed with lace, feathers, and fur.

The Pelisse 1810s–1820s

The first coat

The chemise dress, made of light fabrics and ideally exposing as much décolleté as possible, presented problems for the health of fashionable ladies in the northern European climate. It was essential to find a solution to the need for protection from the weather without spoiling the classic lines of the *robe de mode*. Outdoor garments that were more tailored than the cloak began to appear at the end of the 18th century. The sleeved pelisse, the spencer jacket, and the redingote all rose in popularity, although the elegant shawl was first choice for an extra layer and the heavier cape or mantle shielded the wearer against extreme conditions.

ELEMENTS OF FASHION

- *tailoring and sleeves following the lines of the dress*
- *reticule purses, often in novelty shapes*
- *silk, velvet, kerseymere, merino, plush*
- *passementerie trimmings*
- *fur linings*
- *collars and raised necklines*
- *woven shawls*

The coatdress, ca. 1810

Formerly a half-length outdoor covering with no lapels, by the 1820s the pelisse was a full-length coatdress. The redingote had been developed from the man's riding coat into a practical dress, the lines of which were adapted into a coat as skirts became fuller in the mid-century. There was less distinction between tailored day dresses and outdoor garments than in modern times.

Construction, ca. 1825

The pelisse coat was often lined with fur or padded during winter, but the lines of the dress it followed made a small reticule (or ridicule purse) necessary instead of pockets. Originally open, this coat developed into the buttoned pelisse robe and later the redingote. These garments were at first too complicated for the female dressmaker and had to be cut by a gentleman tailor.

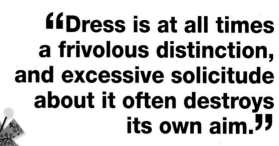

> **"Dress is at all times a frivolous distinction, and excessive solicitude about it often destroys its own aim."**
>
> JANE AUSTEN
> *NORTHANGER ABBEY*, 1818

Ornamentation for warmth, ca. 1820
The low, open neckline of the day dress was often filled in with a kerchief or chemisette, while the outdoor garments sought to cover the area with a large collar or, during the Romantic era, a ruff. Ornamentation on the pelisse was often appliquéd or ruched to add weight. There was a vogue during the war with France for military trimmings with braiding and fur trim on heavyweight wools.

The woven shawl, ca. 1820
Handwoven cashmere shawls from India were costly fashion accessories and demand prompted machine-loom factories in Norwich, England and Paisley, Scotland to open. The designs copied the Indian cone patterns from Kashmir and were given the name of the Scottish town where they were crafted. The fabric ranged from woven silk and wool mixes to cotton prints and became accessible to every budget. Shawls retained their appeal throughout the 19th century.

Gothic Romance 1820s

Gothic medieval influence

By the second decade of the 19th century, the classical influence had begun to be replaced by details borrowed from medieval costume, which was termed "Gothic" in style.

This heralded the burgeoning Romantic period. Romanticism, taking its lead from the cultural movement that included writers Lord Byron and Sir Walter Scott, was concerned with the fantastical and sublime. The imagination was encouraged to take free rein and the prevailing mood resulted in fashion changing from the simple lines of the Greco-Roman aesthetic to a taste for the exotic. The Romantic feminine ideal was as pale and delicate as a tragic historical heroine.

ELEMENTS OF FASHION

- elaborately curled and looped hairstyles
- ferronières (jeweled headbands) for evening
- checkerboard patterned fabrics
- hats and bonnets profusely trimmed with feathers, ribbons, and flowers
- belted narrow waists
- Anglomania in France
- Italian quilting
- Turkey red

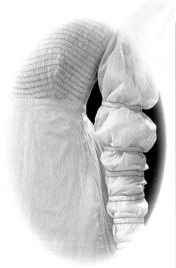

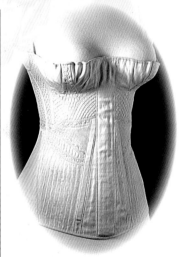

Sleeves style, 1819–20

The Gothic influence was apparent in such medievalist touches as long sleeves bound by cord. The Romantic era broadened its pillage of history: sleeves were slashed in imitation of Tudor style, ruffs and Vandyke points adorned collars and padding, and Elizabethan flouncing and ruching were also used to give the wearer the impression that she belonged in the historical novel.

Return of the corset, 1820–30

To allow for increased ornamentation on the bodice, there was a gradual dropping of the waistline, and at the height of the Romantic period in the 1820s, the waist returned to its natural position. This, in turn, resulted in a reinstatement of the corset. Despite several bids for freedom, the female form was not to achieve its natural state again for nearly a century.

Essential headwear, 1818–30

Turbans had come into vogue in the First Empire after Napoleon's expedition to Egypt and remained suitable attire for married women. During the Romantic era, hats and caps (top example, 1818–23), for indoors and out, became larger and more ornate, which also helped to give the impression of a smaller waist. Women's hair was elaborately curled and arranged and hats and bonnets (bottom, 1825–30) had expanded crowns and brims to accommodate the new hairstyles, such as the Apollo knot.

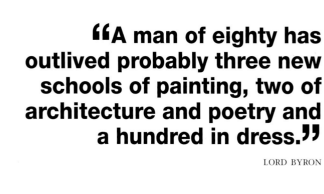

> **"A man of eighty has outlived probably three new schools of painting, two of architecture and poetry and a hundred in dress."**
>
> LORD BYRON

The new silhouette, England, 1825–30

As the waist became once more tightly laced, the effect was accentuated by making the skirt wider and the shoulders broader. Sleeves were no longer set to give the impression of a tiny frame, but the bodice was paneled to provide more shape, with a décolleté cut straight across and the sleeves puffed out at the shoulder. The new dress style often had a waist-cinching belt or the bodice dropping into a V shape.

Bridal costume, Paris, 1825

This silk wedding dress illustrates how, by mid-decade, the effect of the widening of skirts was accentuated by weighting the hem with rows of ruched flounces. Darts were introduced for the first time to give a smooth bustline, and these, together with the low, oval neckline, drew the attention to the waist, which was the obsession of the era. Lace fichu-pelerines often covered the shoulders.

The Gigot Sleeve 1830–1837

Enormous sleeves, widening skirts, rising hemlines
The beginning of the 1830s saw the fashions of the previous decade explored to their extremities. The skirt hem was still weighted with batting but the ornamentation was moved up to knee height, which increased the horizontal effect of the line. Skirts became shorter and, with a glimpse of ankle and a narrow waist, the new brightly colored dress lent its wearer a flirtatious youthfulness. The oversized gigot sleeve (known also as the leg-of-mutton sleeve), full from the shoulder, with a narrow lower arm to the cuff, was the manifestation of this mood of exuberance and became so large that it no longer sufficed to use a stiffened muslin lining, and stuffed pads attached to the arms were used to support them.

❝Dress consists not so much in the garment as in the way it is worn.❞

HONORÉ DE BALZAC
TRAITÉ DE LA VIE ÉLÉGANTE, 1830

▶ **Extreme silhouette, ca. 1830**
Aptly, the influence of Romanticism in this illustrated Valentine's card of 1830 is very much in evidence, but the lady's pelisse robe demonstrates how sleeves had started to expand. The pelisse as outerwear began to be phased out as sleeves became too big for coats to fit over them. The design was incorporated into a day dress and shawls became larger and more square to accommodate the gigot sleeve.

Fullness in the lower sleeve, 1836

By the second half of the 1830s, the extremities of the huge sleeve had reached their limits and sleeves had begun to deflate and move down the arm. The bodice lengthened and was even more structured, while the width of the skirt, pleated into the bodice, had to be supported with petticoats. The skirt dropped back to floor length and became more sedate.

ELEMENTS OF FASHION

• *shoulders and décolletage exposed by pull of heavy sleeves*

• *the burnous (oriental hooded mantle) for evening*

• *low, square-toed leather slippers or elasticated boots*

• *pelerine to emphasize shoulders*

• *brocades (18th-century gowns recut) and starched petticoats*

Pattern, ca. 1835

The 19th century saw technological developments in dye chemistry that revolutionized textile printing. There was a better understanding of the process and patterned fabrics became widely available for the first time. Extravagant dress ornamentation started to be replaced by simpler gowns in woven and printed patterns, particularly in light wools and cottons. However, white muslin trimmed with lace was still deemed most suitable for very young ladies.

Short sleeves, ca. 1828

This dress shows how the puffed sleeve of the 1800s began to take on a fullness, which developed into the beret sleeve, which was cut in a complete circle. By the mid-1820s, short sleeves, for formal wear, could be augmented with a covering of a long, transparent gauze oversleeve cut in the gigot shape. By the 1830s, shortly after this dress was made, width would also be added by means of elaborate shoulder ornamentations.

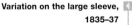

Variation on the large sleeve, 1835–37

The gigot sleeve was the most characteristic style of the large-sleeve fashion of the 1830s, although other full styles were known as *à l'imbécile* or *à la folle*. The fullness here begins with a drop from the shoulder to avoid disturbing the line of the scoop of the neckline.

23

The Early 19th-Century Male

The dandy

The English dandy and his French counterpart, the "incroyable," first came into evidence in the 1790s. He was a gentleman who applied the dictum of restraint as the foremost principle of male sartorial elegance. This restraint distinguished him from the macaroni—the overdressed fool—of the 18th century.

Top hat
The dandy popularized the top hat for men, phasing out the previously universal tricorne. Originally made of felted beaver fur, it used silk hatter's plush from 1800. After Beau Brummell's influence waned, the hat shapes of English dandies became more pronounced with flaring crowns and wider brims, while the top hat of the incroyable was fantastical in its extremes.

The Beauties of Brighton, Alfred H. Forrester, 1826
A parade of the follies of fashion at a popular resort. Forrester has included his self-portrait, chin in hand, at the extreme left. Every type of extravagance in contemporary costume is caricatured here, offset by the ornate domes of Brighton Pavillion, in England, itself in the background.

Silhouette of superiority
The impression that the dandy desired to give was one of superiority through sartorial finesse. Brummell was known as an arrogant wit, but others had to rely on the high collar, which could impair the movement of the neck, to lend them hauteur. A streamlined Apollonian physique and upright posture were also aided by stays and padding.

Collar and cravat

The dandy's immaculately clean linen shirts were crowned by a high starched collar around which was tied a neck cloth or cravat consisting of a large folded square of lawn, muslin, or silk. Various names were given to differing versions: the Napoleon; the American or Yankee; the Osbaldeston; or Barrel. In France, the collar became so high that the cravat could cover the mouth.

Dress coat

The dandy's dress coat was tailored from dark, good-quality plain cloth with no ornamentation except gilt buttons. The shape, adapted from the English hunting coat, had knee-length tails at the back, cut away at the front. It was always worn with vest and breeches of a different color and the collar, which stood up at the back, was usually made of velvet.

Breeches

Light-colored knee breeches were worn to contrast with the dark cloth of the coat in the daytime with knee-high boots— the rain boot after 1815. For the evening, darker breeches were worn with silk stockings and pumps. Both were tightly fitting. Brummell popularized close-cut pants which ended above the ankle, but wider *à la turque* pants were also worn.

Beau Brummell 1778–1840

George Bryan "Beau" Brummell, whose name became synonymous with masculine elegance, was in a prime position to become influential in the development of men's costume in Regency England as friend, and confidant, to the prince regent.

Brummell was not an aristocrat but was born into elevated surroundings, the son of the private secretary to Lord North. An education at Eton and Oriel College, Oxford, served to develop a taste for privilege in Brummell. On his father's death in 1794, he received a large inheritance and moved to Mayfair, a fashionable part of London.

Brummell became friends with the Prince of Wales, who was to become King George IV, after meeting him by a chance encounter at an attraction farm in London's Green Park run by Brummell's aunt. Prince George, whose capriciousness matched that of Marie Antoinette, was amused by Brummell and for a time graced the elegant commoner with his favor. Brummell was appointed to a position in the army but his main function was to provide the prince with sartorial advice.

It is a misconception that dandyism was the pursuit of masculine finery. Brummell, as the original dandy,

Born
London, 1778

Manifesto
Arbiter of refined style in men's fashion in Regency England.

advocated refined understatement of dress. Any garment considered to detract from the excellence of cut and tailoring was removed as excessive. The lace ruffles, jewels, embroidery, and buckled shoes of the previous century were all dismissed as fripperies that served to avert the eye from the ill-fitting costumes of the aristocracy.

Beau Brummell's wardrobe was pared down to a plain white linen shirt, a coat in a dark, single color, a light vest and tight-fitting knee breeches or pantaloons worn with riding boots and a starched white neck cloth. All elements were of the finest quality possible, and Brummell's appearance was testament to British tailors, who were rapidly becoming recognized as the most skillful in Europe. This did not mean that Brummell was a man without vanity— despite his abhorrence of vulgar ornamentation, he prided himself on the fact that he could require five hours to dress. The simplicity took time. A gentleman, he thought, should be so scrupulously clean that there is no need for perfume, and he would only appear clean shaven and with neatly clipped and curled hair.

The spotless white linen shirt of the dandy had a high collar that rose to the chin. The neck cloth that was

"I cannot be elegant since you have noticed me."

BEAU BRUMMELL

wrapped round this was the single outward show of peacockery that Brummell afforded. The tying of the cravat was an art, and Brummell was known to have his valet perfect this task at the expense of huge laundry bills and many wasted hours.

Beau Brummell's sharp wit and eagle eye for detail secured his place at the top of the sartorial ranks who regarded discipline of dress as their code of honor. He had not so much allegiance to the army, however, and soon tired of his appointment. It was only a matter of time before his wit turned to arrogance and he quarreled with his friend the Prince.

In 1816, Brummell was forced to flee to France to escape his debtors. Friends secured him an appointment at the consulate in Caen, but in 1835 he was finally imprisoned for debt and died alone in Caen's asylum in 1840.

With the departure of Brummell, the English dandies lost their greatest regulator and general. The sobriety that was so important to Brummell began to be modified in various ways— his elements of perfection became exaggerated to the point of caricature. Cartoonists fell upon the more extreme fancies of the gentlemen and savagely depicted the dandies as ridiculous corseted figures with tiny heads sunk into neck-bracelike collars, supporting huge funnel hats.

It is widely believed that Beau Brummell's contribution to fashion was to make sartorial excellence possible for all gentlemen to achieve and not simply the domain of the aristocrat. In 2002, a statue of Brummell was erected in Jermyn Street in London, the heart of the district traditionally occupied by gentlemen's outfitters.

Beau Brummell understood that the devil was in the detail. Knowing the value of line in fashionable dress, he was credited with introducing the pant strap so that pantaloons were pulled taut and wrinkle free. It is also said that he recommended polishing his boots with champagne. Brummell's vest was understated and his coat was invariably a stylish dark blue and cut from the finest English broadcloth. His top hat, the correct headwear for the day, was shined and he was never without the fashionably correct cane.

Early
Victorian

Introduction

The fashionable world of Britain in the 1830s had encapsulated flamboyance and romance. In the early Victorian period, frivolity of dress was to become frowned upon and the mood was to dictate an air of gentility.

In 1840, the new Queen Victoria married Prince Albert of Saxe-Coburg. The royal match set the standard for the values of the times: domesticity and the family were prized and reflected in female dress, which became demure and modest to suit the passive role of the "little woman" in the home.

In social terms, the ideal of the woman in the home was indicative of a shift at that time. The development of the middle class, which had resulted from the economics of the Industrial Revolution, had produced a generation that desired to display its success conspicuously and found it necessary to find its place in society. The genteel wife of a prosperous husband was expected to preside over the housekeeping, manage the "help," and produce children without a thought of the life of work that had been the fortune of her forebears.

Social change and its effects

Industrialization and urbanization caused a precipitation of sociological development. The factories and textile mills needed labor, which brought about squalid, overcrowded living conditions and poverty in the cities. The plight of the beleaguered workers versus the wealthy industrialists prompted the organization of labor as well as riots and uprisings. In 1842 England, there was a general strike by the cotton workers, and the mill owners were forced to contemplate reform as well as production.

Progress came at a price for traditional crafts: skilled lace and shoemakers faced replacement by steam machinery and the Luddites fueled further unrest and uprisings.

However, for the new middle-class Victorians, this time of turmoil was also one of excitement and fresh opportunity. Steam power facilitated the development of the railroad system and the new-found speed and ease of travel brought with it the possibility of vacations for the recently monied class.

Prince Albert was a champion of 19th-century progress, and in 1851 he masterminded the Great Exhibition, held in the specially constructed Crystal Palace in Hyde Park, London, which displayed the products of invention and innovation from Britain and around the world. Albert used the profits of the exhibition to advance science, the arts, and the national museums, and to fund the Imperial College and the Royal Albert Hall.

The national taste for the modest grew into one for opulence and wealth as the 1840s became the 1850s. Already exposed to the international tastes on display in the Crystal Palace, English women turned their sights again on Paris. With the establishment of the Second Empire of Napoleon III in France, imaginations were fired by Empress Eugénie's influence on fashion.

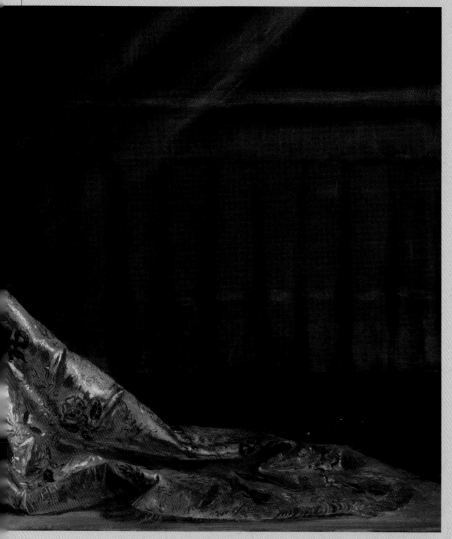

The robes for a state coronation were— and still are—manifold and richly ornate with complex significance. By contrast, Queen Victoria, painted wearing her coronation robes by Charles Robert Leslie in 1838, was personally less interested in sartorial grandeur—to the point where it is said that Empress Eugénie once expressed anxiety that the people of Paris should make fun of the Queen's clothing during a state visit to France.

The New Queen 1837–1840s

A sense of duty

The ascension of Victoria to the throne in 1837 marked a change in social outlook, because although the new queen was lighthearted and young, her sense of duty was not casual. The somber morality of the 1840s contrasted directly with the frivolity of the previous decade and was reflected in dress. Hair began to be arranged simply and neatly, the enormous sleeves were deflated and moved down the arms, and ornamentation and color were less flamboyant. Skirts dropped to the floor again, with a new weight and volume that caused women to move with a careful elegance.

▶ Polka dress, ca. 1840

The Victorians loved dancing, which the young queen helped to popularize by giving evening concerts. She particularly enjoyed waltzing with Albert, but in 1840 a craze for the polka swept the nation. The polka proved to be a great social leveler, danced in saloons, community outdoor areas, and at court balls. Evening dresses generally still had short sleeves during this period, in contrast with sedate day dresses.

ELEMENTS OF FASHION
• *the polka jacket*
• *lace collars*
• *softer pastel colors*
• *the first crinoline: a petticoat stuffed with horsehair*
• *wider skirts, flounced and gauged into the bodice*

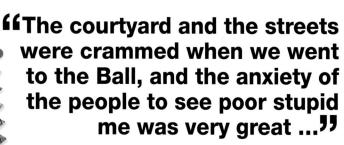

"The courtyard and the streets were crammed when we went to the Ball, and the anxiety of the people to see poor stupid me was very great ..."

VICTORIA, PERSONAL JOURNAL,
MAY, 1937

Royal tartan, ca. 1840
Victoria and Albert bought Balmoral Castle in the Scottish Highlands in 1848, embracing the idea of healthy highland pursuits in a grand Scots baronial style.
The prince personally oversaw the interior design, making much use of tartan. Albert designed the Balmoral tartan and the queen designed the Victoria, which the family wore while spending time in Scotland. The royal preference prompted the use of the fabric in fashion for the first time and it also became popular in the United States.

Gauged bodice, 1840
At the beginning of the Victorian period, skirts were set onto the bodice in pleats or gathers, but as the width of skirts grew, after 1841, a new method was developed by closely pleating the lined fabric and sewing alternate pleats to the bodice. This alleviated any bulkiness and helped maintain the shape of the skirt. The so-called "gauging" system required a lengthened bodice, which became characteristic of the era.

Flounces on a French wedding dress, ca. 1840
Skirts grew wider from 1841 and a new fashion for flounced skirts developed. These further emphasized volume where there was already an abundance of fabric to be pleated into the waistband. Flounces were often manufactured "*à la disposition*"—woven or printed specially so that bands of pattern encircled the skirt. The width of the skirt was supported with multiple petticoats of various fabrics and weights.

The Early Victorian Female

The little woman

A notable aspect of Victorian society was the growth of the middle class as a result of the Industrial Revolution, and the subsequent development of the country's infrastructure. Prosperous businessmen, merchants, and salaried professionals moved to the new suburbs. Status required that their wives were models of domestic virtue: quiet, decorous, delicate, and inactive.

The sleeve and bodice

By 1845, the sleeve was cut simply and straight. The longer-cut bodice was rigidly boned and, together with the corset, augmented the restrictive qualities of the upper part of the early Victorian dress. Combined with the heaviness of the huge skirt over multiple petticoats, this was ideal garb for the model passive female.

The bonnet

The flirtatious and ornate hats of the 1830s had given way to the close-fitting poke bonnet by the 1840s. The neatly proportioned bonnet tied under the chin and lent the wearer a modest, private air. It was impossible to see the face of a woman wearing a bonnet unless looking at her from directly in front—or, indeed, for her to look anywhere but straight ahead.

Demure silhouette

By the 1840s, women's dress was the measure of propriety, and fashion served to conceal in a uniform way. The shape of the bonnet was often hidden under veiling and the shape of the bodice was hidden under a shawl, rendering the waist undetectable. In this way, the entire outdoors silhouette resembled an inverted V shape while the skirt length made it seem as if women glided instead of walked.

Child's dress

Little girls still wore a miniature version of their mothers' dresses, with the same lengthened bodice and V-shaped waist. The bonnet was also modeled on the headwear of their mothers, while skirts came no farther than the tops of their buttoned boots, revealing their long, white drawers. Fabrics, such as silk, wool, and velvet, in darker colors were used, as they were for adults.

Dainty feet

If visible at all, feet were made to look as small as possible. Shoes were unheeled silk or crepe slippers and leather or cloth half boots for walking. Tiny feet were associated with the genteel image of contemporary woman and her physical delicacy. This daintiness was also desired in a woman because Queen Victoria herself was very small.

Hand-tinted fashion plate, 1840s

Magazines were not treated as disposable items in the 19th century. Periodicals, such as the *Ladies Cabinet* in England and *Godey's Lady's Book* in the United States, were not just a reference for fashions of the day, but valued for their artistry. Jules David began to use backgrounds as context for his illustrations in the Paris *Moniteur de la Mode* in 1843.

The Bloomer 1850s

Suffrage and emancipation

In the mid-19th century, education was becoming more accessible for women, especially in the United States where public colleges accepted female students. Women were starting to become aware of a world outside the home and some were daring to ask questions about their place in society. Occasional individualists had been seen in pants, notably the Duchess of Montrose, who wore them for shooting in 1847, and the French novelist George Sand, who defied convention in a man's suit. However, it was the American suffrage and temperance campaigner Amelia Jenks Bloomer who first brought pants for women to the attention of the general public.

American influence
The dress reform costume that Amelia Bloomer advocated consisted of a tunic dress with a bodice like that of a conventional dress of the day, a wide skirt that finished a few inches below the knee, and a pair of wide baggy pantaloons, caught into a lace trimming at the ankle. Bloomer brought her costume to Britain in 1851, but was met with widespread ridicule and was mocked by the satirists.

Bloomer waltz, costume for summer, ca. 1851
The illustration from the cover of a "Bloomer waltz" shows a woman wearing not only the daring rational dress garb, but also breaking convention with her choice of hat. Younger women started to wear practical hats for informal occasions, and by 1854 the wide-brimmed straw hat was fashionable at summer resorts, although regarded as immodest. Women were still expected to wear a bonnet to church.

"The costume of women should... conduce to her health, comfort, and usefulness... it should make [her personal adornment] of secondary importance."

AMELIA JENKS BLOOMER

Punch magazine, 1851

"Bloomerism" did not escape the attentions of the cartoonists of the day, who depicted this new American custom as a dangerous precedent to adopting other male-only habits and as an affront to the sensibilities of a genteel Englishwoman.

ELEMENTS OF FASHION

- *baggy pantaloon bloomers*
- *tunic dress*
- *silk trimmings*
- *wide-brimmed hat*
- *indifference to ridicule*

Trimmings, ca. 1855

Pant outfits were considered by the few women who wore them to be as becoming as conventional dress. Although Bloomer and other radicals denounced boning, the waist was mainly constricted in the way that fashion demanded, and trimmings, which were on the increase in the 1850s, were not spurned. Machine-made silk fringes were extremely popular and followed the lines of the bodice.

Full bloomer costume

Pants for women did not become a fashion, but Amelia Bloomer continued to travel and lecture for several years in the hope that women interested in suffrage would adopt this sensible garb. Bloomer did concede that the crinoline was a much more suitable alternative to the hugely hampering petticoats and it was not until the 1890s that women finally started to wear bloomers for the purpose of bicycling.

CHRONOLOGICAL CATWALK
The Early Victorian Male

Savile Row

In 1846, Henry Poole expanded his family business and opened the first tailor's shop on Savile Row in London, beginning the long tradition of the Savile Row suit. Such was the reputation of English tailoring that within forty years Pooles were dressing nearly all the male crowned heads of Europe. Savile Row became synonymous with custom-made menswear exquisitely tailored from quality fabrics with unrivaled skill.

Tailored silhouette

The frock coat had begun to be less severely padded and pinched in at the waist by mid-century, in the same way that women's fashion had become less flamboyant. The collar was still held against the neck by the tie, but was again less of a statement. Only hats became more extreme, with the top hats worn with formal dress continuing to become taller, reaching the narrow stovepipe shape in the 1850s. A slim, elegant leg was accentuated with tapered pants and neat shoes.

The bow tie

The neck cloth favored by the dandy during the earlier part of the century had been through a fashion of patterned fabrics throughout the 1820s and 30s, but had settled into a solid color by the 1850s. In mid-century, the cloth was narrowed into a band to make a tie, with the ends becoming the more pronounced section to define the bow.

Black and brown coat and vest

Menswear had also turned towards the somber look after 1837. Plain, dark colors for the fashionable frock coat worn during the day were not only the mark of gentility, but also necessary in the industrial age, when soot hung in the air. However, the vest still allowed for some pattern, and was often produced in tartan.

Checked pants

Pants had now taken over from breeches in the fashionable gentleman's wardrobe, although the latter were still worn in the country. Often checked or tartan, pants were cut relatively tight and straight, with a strap under the instep. Baggier peg-top pants were an alternative worn by the "swells" toward the end of the 1850s.

Oxford shoes

The Oxford shoe, also called the Balmoral, originated in Scotland and Ireland and was initially a half boot. The Oxford eventually became a low-cut shoe, known as a brogue. Northampton was the center of the British shoe industry and in 1857 its shoe makers opposed industrialization, although by 1861 the Turner factory was producing 100,000 pairs a week by steam-powered machine.

The Gazette of Fashion, custom-made tailoring, 1852
Four types of coat were required for the early Victorian gentleman's everyday dress. A morning coat was worn for formal day occasions, and the single-breasted fitted frock coat for business, usually over a colorful double-breasted vest, perhaps with an overcoat, while a dress coat was favored in the evening. Savile Row became a stalwart of the British fabric industry, using English wools and Scots tweeds and tartans.

The Bowler Hat 1850s

Safety first

The bowler hat was invented in 1849 by James Lock on the request of William Coke, an English landowner who wanted a hard hat to protect the heads of his gamekeepers. Lock devised a felt-covered, domed hat that was hardened with shellac. His prototype was made up by Thomas & William Bowler, hatmakers in Southwark, London. On being shown the hat, William Coke stamped on it. The hat passed his test and became known as the Coke. The company went on to produce over 60,000 hats annually to meet the demand in Britain and other parts of the world and in due course the design became widely known as the bowler.

"Live life, do your work, then take your hat."

HENRY DAVID THOREAU

Social leveler, ca. 1865
Before the advent of the bowler, hats denoted social distinction among men. A top hat was the accepted headwear for a gentleman, but when the bowler first made an appearance it was quickly taken up as a casual alternative. For the lower classes, the bowler was seen as neater than their usual cloth caps and rapidly became adopted by men of every social denomination.

"A Debonair Character," *Vanity Fair*

This cartoon of Napoleon IV by "Spy" shows the Prince Imperial sporting a bowler. In the mid-19th century, what had started as a design for a safety hat became a fashion item. Since then, the hard-wearing, practical but stylish functionality of the bowler has been adopted by a variety of professions, from city gent to market trader to dressage rider.

The 19th-century "down-and-out" character

Although mostly used these days as a fashion item, the numerous associations of the bowler hat have contributed to its iconic status. More than sixty years after its invention, Charlie Chaplin used the hat as his trademark when he developed his "little tramp" alter-ego. By then, the hat's inclusion in the tramp's persona clearly indicated his aspirations to respectability.

ELEMENTS OF FASHION

• *hard, domed crown*

• *small, upturned brim*

• *ribbon trim*

• *black felted finish*

• *often paired with a rolled-up umbrella, cane, or a characteristic smile*

The derby, ca. 1850

In the United States, the bowler came to be known as the derby, and was just as much the people's choice as it was in Britain. In particular, the derby was worn by pioneers in the West in the 19th century—in fact, somewhat more than the cowboy hat—and was taken up by both the European settlers and indigenous Native Americans.

Henry Creed 1824–1914

The House of Creed is known as a heritage perfume brand, but the company that produced the famous Green Irish Tweed scent has its roots in the history of tailoring.

James Creed arrived in London from Leicester in 1760, and launched an offensive to befriend the valets of gentlemen of fashion. This strategy secured him a number of wealthy clients and he was able to open a shop offering alterations and repairs. In time, this became a family business as James's son, also James, and his son Henry were trained tailors. It was Henry Creed, James Creed's grandson, who truly advanced the fortunes of the dynasty.

By the 1840s the business was flourishing and Henry Creed received the advantages of a good education and travel before settling into his apprenticeship and the life of a tailor. Consequently, Henry was elevated to a consort of the *beau monde*. One of his best clients was the Comte d'Orsay, a notorious dandy who had written a

Born
Leicester, 1824

Manifesto
To dress the royalty and aristocracy of Europe

fashion column in London's *Daily News* in the 1830s. The comte introduced his tailor to the French and the English aristocracy. At this time, the French royal family were exiled in England and Henry Creed was commissioned to make riding habits for both Empress Eugénie and Queen Victoria.

In 1840s' France, a small wave of rebellion had appeared against the notion of the demure and meek woman. The female French equivalent of the dandy had been dubbed "la lionne" (the lioness) and was rich, married, handsome, and independent. The lionne reveled in hunting, shooting, smoking, and drinking, but her independence was symbolized by her horsemanship. Women who were captivated by the spirit of the lionne took up riding for a taste of freedom, and the "amazones," or habits, with their slightly masculine tailored bodice, became a wardrobe necessity.

Queen Victoria, with her Balmoral taste, appointed Creed as official supplier of tweed tailoring to the royal household. The quality of the cloth was a principal factor in the success of the House of Creed, encapsulating as it did *"le style anglais."*

In 1854, Creed opened on the Place de l'Opéra in Paris, bringing English tweed tailoring to the Second Empire

> **❝ ... the true dandy was not the most foppishly dressed, the most stylish, the most flash-mannered; he was primarily an artist of talent.❞**

COMTE D'ORSAY

of Napoleon III. His business prospered on both sides of the English Channel, in time serving all the courts of Europe, and Henry Creed commuted between the two countries. He married Eleanor Southey, sister of the Romantic Poet Laureate Robert Southey, and the family line continued with his son, another Henry.

In 1871, Henry Creed the elder, alarmed by the fall of France and the imminent threat to his business, traveled to Paris and was wounded in a clash between political rivals. His grandson Charles Creed wonders in his autobiography whether it was his apolitical attitude or his spirit of enterprise that saved his life, but Henry Creed lived to witness his own son Henry succeed to the House of Creed.

The Singer sewing machine and the department store had revolutionized the fashion system for women, but it was Henry Creed the younger who provided an alternative to the gown. While being fitted for a suit, the Duke of Alba commissioned Creed to make a matching outfit for his wife, and the female "tailor-made suit" was born. The tweed tailored suit became a womenswear staple for the first half of the 20th century. Indeed, during World War I, a Creed suit was

the chic way to express the utilitarianism of austere times— the spy Mata Hari was shot in one.

The fortunes of the House of Creed peaked after Charles Creed was demobilized following World War II and went on to profit from the 1950s taste for haute couture and the attention that Paris-based designers received from the United States. The demise of couture resulted in the concentration of the perfumery business in Paris, which retains its unmistakable British cachet.

Primarily used for gentlemanly outdoor pursuits, such as for this hunting coat for Lord Forester in 1851, tweed gradually became assimilated into the fashionable world with the rise of the House of Creed. In 1912, the Linton Mill in Carlisle, England, opened and became a supplier for the House of Creed. Linton became synonymous with understated, fine cloth in the insider trade and became suppliers to Molyneux, Chanel, and Jean Muir among others.

Haute Couture

Introduction

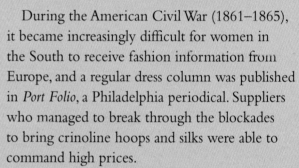

During the second half of the 19th century, power shifted across Europe. The Congress of Vienna reestablished monarchies across the European continent and, by the mid-1860s, Napoleon III's Second Empire was well established in France. The spirit of the age was materialism, as the new ruler followed the example of his uncle, Napoleon I, and sought to present Paris as a grand, suitably imperial city.

One of the maxims of such an implementation of power was the conspicuous display of wealth. Empress Eugénie, who possessed a genuine love of fashion, was a natural figurehead for such pageantry, and it was her patronage of the House of Worth that encouraged the introduction of the haute-couture system that still exists today.

The origins of the couture fashion system

Eugénie's fashion influence radiated—via fashion magazines, such as Samuel and Isabella Beeton's *The Englishwoman's Domestic Magazine,* and *La Belle Assemblée*—to the rest of Europe, and overseas to the United States. In fact, it was Eugénie's love of the flamboyant crinoline that kept it in fashion, against the better judgment of the discerning Charles Worth, who could not afford to lose such a valuable client.

Englishwomen, too, fell under the spell of the crinoline, although Empress Eugénie may have been thought a little too fast when reports of the moral shortcomings of the Second Empire crossed the English Channel—she was reputed to have worn black eyeliner.

During the American Civil War (1861–1865), it became increasingly difficult for women in the South to receive fashion information from Europe, and a regular dress column was published in *Port Folio*, a Philadelphia periodical. Suppliers who managed to break through the blockades to bring crinoline hoops and silks were able to command high prices.

Couture was the top of the fashion system, supported by a few wealthy international clients —the royal families of Europe, who were able to reestablish after the Congress of Vienna convened in 1815, and the banking dynasties of the United States—but for the ordinary woman opportunity also broadened. Steam power introduced machinery that could knit stockings and gloves, making mass-produced accessories more affordable. Partially ready-made clothes became available for dressmakers to fit and finish, while drapers and department stores had made-to-order departments for the middle-class woman whose new-found leisure time afforded her the pleasure of shopping.

The arts and motifs of Japan and China had a profound impact on Europe from the second half of the 19th century. Designer jewelry started to make an appearance during the 1860s, including this enameled piece created by the Paris jeweler Falize. The firm used Japanese prints as a source of inspiration, and Hokusai's *Manga*, an encyclopaedic collection of images illustrating every aspect of Japanese life.

The Singer sewing machine, introduced in 1851, was not altogether an instrument of liberation. Ready-made clothes had started to be produced in London's East End and in the manufacturing areas of other cities, which extended the exploitation of factory workers into sweatshops. The Singer had been intended for domestic use, but poorly paid seamstresses worked long into the night in their homes, sewing piecework to make ends meet.

The beautiful Empress Eugénie sparked a new craze among the wealthy and socially aspiring for the cage crinoline. She favored the creations of Charles Frederick Worth and her patronage afforded him unprecedented influence over women's day and evening wear. Eugénie's excessive style of dress made her a fashion icon of the 19th-century *beau monde*, as her ill-fated role model, Marie Antoinette, had been a century earlier.

The Crinoline Cage 1850s–1860s

Instrument of liberation

The dress width of the 1850s was becoming problematic as women struggled under the weight of as many as six petticoats. While this prompted debate on the ridiculous aspect of fashion, women wavered between the retrospective move of taking up a hooped skirt support like the 16th-century farthingale and the possibility of achieving the desired silhouette with relative comfort. The first crinoline at the end of the 1830s had been made of horsehair, but it was not until 1856 that an American, W. S. Thomson, patented a metal cage structure for sale in the United States, Britain, and France.

> **"A visitor from Mars contemplating a man in a frock coat and top hat and a woman in a crinoline might well have supposed that they belonged to different species."**
>
> JAMES LAVER
> *THE CONCISE HISTORY OF COSTUME AND FASHION*, 1979

ELEMENTS OF FASHION

- *light, steel-hooped frame support*
- *pantaloons for modesty*
- *pagoda sleeves with "engageante" undersleeves*
- *brighter colors*
- *black lace shawls*
- *brocaded and warp-printed silks*
- *porkpie hats*
- *braided and colored underskirts*
- *front-fastening jacket bodice with basques*

The desirable dome, ca. 1864
The crinoline cage proved such a revelation of liberation that its popularity grew among gentlewomen and working classes alike. The desire for a huge domed skirt was so widespread that it was unthinkable at that time to wear an unsupported skirt, despite the disapproval of some women, such as Florence Nightingale and even Queen Victoria. Skirts became less flounced as the width was already achieved with the cage, which made them even lighter.

Fashion first, ca. 1860s

It became a favorite among cartoonists to demonstrate the pitfalls of the crinoline fashion. In order to preserve modesty while out walking, because the swaying skirts could easily be caught by the wind, long linen or red flannel pantaloons were worn with colored or hooped stockings. Skirts could be looped up using an internal rigging device for walking or playing croquet, and decorative petticoats were worn underneath.

Steel cage, ca. 1860

The Bessemer steel process advocated using sprung steel or watch spring, resulting in a cage that was lighter and easier to move in, and Thomson's patent connected the hoops with tapes to ensure the desired dome shape. By 1859, there was enough steel wire being produced in Sheffield, England, to produce half a million crinolines a week. These cages were inexpensive enough for women of all social classes to buy.

Aniline-dyed silk, ca. 1858

Moiré, or watered silk, was particularly popular with older women because it reinforced an air of luxury in female dress at the time. The use of the fabric also contributed to the reduction of flounces on the skirt as it was too stiff for this purpose. In 1856, the first aniline dyes were available, which allowed for a brilliance of color, and dresses were made in startlingly bright hues.

Charles Worth 1825–1895

A Lincolnshire boy, Charles Worth was apprenticed at the age of 13 to the London firm of drapers Swan & Edgar. Here, he was first introduced to French fashion while unpacking the imported Paris styles. The young Worth also started to visit the National Gallery in London and found himself fascinated by the historical costumes depicted in its portraits. After a spell at Lewis & Allenby, silk mercers to Queen Victoria, Worth decided that Paris was the place to continue his career. In 1846, employed by Maison Gagelin-Opigez, a high-end silk mercer, he met a salesgirl, Marie Augustine Vernet, who was to become his wife. After a court train designed by Worth for the company won a first-class medal in the Exposition Universelle of 1855, Worth left Gagelin-Opigez to set up as a designer working under his own name. He joined forces with the wealthy Swede Otto Gustaf Bobergh, and the House of Worth & Bobergh opened at 7 Rue de la Paix in 1858.

Born
Bourne, Lincolnshire

Manifesto
To transform the "decoration of women" from a cottage industry into the world's first fashion empire

> **❝ ... when I meet ladies who know that dressing is an art, I take very great satisfaction in having them as patrons.❞**

CHARLES FREDERICK WORTH
HARPER'S BAZAAR, DECEMBER 1877

Marie Augustine Worth, aware of the strong influence that Empress Eugénie and her courtiers had on fashion in Paris, was determined to win their custom for her husband. Marie took some of Worth's designs to the wife of the Austrian ambassador to France, Pauline, Princess von Metternich. Knowing the mind of the fashion-conscious woman, Marie was sure that when Eugénie saw the princess in a Worth dress, she would be unable to resist asking its provenance. Her patronage guaranteed Worth a unique position as designer to the crowned head of state, who could decree the length of a hem on a whim.

While Worth may have found his creative abilities compromised by Eugénie's devotion to the crinoline, he dutifully produced ever grander outfits to suit her taste. Subsequently, he discovered that he held sway over other society women who desired a Worth dress. He was famously rude and arrogant and imposed his stylistic choices on his female client, instead of listening to her opinion.

The crinoline achieved its widest point in 1860 and then underwent various modifications as the volume shifted to the back, to form first the half crinoline and ultimately the bustle. Worth had attempted to outmode the crinoline in 1864 by introducing a skirt with a train that was lifted under the waist with horsehair padding, but in reality the shift in style took at least until the end of the decade.

Worth's collections always sought to attract the eye of the empress and so were of luxurious fabrics and romantic interpretations of historic dress, especially for the masquerades Eugénie was so fond of. However, his cut and fit were exemplary, and he had no want to distract the eye from this by excessive trimming.

As well as aristocracy, Worth gained celebrities of the time as his clients, including the stage actress Sarah Bernhardt and the soprano Nellie Melba. This set the scene for the fashion system of the 20th century as royal customers became less prominent.

Worth had already pioneered the practice of producing dresses with interchangeable bodices, and in the 1860s he introduced the tunic dress, a knee-length dress with a longer skirt underneath. Here, he was ahead of his time. The tunic dress did not become universal fashion until Paul Poiret's interpretation in the early 20th century. More acceptable was the innovation of the crinolinette, a shorter crinoline, which the active Empress Eugénie and her ladies-in-waiting adopted for walking and ice-skating in the Bois de Boulogne.

In 1870, the House of Worth was flourishing and the partnership with Bobergh was dissolved. Defying the effects of the Franco-Prussian War and the siege of Paris, and surviving Worth's death in 1895, the business expanded to London. Worth's sons, Gaston and Jean-Philippe, ensured that the company's influence and ingenuity were retained under their control. In 1910, Gaston Worth founded the Chambre Syndicale de la Haute Couture, which served to protect copyright and the industry's standards. Jean-Philippe followed the model of couture branding set by Chanel and launched Les Parfums Worth in 1924.

The Worth Dress 1858

The salon

While Napoleon and Josephine Bonaparte had favored Louis-Hippolyte Leroy as their tailor during the Second Empire, it was Charles Frederick Worth who was the chosen one during the reign of Napoleon III. Empress Eugénie became a valuable client and this status enabled Worth to dictate the terms of sale. The House of Worth was the first establishment of haute couture. Instead of a dressmaker coming to their homes, women visited the salon and dresses were made to measure for them with a series of fittings, initially on a muslin or linen toile. Worth became the first designer to produce seasonal collections that were then shown to clients, instead of working to request.

> **"Empress Eugénie did not bring ... all the aplomb and seriousness about little things which are early inculcated on ladies brought up to the profession of royalty."**
>
> ELIZABETH WORMELEY LATIMER, *FRANCE IN THE NINETEENTH CENTURY*, 1892

ELEMENTS OF FASHION

- *the changing shape of the skirt*
- *buttoned ankle boots*
- *shorter, front-fastened corsets*
- *circular capes*
- *gored skirts for greater fullness at the hem*

Followers of fashion, 1850s

Artist Franz Winterhalter (1806–1873) was a portrait painter for the aristocracy during the 19th century whose popularity grew during the Second Empire, when he became a favorite of Napoleon III and Empress Eugénie. Known as the "Painter of Princes," Winterhalter portrayed female royalty in a romantic light, paying such great attention to the fashions of the day that the off-the-shoulder crinoline is often associated with his name.

Taffeta

Robert Louis Stevenson (1850–1894) wrote "Auntie's Skirts," a poem about the rustling sound of a woman's dress, which appeared in his *Child's Garden of Verses*. Taffeta, the stiff, yarn-dyed fabric woven from silk, popular for its iridescent sheen, was responsible for the childhood memories from the 19th century of the mysterious rustling that followed ladies as they walked.

Mantelette, 1858

Toward the end of the 1850s the crinoline was a beehive shape with a tightly corseted and boned bodice. Ordinary coats could not be worn over this; instead a wide shawl or mantelette—a hybrid between a jacket and a shawl—was the usual outdoor wear. Bonnets were smaller and worn on the back of the head and the effect was of a triangular silhouette.

Crinoline, ca. 1862–1865

The crinoline became the sartorial symbol of the Second Empire. Empress Eugénie's preference for the style had set the fashion and the huge skirts and lavish, romantic trimmings echoed the material extravagance of the era. By 1865, fashion had begun to change and the central dome of the hoop had changed shape and had moved the volume to the back of the skirt, leaving the front straighter.

Court dress and train, ca. 1860–1865

Worth's couture system was an important part of the burgeoning fashion industry, but at this level it was still an exclusive business. Court dresses required trains and Worth's first achieved notice when a court train that he designed won a first-class medal at the Exposition Universelle of 1855. It was, however, the Russians and Americans who spent enough at the House of Worth to keep it financially successful.

CHRONOLOGICAL CATWALK
The Mid-19th-Century Female

The fashion-conscious woman

After the sewing machine was patented in 1846 by Isaac Singer, fashion reached beyond the realms of the rich, as middle-class women tried to emulate couture styles with their own dressmaking skills. In 1860, Samuel Beeton's *Englishwoman's Domestic Magazine* was selling women's paper dress patterns by mail order, and in 1863 Ebenezer Butterick did the same for menswear in the United States, expanding to dresses in 1866.

Exaggerated hourglass silhouette

The cut-across décolleté, pinched waist, and huge, swinging hooped skirts were coquettish in the extreme and an ultrafeminine contrast to the trim frock-coated gentleman. By the beginning of the 1860s, the crinoline had reached its most extreme width and her skirts made it impossible for a lady's escort to walk by her side. The top half of her body was simply unreachable that an extended fingertip was the only possibility for a decorous kiss.

Pantalettes

Another example of the odd ideas required by 19th-century decorum, pantalettes were a version of the pantaloons that were worn under the crinoline. Children's lace-trimmed pantaloons were an ostentatious mark of gentility, and in order to make these garments more affordable, pantalettes were devised, which were tubes of white linen fastened with garters just above the knee.

The bertha

Evening dresses were always décolleté and even children's dresses exposed the shoulders. A capelike trim called a bertha was often attached to the top of the dress and covered the top of the bust and upper arms. It was usually a flirtatiously decorative addition of lace and ribbon, but also served as a nod to modesty during the inconsistent Victorian era.

Fashion plate, 1860

The Englishwoman's Domestic Magazine, started by Samuel Beeton in 1852, was the first inexpensive magazine for middle-class women. It carried socially forward-thinking articles on domestic and other matters for women and from 1860 collaborated with the Paris magazine *Le Moniteur de la Mode* to publish color plates of Paris fashions with enthralling descriptions.

Dress decoration

The opening of Bon Marché in 1852 in Paris heralded the global advent of the department store, and by the 1860s women could buy an entire outfit under one roof. Ready-made clothes now became more freely available but were still made to last by changing the trimming for the latest fashions. Worth's designs sent customers to the notions department to try to replicate his ribbon embroidery for themselves.

Hairstyles

Fashionable ladies wore their hair in a low chignon in the early 1860s, often with side ringlets for evening. By the mid-1860s, the chignon had started to rise up the back of the head. The bonnet became smaller and worn farther back as this hairdressing change required, until the end of the decade, when bonnets had to be abandoned for hats.

Designer Jewelry 1860s–1870s

Items of ornament, objects of desire

The implementation of the haute-couture fashion system in the 1850s and 60s was indicative of the consumerist society established by the elite at this time. Accessories and other luxury items also became part of this, and designer jewelry houses were frequented by the international wealthy. After Prince Albert's death in 1861, Queen Victoria's extended mourning inspired the English fashion for jet, but 19th-century jewelry was typically ornate. The discovery of diamonds in South Africa, sapphires in Kashmir, opals in Australia, and gold in California made jewelry more affordable and the middle classes could buy semiprecious interpretations from the new department stores, while glass and paste were used for cheaper substitutes.

ELEMENTS OF FASHION

• *15-carat, 12-carat, and 9-carat gold introduced in 1854*

• *rose-cut, table-cut, and cushion-cut diamonds*

• *styles inspired by 19th-century archaeological findings*

• *machine-made jewelry introduced in 1850*

• *Kimberley diamond mine founded in South Africa in 1871 prompted a desire among the wealthy to buy diamonds*

• *"Language of flowers" matched by colored jewels to reveal a message*

▶ **Necklace, Alexis Falize, 1867**
Nineteenth-century jewelry often displayed topical themes. The Romantic period had a fascination with nature and symbols of Eden and in 1835 the appearance of Halley's Comet inspired jewelers. This necklace by French jeweler and goldsmith Alexis Falize is one of the pieces that he made under his own name after supplying Tiffany and Boucheron. It displays the interest in Orientalism generated by the succession of international exhibitions.

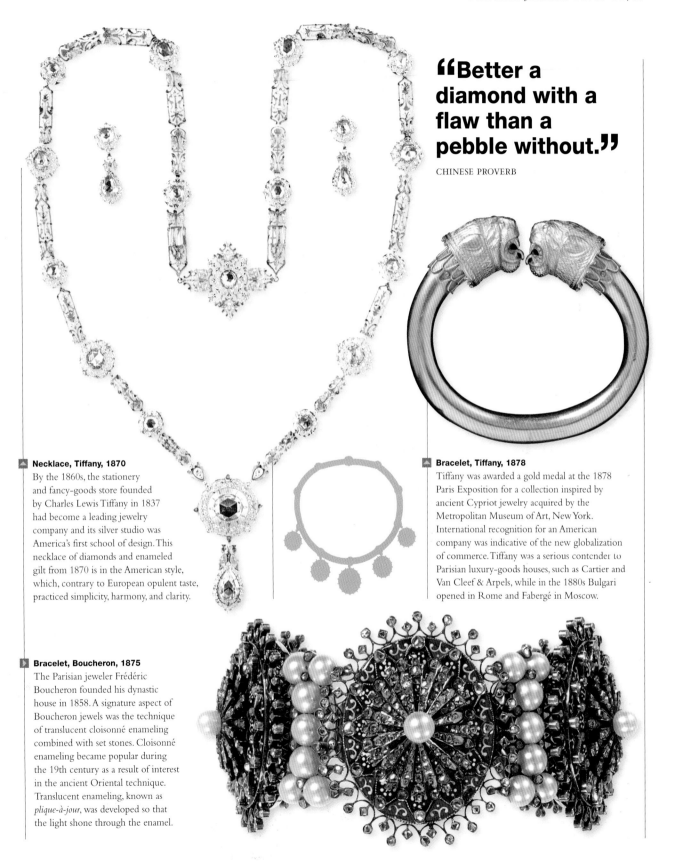

"Better a diamond with a flaw than a pebble without."

CHINESE PROVERB

Necklace, Tiffany, 1870
By the 1860s, the stationery
and fancy-goods store founded
by Charles Lewis Tiffany in 1837
had become a leading jewelry
company and its silver studio was
America's first school of design. This
necklace of diamonds and enameled
gilt from 1870 is in the American style,
which, contrary to European opulent taste,
practiced simplicity, harmony, and clarity.

Bracelet, Tiffany, 1878
Tiffany was awarded a gold medal at the 1878
Paris Exposition for a collection inspired by
ancient Cypriot jewelry acquired by the
Metropolitan Museum of Art, New York.
International recognition for an American
company was indicative of the new globalization
of commerce. Tiffany was a serious contender to
Parisian luxury-goods houses, such as Cartier and
Van Cleef & Arpels, while in the 1880s Bulgari
opened in Rome and Fabergé in Moscow.

Bracelet, Boucheron, 1875
The Parisian jeweler Frédéric
Boucheron founded his dynastic
house in 1858. A signature aspect of
Boucheron jewels was the technique
of translucent cloisonné enameling
combined with set stones. Cloisonné
enameling became popular during
the 19th century as a result of interest
in the ancient Oriental technique.
Translucent enameling, known as
plique-à-jour, was developed so that
the light shone through the enamel.

CHRONOLOGICAL CATWALK
The Mid-19th-Century Male

The rise of the ready-made

The introduction of the sewing machine brought a significant increase in the production of ready-made menswear. Brooks Brothers opened in New York in 1818, emphasizing the importance of the quality and fit of their suits. In England, ready-mades did not have the same reputation and menswear stores selling factory and cooperative-made clothing only increased after the fashion changed in the 1860s.

The Albert top frock

The more formal frock coat was still widely worn in the mid-19th century by gentlemen who preferred to patronize their tailors. In the 1860s, various tailored garments were named after Prince Albert, including the double-breasted frock coat, which became the accepted wear for business in Britain, Europe, and the United States, worn with either a bow tie or cravat.

The short coat

The short or sack coat had started as the garb of the working man who needed serviceable clothes and had neither the time nor money to visit a tailor. With improved ready-made clothing, the coat became finer and better fitting and was accepted as informal wear, worn as part of a suit with matching or contrasting pants, and suitable for morning wear and country or sporting pastimes.

Introduction of the suit, 1866

A group of Oxford students posed for this photograph. Before the mid-19th century, it was unusual to have coat, vest, and pants cut from the same cloth. The word suit comes from the French verb *suivre*, meaning "to follow," and in a literal sense, the pants follow the fabric from which the jacket is cut. A mid-19th century precursor to the lounge suit was the "ditto suit."

Informal silhouette

The silhouette became generally much more unstructured for men by the second half of the 19th century. The short coat would eventually become the lounge suit and was a recognizable modernization of menswear. The frock coat softened and became the "ditto suit" with matching pants and vest, a style particularly favored in the United States—Abraham Lincoln, for example, preferred the "ditto suit."

The Four-in-Hand tie

As the Industrial Revolution had changed the shape of the coat, a new tie was needed. Like the hat, this design came from working origins and the Four-in-Hand tie, so-called because it resembled the reins of a carriage, was adopted as a comfortable and easy alternative to the cravat, which did not suit the fashion of the informal short coat.

The billycock

The ubiquitous top hat was also not appropriate for wearing with the lounge suit, as the short coat and pants came to be known. This increased the popularity of the derby or bowler, also known as the billycock. The billycock appeared in brown, white, and gray as well as black and became the everyday staple as the suit was more widely adopted.

Japonisme 1860s–1870s

Eastern art and design

Prince Albert's brainchild, the 1851 Great Exhibition, started an exchange in innovation and international trade that was continued with the international exhibitions of the 19th century. These events acted as catalysts for the broadening of collective European horizons and a growing interest in Eastern cultures, which led to the study of Eastern art by Western architects, artists, and designers. The 1867 Paris International Exhibition established the Oriental influence on fashion. To meet the interest, Japan started to export handcrafted japonaiserie, made specifically for the European market, and in 1878 the English industrial designer Christopher Dresser was invited by the Japanese government to travel to Japan to advise on their art industries.

Oriental influence, 1864
Japanese art and design were key influences in the 19th-century Aesthetic art movement of which James Abbott McNeill Whistler (1834–1903) was a leader. Many of his paintings from the mid-century period reveal this interest. In his 1864 *Caprice in Purple and Gold*, his mistress, seated before a folding screen, wears a kimono. Artists of this movement were also involved in textile design, often using Asian motifs.

ELEMENTS OF FASHION

- origin of 19th-century fashion for cloisonné enamel
- fans used in dress and as wall decoration
- decorative symbolism found in kimono patterns
- satsuma ceramic buttons
- embroidered silk
- Oriental screens for dressing

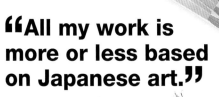

"All my work is more or less based on Japanese art."

VINCENT VAN GOGH
1888

Boudoir attire, ca. 1850–1880
In 1853, the U.S. Navy put pressure on Japan to open her ports to the West. This prompted an attempt to Westernize life in Japan to contend with her aggressors. For the first time, the T-shaped garment was termed a "kimono" to differentiate it from Western clothes. Exports of kimonos to Japanese-crazed Westerners ensued, who saw them as boudoir attire, whereas in Japan they were integral to the cultural propriety.

Bamboo and silk leaf fan, ca. 1850–1870
The traditional folding fans called "*ogi*" fans in Japan were extremely popular in the West in the 1860s and were a more affordable way of adding a touch of japonisme to an outfit. The fans were often printed in the "*ukiyo e*" woodblock style, but European artists also started to experiment with painting on the folding sections. Original Japanese fans, with carved and inset ivory guards, became collectors' items.

Kimono silk, ca. 1860s–1870s
The kimono is constructed from a single bolt of cloth. Everyday cloth could be woven on home looms in Japan, but the more elaborate silks were the heart of the Japanese textile industry, which was run by men from speciality workshops for weaving, dyeing, and embroidering and centered around large drapery stores. The symbolism on this red silk crepe fabric illustrates a traditional folktale of dragons that live in the mountains.

The Belle
Epoque

Introduction

The period that saw the transition from the end of the old century to the beginning of the new was one where the observer of fashion can pinpoint the start of the modernization of dress. This is particularly true of womenswear, and not only do the changing styles start to resemble the recognizable shapes of contemporary fashion, but they also chart the journey of the woman's quest for social equality.

From 1870 to the early 1900s, the silhouette changed from the first bustle, which echoed the shapes made by the 18th-century panniered skirts, to the longer, tighter skirts with a train, and on to the exaggerated S-bend corset and monobosom that supported a wealth of trimmings.

It is not in the history of haute-couture gowns, however, that the dawning of emancipation from woman as chattel is apparent; rather in the masculine tweed suits adopted by the middle-class women who had started to earn their keep as governesses, sales girls, and typists. The tailor-made was requisitioned by this new workforce from the *tailleurs* worn by upper-class women for traveling and country pursuits, and was indicative of a paradigm shift that released women from the home.

Leisure activities, which had previously been the privilege of the upper social echelons, became more universal as the women who had been the children of the newly established middle class grew up. These offspring of the newly socially elevated had expectations of their world and embraced a lifestyle that permitted education, sports, and fun. Clothing had to fall into step.

The taste for decadence

High society, meanwhile, was dictating decadence. Edward VII had succeeded to the English throne in 1901, a playboy whose world was a social calendar of excess. Conspicuous consumption was a prerequisite in a society that revolved around the appetite and rejected moderation.

The corseted hourglass figure, much admired and appreciated by Edward, was the feminine ideal, and the lavishness of a woman's dress was a

display of wealth. Belle Epoque Paris was fueled by champagne and licentiousness—the underwear of noblewomen was as decorated as that of the capital's prostitutes and as frilly as the can-can girls' at the Moulin Rouge.

In 1892, the magazine *Vogue* was launched in New York, in time to see the waistline rise into the directoire line during the early 20th century, and women begin to stand straight and tall. Then, by the second decade, a wave of artistic

exploration in Europe guided fashion from flaunting opulence to expressing new ideas of exoticism, modernism, and decoration.

By the end of the 19th century, fashion extended to a much wider social range. The fashion-conscious, middle-class woman, whether employing a dressmaker or making her own clothes, could buy publications, such as the American Butterick's *Ladies' Quarterly of Broadway Fashions*, study the new styles, and mail order the corresponding paper patterns, which were also catalogued in the magazine.

The Bustle 1870–1885

From horsehair padding to steel contraption

Throughout the late 19th century the female form continued to be shaped by wire or padding. By the end of the 1860s, the short-waisted bodice became longer and the basque of the jacket bodice lengthened and was worn over an overskirt that was looped up at the back. This was known as the cuirass bodice. The polonaise bodice was also popular, an adaptation of 18th-century dress, which extended out from the waist to the knee and was worn over an underskirt. A colorful striped or printed cotton version was the "Dolly Varden," named after a character in Charles Dickens's *Barnaby Rudge*, set in 1780, and worn with a shepherdess-style straw hat.

The crinolinette, ca. 1870

As the exaggeration of the skirt moved toward the back, the dress required a different kind of support. The half crinoline, or crinolinette, was a petticoat that was straight at the front and still hooped at the back, sometimes with a series of horsehair pads just under the waist to support the looped-up skirt. Fifteen years previously, the cage crinoline had freed women from a similar burden.

French fashion plate, 1873

Although Paris fashion plates had been a point of reference for English ladies for a century, haute couture reinforced the accepted authority. The last quarter of the 19th century saw a big increase in couturiers opening salons. One of these, the House of Doucet, became a favorite of actresses for the romantic double-skirted costumes inspired by 17th- and 18th-century, opulent-era paintings in pastel lingerie colors.

The bustle pad, ca. 1875
By the 1870s the crinolinette had become the bustle, which was a separate undergarment in its own right. It was referred to in fashion journals either by the French term "*tournure*" or as a "dress improver." The back of the double skirt was draped over the top of the bustle, which was either of horsehair or cotton eiderdown construction filled with down and secured with tapes.

"My trousseau cost more than my sister and I had ever spent in all our lives put together."

ALEXANDRA OF DENMARK, ON HER MARRIAGE TO EDWARD VII, 1863

The new phantom, 1884
As with the crinoline, the bustle underwent two incarnations. After the early 1870s, the Grecian bend, with the long corset throwing the bust forward and the hips backward, narrowed into a slimmer line at the end of the decade. The mid-1880s bend boasted a rigid projection, and "scientific" folding frame, known as the "new phantom," was conceived as support. Like the earlier crinoline cage, the frame was also perceived to be better for its wearer's health.

Alexandra wearing the Princess line, 1870s
The alternative to the separate bodice and skirt was the princess line, a one-piece dress cut without a waist seam, but with vertical seams to emphasize the line and fitted over the bustle. It was said to have been invented by Worth for Princess Alexandra—although the Princess robe first appeared in the 1840s, it was not adopted by fashion until thirty years later.

ELEMENTS OF FASHION

- high heels

- dresses cut in two different, brightly colored patterns

- tiny hats, perched on top of enormous chignons of curls

- false hair pads called "scalpettes"

- the "Jersey dress"— a knitted costume popularized by British actress Lily Langtry

Rational Dress 1880s–1890s

Artistic and aesthetic dress

While the late 19th century was a time of excess and exuberance, there were those aligned to the alternative arts movement who wanted to express their aversion to the contemporary commercialism. One of these, the aesthetic movement, a group of artists and writers who developed the "cult of beauty," was satirized over its attempts to manifest its ideas in dress. Modern fashion was seen as ugly, vulgar, and restrictive. Artistic beauty should be incorporated into everyday life as sensual pleasure. The Pre-Raphaelites wanted to revive traditional crafts from before the Industrial Revolution and believed that art should be functional. Both groups agreed on the rejection of the corset.

ELEMENTS OF FASHION

• underwear weighing no more than seven pounds

• art-needlework embroidery

• Renaissance slashed sleeves

• Oscar Wilde's aesthete's costume of velvet knickerbocker suit

• wideawake hat and floppy bow tie for men

Artistic dress, 1880

Dante Gabriel Rossetti and William Morris were two of the original members of the Pre-Raphaelite Brotherhood, from which the aesthetic movement developed. *The Daydream* (1880) by Rossetti, for which Morris' wife, Jane, was the model, demonstrates their interest in medievalism. Women associated with the group adopted the loose, flowing gowns based on dress depicted in art of the Middle Ages. Artistic dress represented natural purity and craftsmanship.

"Have nothing in your house that you do not know to be useful, or believe to be beautiful."

WILLIAM MORRIS DICTUM, 1882

Peacock-feather motif, 1887
The Silver Studio was a commercial textile design studio founded in 1880 by Arthur Silver in west London. It became well known for its art nouveau fabrics and wallpapers, popular throughout Europe and in the United States. It was also commissioned regularly by Liberty & Co., and some of this London department store's most recognizable house textiles were products of Silver Studio design, including the iconic peacock pattern.

Silver waist clasp set with opal, Oliver Baker, 1899
Liberty made the handcrafted decorative arts fashionable in London and, in the 1890s, Arthur Lasenby Liberty started importing silver and pewter and employing metalworkers, such as Oliver Baker, to design the Cymric jewelry line that launched in 1899. This was opposed by arts and crafts stalwarts, such as C. R. Ashbee, founder of the Guild of Handicraft in 1888, for being machine-made. Baker had formerly worked for Ashbee.

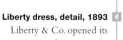

Liberty dress, detail, 1893
Liberty & Co. opened its costume department in 1884. Its director, Edward William Godwin, was in agreement with Morris's arts and crafts dictum and the store's in-house clothing challenged Paris fashions. Natural dyes, rather than aniline, were used and clothing was decorated with embroidery in the art needlework style. Smocking was an example of a handcraft whose beauty had a purpose—to create shape in a garment.

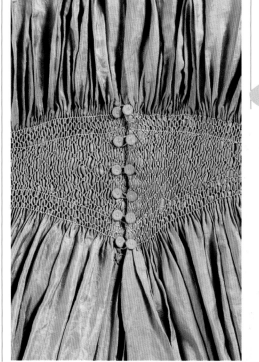

The health corset, 1890s
Although advocates of rational dress had largely been dismissed as eccentrics since Amelia Bloomer, dress reform was becoming less of a minority practice as the century closed. In 1884, the first shop selling Dr. Jaeger's Sanitary Woolen System opened in London, promoting the health benefits of wool worn next to the skin. The so-called health corset, which was reinforced with cording, was sold as an alternative to the boned corset.

The Active Woman 1890s–1900s

The Gibson girl

The Gibson girl character was created by the graphic artist Charles Dana Gibson and appeared in his illustrations from 1890 until 1910. A representation of the free-spirited, active young American woman, she was depicted as attractively modern—tall, poised, with hair piled high, and lithe curves under a crisp blouse. L. M. Montgomery wrote *Anne of Green Gables* with a picture of Evelyn Nesbit, one of Gibson's models, pinned to her wall. Gibson's girl gripped a generation and was used to market clothing, including corsets, and a myriad of household wares.

> **❝It would give me such a thrill, Marilla, just to wear a dress with puffed sleeves ... I'd rather look ridiculous when everyone else does, than plain and sensible all by myself.❞**

L. M. MONTGOMERY
ANNE OF GREEN GABLES, 1908

▶ Modest emancipation, 1898

Advertisements depicting stylized illustrations of women enjoying outdoor pursuits after the Gibson girl model inferred exuberance, but women were still expected to be covered from head to toe. Leisurewear, based on the lines of tailored menswear, consisted of tweed jacket, bell-shaped skirt, and a shirtwaist, or masculine-cut blouse, often with a collar and tie, topped off with a straw boater.

▶ The Gaiety girl, 1895

In the same way that the Gibson girl personified youthful exhilaration for the American woman, in England the Gaiety girl, a character in a musical comedy show, was the popularized notion of young, fun, but respectable beauty. In the 1890s, musical comedies were a way for couturiers to showcase their clothes and the elevated chorus line wore the latest fashions, including bathing attire.

The hourglass ideal, ca. 1906

Belgian-born actress Camille Clifford first achieved fame when she won a magazine contest to find Gibson the perfect hourglass embodiment of his "girl." Clifford modeled for Gibson and then debuted on the stage as the ideal combination of vivacity, luminous skin, sparkling eyes, luxuriant hair, heavy bust, tiny waist, and swirling skirts that was the feminine personification of the spirit of the age.

Sportswear, 1890s

Bicycling became all the rage during this period, and the now openly active woman embraced the pastime as well as golf, lacrosse, hockey, and tennis. The rational dress movement had prompted various developments in sporting costume for women by the 1890s, including wider flared skirts, which facilitated movement and belted blouses with huge puffed sleeves. Eventually, bloomers became appropriate attire for the young lady bicyclist.

ELEMENTS OF FASHION

- *leg-of-mutton sleeves*
- *A-line skirts*
- *wasp waists*
- *tunic bathing costumes with sailor collars, worn over long panties*

The Empire typewriter, 1897

The image of the Gibson girl became a role model for young women striving to embrace their new emancipation while retaining femininity and elegance. As opportunities opened for women in the workplace and colleges, plainer dresses, tailor-made clothes, and chesterfield coats were incorporated into everyday wear as a practical, more professional alternative to the ornate fashions and confining capes and cloaks of the era.

The S-Bend Corset 1890s–1900s

Excess and extravagance

The corset was the subject of a division of opinion in fashion by the end of the 19th century, but the artistic community, although exercising considerable stylistic influence with art nouveau and Orientalism, was no match for frivolity. During the belle epoque, or Gilded Age in the United States, the rich enjoyed extreme luxury and the symbol of this life of privileged excess was the S-bend corset. The S-bend was originally conceived as a health corset, to take pressure off the abdomen by throwing the bust forward and the hips back, but became the framework for the ornate fashions of the late 1890s and 1900s.

"Fabiola," day dress, Jeanne Paquin, 1903
The decadent age was mirrored in the sexually suggestive lines of the S-bend, which emphasized the female line in primitive caricature. This design by Jeanne Paquin, who opened her house in 1891, shows how couture glamorized this silhouette with a tiny waist and lavish volume in the sleeves and hem. As the excesses of society grew, so did the enormous and heavily decorated hats and hairstyles.

Edward VII and the Cornwallis family, 1897
The Edwardian lady was stately, and deportment—aided by corsetry and high, featherboned collars, numerous petticoats, and dancing lessons—was a mark of good breeding. Society had widened, however, with Edward enjoying the company of Jewish and South African millionaires, actresses, and American heiresses as much as aristocracy. Money mattered almost as much as nobility, and skirts with a train indicated wealth and servants.

"The wise woman with a limited dress allowance will invest a great deal of it in underwear."

MRS. ERIC PRITCHARD
THE CULT OF CHIFFON, 1902

Visiting gown, Lucile, 1905
Convention expected the wealthy upper-class woman to change her clothing for every event of the day. Her wardrobe required tweeds, blouses, day dresses, tea gowns, outfits for different leisure activities, including motoring coats and veils, evening gowns, and ball gowns.
Lady Duff-Gordon opened Maison Lucile in London in 1894, later expanding to Paris and New York, due to her success in supplying the requirements of her fashionable clientele.

Tea gown, House of Rouff, 1898
Lace was an important part of the Edwardian wardrobe and trimmed both day and eveningwear. For mid-afternoon, a tea gown, or *peignoir*, was worn to receive guests. It was loose, flowing, and extremely feminine, usually liberally trimmed with lace or the more affordable Irish crochet. The lingerie aspect of the tea gown, which was often worn uncorseted, created an atmosphere of daring intrigue in the afternoon.

ELEMENTS OF FASHION

• *sweet pea shades in chiffon, mousseline de soie, and tulle*

• *feather boas*

• *high, boned collars for day*

• *a plunging, off-the-shoulder décolleté for evening*

• *long kid gloves*

• *parasols*

• *frilled underwear and petticoats trimmed with lace*

"A Protest," evening gown, Lucile, 1905
By the early 20th century, the suffragette movement was actively demanding votes for women. The core activists were mainly middle-class women, who were likely to be photographed in tailor-mades. The suffragette colors—purple, white, and green—did infiltrate high fashion. In 1908 London, the high-class jewelers Mappin & Webb issued a catalog of Christmas jewelry in the suffragette shades. Lucile's evening dress with its typically extreme décolleté was for a socially mobile sympathizer of the cause.

CHRONOLOGICAL CATWALK
The Belle-Epoque Male

The casual wardrobe

The popularity of new leisure pastimes initiated wardrobe development in menswear much more than the vagaries of fashion. Driving in an open automobile required weatherproofed coats; swimming precipitated the streamlining of swimwear; while boating led to lighter, less formal clothing. Messing about on the river, in the style of *Three Men in a Boat* (1889) or *Wind in the Willows* (1908), became a casual-wear opportunity for the raffish young man.

Boater
The Edwardian era saw an increase in fashionable styles of hats for men. Edward VII popularized the homburg as an alternative to the derby. The boater was a straw summer hat, originally part of the rowing outfit, but soon became as ubiquitous as the derby.

The casual silhouette
By the beginning of the 20th century, social distinction in menswear was becoming less easy to distinguish. The more leisured classes still wore high, stiff collars, while the boater hat and the blazer were an indication of youthful sportiness. Leisure activities, such as boating, still required buttoned-up coverage from the collar down, although tennis and sailing enthusiasts daringly removed their jackets and even rolled up their sleeves.

Striped blazer
The boating jackets of members of the Lady Margaret Boat Club at St. John's College, Cambridge, in England, were originally called "blazers" because of their bright red color. Gaily striped blazers were subsequently worn in the colors of boat, tennis, or cricket clubs, and the blazer and boater combination was widely adopted as a casual summer style.

Teatime at the Cambridge Mays, **P. R. Craft, ca. 1905**
The "May Bumps," popular races held between the Cambridge colleges, and an annual event from the early 19th century, have long offered an opportunity for spectators to don their most festive casual clothes.

Flannels

Casual white flannels provided the hallmark of the Edwardian male's sporting look. Worn for cricket, boating, tennis, or simply promenading on the sands, loose-fitting flannels were an important prop to the socially mobile young man in pursuit of leisure and were not only lighter and more practical to wear but also broadcast a certain ease of pocket.

Brown shoes

The laced shoe had become popular by the 1900s. First worn for sport, travel, or for summer casual wear, laced shoes gradually replaced the buttoned boot. At the end of the 19th century, shoes became narrow and pointed, but the mass-produced, more comfortable "American model" with a rounded toe took over, and brown or white styles were worn for both sporting and country pursuits.

Paul Poiret 1879–1944

The history of fashion would not have taken the same course in the 20th century had it not been for Paul Poiret. Poiret's innovative skills were great and he was equally adept at harnessing the prevailing mood and self-promotion.

Born in Paris in 1879, Poiret's father was a cloth merchant and apprenticed his son to an umbrella maker when in his teens. Poiret had an interest in fashion from an early age, sketching designs and making dresses for his sister's dolls from scraps of umbrella silk. Such was his confidence that he went to see Madeleine Cheruit at the house of Raudnitz Sœurs, who was persuaded to buy some of his sketches. This launched a career as a freelance designer for many of the *grands couturiers* and in 1896 Poiret went to work at Maison Doucet. There he learned how to cut and drape, developing his own style, which departed from traditional tailoring methods. He emulated Jacques Doucet's personal style as a man of sophistication and elegance and took his advice to absorb the ways of the social elite, dressing in English suits and attending fashionable parties.

After military service, Poiret went to work for Worth, but his modern ideas were too *outré* for their clientele and in 1904 the young designer set up in business under his own name. Doucet

Born
Paris, 1879

Manifesto
To equate high fashion with the arts.

proved to be a valuable friend, and he recommended Poiret to the successful actress Réjane, who became his patron.

In 1905, Poiret married Denise Boulet, a slender 19 year old whose physique was dramatically different from the Edwardian buxom ideal. Denise became her husband's muse and the shape of his designs began to change to favor her figure. By 1906, Poiret was cutting softer dresses with a looser waistline. Madeleine Vionnet was also claiming responsibility for abolishing the corset at this time, and Isadora Duncan was causing a sensation in her Fortuny tunics, but it was Poiret who ensured that his designs received the attention and acknowledgment for this radical departure.

In 1908, Poiret pioneered the idea of publishing a booklet of his designs, beautifully illustrated by Paul Iribe, which aided his position as the most celebrated couturier in Paris. He hosted lavish fancy dress *soirées* at his L'Oasis club, which became so popular that when he launched the lamp-shade tunic for his wife to wear at his Persian Thousand and Two Nights party in 1911, guests who had not complied with the Eastern-style dress code donned outfits that Poiret provided instead of risking being turned away. Publishing a second

"I am an artist, not a dressmaker."

PAUL POIRET

booklet illustrated by Georges Lepape, Poiret denied that he was influenced by Bakst's Eastern-inspired costumes for the Ballets Russes, although interest in the exotic was clearly in the air.

Poiret's confidence was turning to arrogance and when he launched the hobble skirt, the publicity backlash was extreme—criticism from fashion's detractors, excitement from its observers.

In the next few years, Poiret launched a perfume, Rosine, named after his daughter; toured Europe with his collection and mannequins; launched Atelier Martine, named after another daughter, in which to train young girls to work along the lines of the Wiener Werkstätte; and toured the United States. He became concerned about protecting his designs while in the country, and on his return persuaded other couturiers to join the Syndicat de Défense de la Grande Couture Française to protect copyright.

The outbreak of war forced closure on Poiret and he never regained his former hold on the fashion world, which was soon under the spell of the simplicity of Chanel. Poiret's predilection for exotic decoration with feathers and jewels, strongly colored silks, harem pants and feathered halter necklines had translated the zeitgeist into wearable art, but his theatricality fell out of time.

Poiret's lasting legacy was to understand the necessary combination of commercialism and creativity that makes a fashion business successful. His demise demonstrated the ephemeral nature of such a quality within the capricious confines of fashion.

In 1929, Denise divorced the bankrupt Poiret. She did, however, preserve the clothes that he had made in an archive, and documented his other achievements in interiors and decorative arts. As Denise wore Poiret's most extreme designs, the pioneering prototypes have survived the decline of their creator and his eventual death in obscurity in 1944.

Paul Iribe had illustrated the original 1908 booklet, *Les Robes de Paul Poiret*, to promote Poiret's designs. Iribe's *pochoir* style not only became associated with Poiret, but brought the artist to the attention of the fashion world. He also worked with Coco Chanel, the Callot Sœurs, Jacques Doucet, Jeanne Lanvin, and Madame Paquin. Iribe had graduated from the Ecole des Beaux Arts with Georges Lepape and Georges Barbier, when the art and fashion worlds were enjoying a mutual relationship in Paris, and he established a studio producing designs for textiles and applied arts.

The Lamp-Shade Tunic 1908–1914

A fundamental change in fashion

At the beginning of the 20th century, artists, writers, and designers were drawn to and inspired by Paris. The city exuded an air of artistic freedom and possibility that encouraged and embraced innovation. The arrival of the Ballets Russes from St. Petersburg in 1909 inspired a wave of daring experimentation as the new form of dance, music, and costume, and set design excited and amazed Paris. Couturiers were quick to respond to the Russian avant-garde, with Paul Poiret at the helm. The richness of color, outlandish decoration, and exotic cut were interpreted in a fundamental change in fashion that banished the stiffly corseted Edwardian figure.

Costume design, Léon Bakst, 1911
Serge Diaghilev and Léon Bakst were members of the Pickwickians, a group of Russian artists and writers who had worked together since the 1890s to advance Russian art, inspired by the art nouveau movement in Western Europe. As artistic director of Diaghilev's Ballets Russes, Bakst inspired a wave of Eastern influence with his costume designs and scenery for a production of *Scheherazade* in Paris in 1910.

Lamp-shade tunic, Paul Poiret, 1912
Poiret's innovative designs in the early 20th century contributed to the mood of fashion at that time. Inspired by costume designer Léon Bakst's Eastern-inspired designs based on the garb of harem slaves, in 1913 Poiret produced an exotic collection that included turbans, harem pants, and the lamp-shade tunic, which was wired to stand out around the wearer. Russian-born Bakst's richly decorated designs also popularized the ubiquitous fur trim.

"Etonne-moi!" (Astonish me!)

SERGE DIAGHILEV TO JEAN COCTEAU, 1909

ELEMENTS OF FASHION

• *bold use of color*

• *soft, loosely draped shapes*

• *button trimming*

• *overtunics*

• *small, closely fitting hats*

• *kimono coats*

• *harem pants, worn under the skirt*

Repeat pattern on silk, Wiener Werkstätte, *ca.* 1910–20
The Wiener Werkstätte was a workshop that was opened in Austria in 1903 by a community of visual artists with the aim to "make all facets of human life into one unified work of art." By 1905, their output included hand-painted and printed silks. Although the ethos of the group emulated William Morris's arts and crafts movement, the typically geometric print styles of the textile design anticipated modernism.

Delphos gown,
Mario Fortuny, 1912
In the late 19th century, the Spanish painter Mario Fortuny began to work with textiles while studying Italian Renaissance art in Venice. In 1909, he patented his unique way of pleating fabric, which was used to make his Delphos gown; to this day the process remains a secret. The dresses, dyed with vegetable dyes and weighted with Murano glass beads, became a signature costume of the avant-garde dancer Isadora Duncan.

CHRONOLOGICAL CATWALK
The New-Century Female

The directoire gown

By the end of the first decade of the new century, an idealized version of the "*merveilleuse*" dresses of the 1790s were on show at the Paris Longchamp racecourse. These dresses developed into the new Empire line, also known as "Directoire" gown, which was a radical change from the heavily corseted waistline. The early 20th-century Directoire line, however, was not the pristine white purity of earlier incarnations, but a far more exotic interpretation in terms of color and pattern.

Diadem
Hair began to be styled closer to the head, instead of the large puffs and rolls of hair that had earlier supported hats the size of serving trays. For evening wear, the most fashionable headdress was the diadem, an Eastern-inspired tiara, which was often made further arresting by the addition of an aigrette of osprey feathers that stuck straight up from the center of the forehead.

V neck
The V neck was a radical departure as fashion had dictated that the neckline be covered up to the ears during the day for the last two decades. It had been seen as indecent to display a triangular area of flesh beyond the collarbone, although the Edwardian evening décolleté had been extremely deep. The V neck blouse was called the "pneumonia blouse."

The tunic silhouette
A loosened-blouse effect in the top half of the dress softened over the bust and was often exaggerated with billowing tunic shapes, then narrowed to the tubular skirt from above the knees to the feet. The waistline was raised and cinched to give the effect of long, slim legs although the extremities were still considered indecent and coverage extended to well past the ankles.

Sash
The sash emphasizes the raised waistline of the Directoire line. Lucile was one of several couturiers to embrace the Eastern influence in their fashions and produced exotic creations from flowing silks that seemed free of the oppressive corsetry of the previous decade. In fact, although the waist was not cinched, many women had to wear a longer corset to achieve the slimline effect the Directoire required.

Shoes
Heels that had been high in the 1890s were now lowered as the hobble skirt required less demanding footwear. There was an obsession with narrow, petite feet, and, somewhat like Chinese foot binding, some women wore shoes a size too small in which to take their tiny steps. Pumps with Louis heels were popular for day, cut lower on the toe for evening, and fastened with straps for dancing.

Fashionable dress, Lucile, ca. 1910

Gamela, one of the favorite models at
Lady Duff-Gordon's fashion house Lucile,
is shown wearing a dress of the exaggerated
Directoire line, which first metamorphosed
into an inverted cone shape and ultimately
culminated in the hobble skirt. This was
a momentary hiccup in the history of
emancipation, because the original idea
had actually done much for dress reform.
The narrow skirts could only be worn
with one petticoat underneath, instead
of the former multiple skirts and boned
corsetry that were much heavier and
more cumbersome.

Silks, 1910s

Exoticism in fashion was expressed not
only in cut and decoration, but in the
choice of fabric. Silk was popular for its
shimmering properties, ability to drape,
and obvious Arabian Nights connotations.
Gauzy fabrics were used for harem styles
over vivid colors, Eastern-influenced print,
and embroidery. Designers, such as Jacques
Doucet, superimposed shades to try to
recreate impressionist techniques in fabric.

The Hobble Skirt 1910–1914

The exotic shackle

Already known as the maverick of fashion, Paul Poiret's hobble skirt caused an outcry in 1911. Skirts had been narrowing since the turn of the century, but Poiret's interpretation of the trend was sensational. The line of these dresses seemed dramatically unstructured after the curves of the Gibson girl. The draped silhouette fell from a soft bustline and narrowed severely between the knees and ankles, which restricted the wearer to geisha-like minute steps. This was very in tune with the notions of the East that interested Poiret, with the woman as an exotic and glamorous courtesan. As the haunts of the fashionable elite, couturiers sent their mannequins to the Paris racecourses to show their latest fettering creations.

ELEMENTS OF FASHION

- the high-busted Directoire line
- fur stoles and muffs
- cocoon-shape coats
- spats and gaiters
- shorter, curled hair

A fashion for satire, 1911
The hobble skirt was the subject of much public debate, from gentle satirization to papal condemnation. Cartoonists found much humor to be derived from the new fashion, particularly when worn with the huge hats and high, stiff collars, which were even more exaggerated than Edwardian styles. The style was also seen as erotic, with women rendered helpless by their clothing.

Hobble dress, Lucile, ca. 1910
Haute couture was one business that was not dominated by men. As well as Worth, Poiret, and Doucet, there was room for the Callot Sœurs, Madeleine Cheruit, Jeanne Lanvin, and Madame Paquin. Lucile was the originator of the first fashion shows using live models in her salons, although as this photograph shows, her designs were just as limiting to female emancipation as those of Poiret.

"The Hobble Skirt: What's that? It's the speed-limit skirt!"

CAPTION ON A HUMOROUS POSTCARD, 1911

Hobble skirt, Léon Bakst, 1912

The introduction of the tight skirt was at odds with women becoming more active—the suffragette protests were at their height, but the fashionable woman could only take a step of a couple of inches. The effect of encasement was heightened by the collar and long, tight kid gloves that were worn under close-fitting sleeves. Skirts started to be designed with splits, concealed pleating, and artful draping for ease of movement.

Tango dress, Jacques Doucet, 1914

The tango from South America became a huge craze that had a major effect on fashion—Paquin opened a branch in Buenos Aires. The tango dress, often of yellow or orange satin, was lighter and looser with a long central slit in the skirt. The dance moves eventually caused hemlines to rise and dresses were worn over pants, with a transparent overbodice. Tango slippers were fastened with ribbons that crossed from toe to ankle.

Hobble skirt, Jeanne Paquin, 1912

Fur trim was widely adopted after the Ballets Russes exerted an influence on Paris fashion to such an extent that, even in summer, fur bands were used to narrow the lower section of the skirt. Banded petticoats inside the skirt—or even hobble garters, which further fettered the legs—were also worn to prevent the wearer from taking strides that were too long and running the risk of stumbling or even tearing the fabric.

1914
1930

Art Deco &
the Roaring
Twenties

Introduction

World War I was a turning point in women's history and, therefore, in fashion history. Many couture houses closed or called on *Vogue* in New York to help the beleaguered industry in Europe, cut off from its American customers. *Vogue* showed Paris fashions at the Ritz Carlton Hotel in London in aid of war widows. Paul Poiret was called up and, on his return, he discovered that feminine dressing was undergoing radical change.

Vogue was launched in Britain on September 15, 1915, and over the ensuing five years would bear witness to the beginning of the broadening of the fashion system. Women of all classes started to have their own incomes, and mass production in the 1920s facilitated modes to suit all pockets.

Social convention had changed with the coming of age of the wartime generation. Women on both sides of the Atlantic gained the vote during the 1920s. Urbanization reached a climax and the economic boom and fast attitudes christened the decade the "Roaring Twenties."

The fast times of the Jazz Age precipitated a shift in Paris couture as giddy youth replaced elegance and decorum. Music, whether live or played on the ubiquitous gramophones and radiograms, provided a background to fashions for a new kind of woman: one who moved freely for the first time in generations and understood that it was obligatory to have fun.

The Jazz Age

The decade was also a time of Bohemian and artistic intellectualism. Gertrude Stein, F. Scott Fitzgerald, and Ernest Hemingway were part of the Lost Generation, a group of Americans who gathered in Paris after the Great War and mixed with those who frequented the Parisian salons—Cocteau, Picasso, Dufy, Colette, Delaunay. The

decadent Marchesa Luisa Casati was muse to the futurist Italian painter Fortunato Depero, whose compatriot Giacomo Balla designed the ground-breaking futurist suit. In England, the Bloomsbury group started the Omega Workshop and rejected distinction between fine art and decorative art.

The air of flouting conventions, perpetuated by the flappers, filtered down into general behavior so that such actions as applying makeup in public, smoking, and drinking became acceptable for women. These habits became fashion opportunities, and powder compacts, cigarette holders, and cocktail glasses all benefited from art deco design.

Paris *Vogue* launched in 1920, into a flat-chested fashion world where Coco Chanel would indelibly stamp her double-C logo. Legs covered by pajamas for sleeping, lounging, and the beach in 1922 would reach the hiatus of nudity in 1925 as skirts went up and stockings were rolled down, prompting denouncement by the Church in both Europe and the United States.

By 1927, however, the end of the decade was on the horizon. Cloth manufacturers were suffering from the new styles and hems became unevenly longer, using floating panels and trains as devices to get women used to covering their legs again. In 1929, Wall Street crashed.

Coco Chanel was queen of the new guard of couture. By creating designs for women who were not expected to sit still for hours on end, she imbued her clothing with her own spirit and had a hand in shaping the feminine ideal of the age. Chanel embraced modernity, and her long-term influence was instrumental in simplifying the fashionable wardrobe with daring informality.

The Tailor-Made 1914–1918

Fashion follows duty

When war broke out in Europe in 1914, for the first time women in Britain became indispensable in the workplace. For many, this was their first taste of practical clothing, and fashion needed to follow suit.

Women were required to fill places in factories, in fields, and on public transport. Industrial work dictated boiler suits, "Land Girls" wore breeches and puttees, and bus conductors wore ankle-length skirts with masculine-cut jackets with pockets. Long, tailored tunics were worn over skirts. Eventually, some women simply wore a longer tunic and discarded the skirt.

▽ **Jersey suits, Chanel, 1917**
Inspired by the cut and fabrics of menswear, and particularly by functional fabrics, Chanel began to design using jersey in 1916. As she was in the process of launching her business, Chanel was endeavoring to minimize her costs, and jersey was both affordable and suited the simple lines of her designs. This innovation was perfectly in tune with the new austerity and practicality dictated by the war.

❝To dress extravagantly in war time is worse than bad form. It is unpatriotic.❞

POSTER FOR THE WAR LOANS AND SAVINGS CAMPAIGN, BRITAIN, 1916

▲ **Uniformed nurses, early 20th century**
Warwork crossed the social divide—for some it offered freedom, for others a new spending power. However, out of uniform or the androgynous clothing required by farm or factory work, women craved fashion as much as ever and were determined to enjoy the new feminine lines. The riot of entertainment that was intended to distract from the atrocities of the front meant dressing for a full social life.

Barrel-line evening dress, ca. 1916/17

During the war, it became socially acceptable for women to be openly demonstrative toward their lovers, for whom leave was a precious glimpse of pleasure. The effect on fashion was the romantic "wartime crinoline"—a return to a feminine shape with neat waists, flared skirts, and raised hemlines. This silhouette appeared in 1915 and prevailed over both tailored day wear as well as evening wear. It was decried as wasteful and by 1917 it had developed into the barrel line, which curved in at the hem.

Tailored design with military detailing, Lucile, early 20th century

A surge of patriotism during the war years made its mark on haute couture. It was fashionable for women to be involved in some kind of war work, and even those who preferred charity work to driving an ambulance indulged in military pocket detailing on their smart tailleurs. Lucile was known for her romanticism—a suit styled on an officer's uniform did not escape her glamorous touch.

Lady's gabardine suit, England, 1919

The commandeering of the clothing industry by the British government prompted a vast improvement in machinery and manufacture. After the war, the Tailors and Garment Workers Union was formed and an attempt was made to produce National Standard Dress, a multipurpose garment that was intended to reduce the need for domestic production. Gabardine, a wool twill weave invented in 1888 by Thomas Burberry for outerwear, delivered the required practicality for women's dress during wartime.

ELEMENTS OF FASHION

- *bell-shaped skirts*
- *high uniform collars*
- *military-style hats*
- *bow ties*
- *high-laced boots*

Jeanne Lanvin 1867–1946

Born in Paris, the eldest of 11 children, at the age of 16 Jeanne Lanvin was apprenticed first to a milliner and then to a dressmaker in Paris and opened a millinery store in the Rue du Faubourg St.-Honoré in 1889.

In 1895, Lanvin married the Italian count Emilio di Pietro; two years on, their daughter Marguerite was born. Divorce from the count in 1903 forced Lanvin to rely on her business acumen, and when friends and clients started to remark upon the clothes that she made for her younger sister and later her daughter, she made copies to sell in her boutique. This progressed into creating styles for the mothers who bought the little dresses for their daughters. Lanvin became so successful that in 1909 her business joined the Syndicat de la Couture and mother-and-daughter ensembles became her trademark.

Lanvin's first contribution to haute couture was the *robe de style,* a prewar waisted, full-skirted design along 18th-century lines. It fitted exactly with the return to romantic femininity that women felt drawn to in the sentimental atmosphere prompted by the absence of husbands and lovers during World War I. The *robe de style* was so popular that it lasted until the 1920s as an alternative to the drop-waist designs. When war ended, Lanvin, then 51 years

Born
Paris, 1867

Manifesto
To maintain romanticism in women's clothing while independently establishing a successful business model.

old, did not feel that she had to contribute to the fashion expectations of the flappers and her *robe de style* developed into the "picture dress"—a romanticized, softened interpretation of Victoriana—and made full use of trimming, embroidery, and beading in country-garden colors that would become a Lanvin signature.

When the straight silhouette became a prerequisite of the fashionable gown, Lanvin dropped her waists and flared the skirts from the hips, retaining the romantic, floaty feel of her picture dresses. In the 1920s and 30s, she held sway over the nostalgia that existed alongside the chrome-plated age of the machine. Flamboyant, theatrical women loved Lanvin's insistence that the 1920s should not be completely dominated by the Jazz Age, and musical star Yvonne Printemps became an ambassador for her picture frock.

This is not to say that all Lanvin's ideas originated in the past—her creativity matched her dressmaking skills. Before the war, she had been the innovator of the chemise dress. Possibly inspired by the simplicity of the cut of Poiret's designs, the chemise dress was a forerunner of the square-cut silhouette of the 1920s and a strong influence for Chanel. The chemise had originally been a dress for a little girl, but was so

<blockquote>
"When I do not say anything that means that I approve!"

JEANNE LANVIN
</blockquote>

popular with the young that Lanvin had made full-size versions. This marked the onset of a polarization in couture. The up-and-down silhouette of the twenties dress was easy to make at home, and even financially assured young girls were less interested in the lavish creations of the *grands couturiers*—the simplicity of Chanel was the *dernier cri*.

Lanvin was also interested in the Eastern-influences of the prewar period and her evening wear was exotic: lavish velvet and silk creations remained her personal style in decades to come.

Blessed with a head for business, she steadily built House of Lanvin into a strongly established *maison*, appointing herself as innovator for the fashion system in the postwar era. In 1923, Lanvin had her own dye factory to produce her keynote floral colors. In 1924, she expanded into fragrance, and in 1926 instigated the first menswear boutique followed by interiors, fur, and lingerie stores. Lanvin's best-known perfume, Arpège, was inspired by the sound of her daughter practicing scales on the piano.

The romanticism of Lanvin can be seen in the swirling skirts that were a trademark of the house in the 1930s. Control of the company was bequeathed to her daughter Marguerite when Jeanne died in 1946, and the postwar "New Look" designs for Maison Lanvin were faithful to the tiny waist and full skirt of the original *robe de style*.

The Tennis Dress 1919–1929

Sportswear after the war

Sportswear was a significant factor in dress reform in the 20th century, and after World War I it progressed considerably following the success of French tennis player Suzanne Lenglen. The 1920s were marked by economic boom, consumerism, and leisure after the wartime austerity. Girls who had been raised during the socially liberating time of the war expected more equality as young women. They became more competitive in sports and needed clothing to adapt to their more strenuous activities. As the fashions of the decade developed, the slender *garçonne* silhouette required a certain amount of exercise to keep it trim and an appreciation of the body beautiful grew, revealing more than ever before.

Suzanne Lenglen, 1921
Suzanne Lenglen sought to rationalize clothing on court during her reign over the Wimbledon women's final from 1919 to 1926. Discarding both corset and petticoat, Lenglen replaced the established blouse, tie, and long skirt with her signature outfit, designed for her by Jean Patou. The bandeau she wore around her head in place of a hat was instantly copied.

Sportswear, Molyneux, 1924
The Lenglen effect was quickly seized upon by couturiers and widely emulated down the scale of the clothing trade. Short-sleeved, one-piece dresses, or sweaters and pleated skirts, were a breath of fresh air on the court and improved one's game considerably. Suzanne Lenglen, as a celebrity setter of style, conveyed a touch of glamor to tennis and her look was emulated both in sportswear and in mainstream fashion.

ELEMENTS OF FASHION

• *Le Coin des Sports, Jean Patou's sportswear boutique, opened in 1925*

• *"Norwegian suit" for winter sports with ankle-length woolen knickerbockers*

• *bathing rings worn around the neck to protect makeup from water damage*

• *cutaway, thigh-length bathing costumes*

• *gymnastics knickerbockers*

One-piece swimsuits, 1920s

The twenties craze for the beach was more about sun worship and display than health. Chanel promoted the fashion for a tan, and water sports became popular. Both factors resulted in swimsuits that were more streamlined, lighter, and revealed more flesh. In 1920, the Jantzen Company in the United States made the first rib-knit, elasticized, one-piece swimsuit—and fashion was quick to adapt the technology.

Tennis dress, 1926

Used throughout the 19th century for underwear, by the 20th century linen was the natural choice for summer clothing. As activity became more vigorous, the fabric was chosen because it allowed the skin to breathe. This machine-sewn dress, made by a Miss Hepburne-Scott in Scotland, with its simple lines and contrasting colors, is both practical and fashionable, being sleeveless and pleated but cut with the square-neck and geometric-shape detailing that denotes art deco influence.

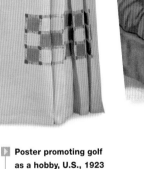

"Women must be able to move, to get into a car without bursting their seams! Clothes must have a natural shape."

COCO CHANEL

Poster promoting golf as a hobby, U.S., 1923

Golf had previously been an elitist sport, but during World War I it became more widely accessible socially to both men and women. The game was still played in tweeds, but by the 1920s golf was in part responsible for the adoption of the sweater or cardigan as everyday casual wear. Edward, the Prince of Wales, is credited with introducing suede Oxford golfing shoes, the baggy plus-four knickerbockers, and argyle socks to the United States.

Golf *by the* NORTH SHORE LINE

CHRONOLOGICAL CATWALK
The Twenties Male

Stage celebrity style

The golden age of entertainment brought style icons under the adoring gaze of the masses. Stage and screen idols, their lifestyles, and their wardrobes could be scrutinized in the countless best-selling magazines, such as *Photoplay*. Douglas Fairbanks looked suave next to Mary Pickford and women swooned over Rudolph Valentino's beauty. Playwright and actor Noël Coward's impeccable taste was much emulated, while many a young man aspired to the apparently effortless good grooming achieved by the dapper Fred Astaire, hoofing on Broadway with his sister Adele.

Brilliantined hair
Immaculate hair was typical of this period on both sides of the Atlantic. Men and boys of all races wore their hair very short with the longer top layers slicked back with tonic, brilliantine or, in the United States, a product called "Murray's Superior Pomade." This haircut inspired the extremely short and masculine Eton crop for women—androgyny was the new sensation in fashionable circles.

Pants with cuffs
The pants of the conservative suit had been a straight, narrow cut, but by mid-decade Oxford bags came in, so-called after the wide pants that Oxford undergraduates wore over their shorts for rowing. These pants became very extreme by the end of the fashion and were worn so loose that they flapped about the leg, while pants in general became wider and were worn with cuffs.

Suit jacket
During the early 1920s, the conservative suit was in style with a high, nipped-in waist and narrow shoulders on a short jacket. A shorter-lived, more exaggeratedly narrowed silhouette was the jazz suit. By 1925, the shoulders began to be squarer and the jacket cut straighter with looser sleeves. Lapels became wider and double-breasted jackets came into style as men stopped wearing vests.

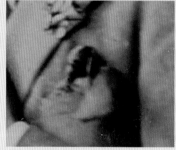

Pocket handkerchief
The handkerchief folded into the top pocket of a jacket is known as a "pocket square." By the 1920s, this had developed into a fashion accessory, with men keeping a second, purely functional handkerchief in their pant pocket. There were many different ways in which the square could be folded, from the conservative one-point fold to the flamboyant reverse puff. The Astaire is a puff with a point on either side.

Dapper silhouette
Dance in the 1920s was particularly important to fashion, and a need for ease of movement made as great a mark on menswear as it did on women's fashion. Together with the rising popularity of sport and a general leaning toward a more casual attitude and increased leisure time, dance led to baggier pants and roomier jackets so that afternoon dances were a relaxed affair.

Fred and Adele Astaire in
Stop Flirting, **1923**
While movies were still silent, the theater and musical reviews continued to be just as popular. The twin obsessions of music and dance meant that Broadway and London's West End were an important part of popular culture. Fred Astaire, with his sister Adele, became a leading stage personality, largely due to his association with the seminal composers George and Ira Gershwin.

The Cubist Print 1922–1929

Avant-garde art and design

Just as art inspired Eastern-style in Paul Poiret, the early 20th-century art movement continued to infiltrate fashion and textiles. Fauvism, the expressionist style that influenced Henri Matisse, had made a strong impression on Poiret's use of color and he collaborated with the artist Raoul Dufy, who designed textiles for him. Fauvism also inspired the artist and textile designer Sonia Delaunay, while cubism, the style developed by Pablo Picasso and Georges Braque, also interested Delaunay in its use of form and construction. In 1925, Delaunay participated in the Exposition Internationale des Arts Décoratifs et Industriels Modernes in Paris, which brought to the attention of the public a style of design that was to become ubiquitous.

Embroidered bag, Hilde Wagner-Ascher, 1925
The embroidered fabric from which this purse is made is the work of the Viennese designer Hilde Wagner-Ascher. Wagner-Ascher was a student of Josef Hoffman, one of the founders of the textiles workshop at the Wiener Werkstätte. The design is typical of the geometric shapes and solid color blocks of the Wiener style, but parallels can also be drawn with Sonia Delaunay's work.

ELEMENTS OF FASHION

- *Russian constructivist textile development*
- *Italian futurist "antineutral" clothing*
- *Vionnet's logo designed by Thayaht*
- *Raoul Dufy textiles for Poiret and Charvet*
- *Chanel No. 5 abstract bottle design*
- *Bauhaus jewelry*

Circular cape by Vionnet depicted in cubist graphic style, Thayaht, 1922
Commercial art, such as fashion illustration, ensured that art styles crossed over into a wider consciousness. Madeleine Vionnet had shown an early interest in cubism, using geometric shapes and seaming in her designs. This stemmed from an aptitude for geometry as a child, although she had left school at the age of 12 to be apprenticed to a seamstress. Her mathematical mind resulted in huge technical developments in cut.

THAYAHT. 22

Writer Nancy Cunard wearing a Sonia Delaunay outfit, ca. 1925

The style of design developed by Sonia Delaunay and her husband Robert was termed "Orphism" by a friend, the poet Guillaume Apollinaire. Delaunay worked with Dada propagandist Tristan Tzara on her "simultaneous dress," devised to express a crossover between fashion, art, and poetry. Delaunay's fashion and textiles studio was highly successful, and many Hollywood stars bought her work, resulting in her style being widely copied.

> **"He who knows how to appreciate color relationships, the influence of one color on another, their contrasts and dissonances, is promised an infinitely diverse imagery."**
>
> SONIA DELAUNAY

London Underground poster, 1924

The bright blocks of color and stylized lines of art deco defined the era. Before the "Expo Déco" of 1925, it was dubbed *jazz moderne,* which instantly aligned the art style with the nightclub world of the bright young things of the 1920s. In its broadest sense, art deco was a manifestation of the atmosphere of enthusiasm, optimism, and vivacity of the decade.

BRIGHTEST LONDON
IS BEST REACHED BY
UNDERGROUND

Cubist-inspired dress fabric, Chanel, 1928

The silk and wool jerseys that were a signature fabric for Coco Chanel were manufactured in the Tricot Chanel factory in Asnières-sur-Seine. Often, the fabrics were used to line coats for matching dresses. Chanel was a renowned perfectionist and preferred to have control over the process, from print design to production, to ensure exclusivity. The factory was renamed Tissus Chanel in 1929 after an expansion into woven fabrics.

Art-inspired fashion illustration, 1927

The interest in decorative arts as a medium in the early twentieth century guaranteed a dialogue between fashion designers and artists. Poiret's bold use of color inspired by the Fauvists and the *pochoir* technique of printing used by fashion illustrators both contributed to the idea that fabric for dress could be considered as a canvas for print design.

Coco Chanel 1883–1971

Coco Chanel, born Gabrielle Bonheur Chanel, provided plenty of detail about her early life, from the conflicting to the fantastical, but it is the consensus that she was born in Saumur, France, in 1883 into an impoverished family and probably grew up in an orphanage.

Chanel's lover, Etienne Balsan, set her up in the millinery business before World War I, introducing her to the English coal magnate Boy Capel, with whom she fell in love. Capel bankrolled her with a hat shop in Deauville, the fashionable resort on the Normandy coast. Chanel's designs were instantly remarkable, her taste being so unlike anything women had worn before. A natural tomboy herself, Chanel did away with all the belle-époque trimmings and created very plain but chic head wear.

Born
Saumur, 1883

Manifesto
To simplify women's clothing with elegance.

By the 1960s, a Chanel suit made of Linton tweed, or wool bouclé, was a signifier of sophisticated chic. A classic suit has the double-C gilt buttons on a collarless jacket lined with contrasting silk, the hem weighted with a gilt chain.

Women started to follow Chanel's example—she stocked men's sweaters in her shop after she had casually put one on and caused a sensation. Taking inspiration from menswear, sportswear, and work wear, Chanel wore Breton striped tops and, as the whole of Deauville followed suit, discovered a signature navy/white color palette.

Setting up a dress shop in Paris, Chanel set about simplifying the silhouette to meet her exacting tastes. She pared down trimming, used lighter fabrics, and simplified lines. As Poiret had done, although never crediting him, Chanel designed clothes to be worn without a corset. She adopted the square lines of Lanvin's chemise dress and made it her own in her revolutionary jersey fabric in navy, cream, and monotone. The dress shop closed at the outbreak of war, but in 1919 Chanel returned to open a couture house in Paris. For daytime, comfortable and relaxed cardigan suits with patch pockets and pleated skirts in soft tweeds created a "poverty de luxe," as Poiret bitterly put it. For evening, Chanel created the "little black dress," (LBD) a garment that its creator maintained was so chic in its perfect simplicity that it was impossible for anyone else to design.

Chanel's arrogance was legendary. She was of the opinion that she *was* fashion. Other couturiers were tolerated patronizingly, hated (Patou), or dismissed (Schiaparelli, whom she referred to as "that Italian artist who makes dresses"). The innovations that Chanel contributed to fashion in the 1920s justified this behavior—at least to herself. Naturally possessing a *garçonne* figure, Chanel made this the only "*ligne*" that could wear modern clothes. She "invented" the suntan, for which the tourism industry was forever grateful. She bestowed her touch on numerous items: boatnecks; sling-backs; two-tone; sweaters and pearls; blazers; peacoats; boaters and berets; crisp white shirts under navy suits; swimsuits; beige; costume jewelry; and bags with gilt chains—all of which became iconic. Chanel's signature was the unstructured, dressed-down, sporty outfit, but the clarity of cut was so perfect that her designs were the epitome of chic. They could not hide behind lavish trimming —gilt buttons were functional and braid served to add contrast.

Chanel's friend Misia Sert, the Polish pianist who ran an artistic salon in Paris, introduced her to Picasso, Cocteau, Diaghilev (for whom she designed the costumes for the ballet *Le Train Bleu* in 1924), and to artist Paul Iribe, who became a lover. More powerful lovers followed—the Grand Duke Dmitri of Russia, the Duke of Westminster—as Chanel mixed with the cream of society. In 1931, she signed a contract with Sam Goldwyn to design for Metro-Goldwyn-Mayer, although after three movies, including *Tonight or Never* with Gloria Swanson, Chanel grew bored and left.

The launch of Chanel No. 5 in 1921 epitomized the Chanel simplicity "de luxe," and set the wheels of the Chanel branding machine in motion.

In 1939, the outbreak of World War II prompted the closure of the House of Chanel and Coco took a German officer as a lover, for which the French condemned and exiled her.

In 1954, however, Chanel's fashion house reopened in the Rue Cambon, and the 1960s saw her reinstated as a doyenne of haute couture.

Launched in 1921, Chanel No. 5 was the first perfume to carry a designer's name. Despite subtle changes to the styling of the brand, the perfume is still synonymous with luxury almost a century later.

"A girl should be two things: classy and fabulous."

COCO CHANEL

CHRONOLOGICAL CATWALK
The Twenties Female

The self-assured woman

While most women could not abandon their families and jobs for a fast-living whirl of cocktails, nightclubs, and the Côte d'Azur, the simplification of female dress was assimilated into everyday wear and a more carefree self-assuredness was the general mood. This was the decade when women won the right to vote and the postwar generation refused to look back to an age of fettering corsetry and demure decorum.

Short hair
In 1913, the couture-dressed ballroom dancer Irene Castle bobbed her hair, but the hairstyle became more radical as part of the twenties *garçonne* look. The slightly waved shingle was a progression of the bob and in 1926 short hair culminated in the Eton crop, so severe that it needed the beauty of a teenage boy to pull it off.

Cloche hat
The bell-shaped cloche hats echoed the sleek hairstyles and were an indication that you had a short, fashionable bob beneath it. Often brimless, the twenties hat hugged the head and came to brow level to emphasize the eyes. As this made it hard to see, the uptilted head became part of the stylized posture of the era.

Up-and-down silhouette
For most of the 1920s, hems hovered around calf length. Only during the mid-decade did the skirt lengths of ordinary women match those of the flappers. It was the silhouette that was universal. Elasticated girdles were worn to flatten figures and the bra started to be developed as a commonplace piece of underwear.

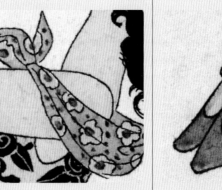

Bare shoulders
The straight up-and-down silhouette was emphasized by the sleeveless evening and day wear endorsed by Chanel, and other designers played with showing more skin with little short sleeves, floating panels, and scarves tied around the shoulders. The obsession with the figure made it acceptable to reveal more skin generally, culminating in black stockings being changed for light beige to give the impression of bare legs.

Bar shoes
The ubiquitous girlish bar shoes that fastened with one or more straps across the instep and low cuban or Louis heels guaranteed a quick, light step. The calf-length skirts of the time meant that shoes worn by the twenties female became more of a focal point and were selected as an accessory to an outfit—Chanel produced a two-toned version that wittily reflected the designer's use of contrasting color.

The illustrated playfulness of fashion, 1924
This hand-colored print, entitled *The Swing*, by 20th-century French illustrator Georges Barbier, appeared in *Falbalas & Fanfreluches*, an illustrated art and fashion almanac published in Paris in the early 1920s, of which only 600 copies were printed. Barbier's illustrations were instrumental in depicting the mood of fashion at one particular moment and were an indication of how illustration was a product of the relationship between art and fashion.

The Charleston Dress 1925–1929

Jazz, jazz, jazz

The Charleston dance may have had its origins in the African-American communities, but the sound of Harlem was resonating all over the world and very soon the Charleston became a global craze in a world hungry for jazz. The fast, frenetic movements, danced solo or in pairs in nightclubs, such as the Cotton Club, showed contempt of strict Prohibition laws, and generated new fashions that were quickly seized upon by the flapper girls, whose main objective was to have fun and appear thoroughly modern. The silhouette was no longer statuesque and stately— the figure required for the Charleston was small, skinny, and agile.

"Let's get out of these wet clothes and into a dry martini."

MAE WEST

The Parisian sensation

The cabaret show La Revue Nègre traveled from Broadway to London and to Paris, and it was there that one of its dancers, Josephine Baker, found work at the Folies-Bergère. Baker, in her diamante banana bikini, was intoxicatingly exotic and the European fashion world was enthralled by the color of her skin. Her witty outfits, frequently composed of little more than feathers, beads, and sparkle, were contrived with movement in mind and came to life with her wild dancing, which became the raison d'etre for the Charleston dress.

ELEMENTS OF FASHION

- *bust minimizers*
- *dropped waists*
- *Helena Rubinstein and Elizabeth Arden beauty products*
- *long earrings offset by sleek haircuts*
- *bangles on the upper arm and long strands of beads*

Androgynous accessories and the Eton crop, 1927

Leisure pajamas had become popular and Marlene Dietrich showed women how to retain allure while dressed in a man's suit, but the Eton-crop hairstyle and collar and tie paired with a painted face and jewelry presented a more overtly sexual message. For most, the experiment with androgyny waned when the English novelist Radclyffe Hall's lesbian novel *The Well of Loneliness* became the subject of an obscenity trial in 1928.

Flapper sashays for fashionable French society, 1928

Flappers needed no support structure in their dresses and even stockings were rolled down and held in place with garters to avoid the suspender-belt line. The *grands couturiers* struggled to keep up with the new fashions. Paul Poiret was baffled by the young, with their skimpy styles and one-piece "teddy" underwear, and the houses of Doucet, Dœuillet, and Drecoll closed their doors.

Madame se meurt, Madame est morte

SACHA ZALIOUK

Ève Adamisée

The flapper face, 1920s

With the advent of movie, attitudes to cosmetics relaxed. Max Factor began marketing a range for the public in the 1920s, and for the first time this was called "makeup" outside the theater. Advertisements claimed that it could make "every girl look like a movie star." Clara Bow's "It girl" cupid's bow lipstick, Louise Brooks's perfect bob, and Pola Negri's finely penciled brows were widely copied.

Velvet dress with gold beading, Voisin, ca. 1925

The nature of the Charleston meant that it was essential for the dancer's legs to be as free as possible. Flappers started to wear dresses that were much shorter with fringed or streamered skirts, which gave the illusion of length and the fashionable tubular style, but which moved with the dancer. Another dance, called the Shimmy, brought in dresses made from layers of fringing that quivered with the wearer.

Madeleine Vionnet 1876–1975

Like Chanel, Madeleine Vionnet had a hard early life—born in Aubervilliers, France, in 1876, her mother left when she was three and she was sent away to school at an early age. Like Lanvin, Vionnet was apprenticed to a dressmaker at the age of 12. She married young, suffered the death of a child, and by the age of 20 was divorced and working in a London tailoring workroom.

In 1901, Vionnet started to work for the designer sister of the Maison Callot Sœurs, Madame Gerber, making her *toiles*. It was under the influence of Madame Gerber that Vionnet progressed from tailoring to mastering haute couture. Already, she had started to put her own stamp on her work, preferring simplicity to the ornate lace ruffles of the Callot style. Vionnet moved away from the boned and stiffened high collars to softer draping.

In 1907, Madeleine Vionnet went to work for Jacques Doucet and pioneered mannequin parades using models wearing only sandals or barefoot. Influenced by the dancer Isadora Duncan, she made the girls abandon their corsets, presenting the designs "in their own skin," as she put it. Vionnet always maintained that she, not Paul Poiret, was responsible for the abolishment of corsets, but this seems a moot point between a handful of

Born
Aubervilliers, 1876

Manifesto
To be a "*puriste de la mode.*"

designers in Paris at the time, and in hindsight it is easier to recognize that this bid for freedom was in the atmosphere of the era.

In 1912, Vionnet opened her own house, but the onset of war forced closure just as she was establishing herself. She did not manage to reopen until 1922, albeit in grand style on the Avenue Montaigne, where the luxuriously austere apartments of the *salon* showed her garments to her preferred minimalist effect.

Vionnet did not share Coco Chanel's notion that all should be pared down to nothing. It was her mastery of innovation in cut that separated her from her counterparts and made her "the designer's designer." Vionnet's clothing ingeniously gave an illusion of simplicity, but her revolutionary way of manipulating fabric made her a pioneer of the 20th century.

Shying away from working from sketches, or cutting on the flat, Vionnet conceived her designs on a miniature articulated wooden artist's model, handling the fabric in a fluid way so that on the body it hung in sinuous folds. This was achieved by Vionnet's technique of cutting on the bias, and indeed the bias cut has proved indispensable for following a woman's natural curves ever since. Vionnet declared that she was concerned primarily with clothing a woman's body and that her greatest achievements had been possible through a reaction against fashion.

The bias cut could be used for entire dresses or parts of dresses—a signature was skirts ending in handkerchief points or tiers of bias-cut petals. Diagonal seaming and fagoting were employed to piece dresses that seemed classical in their execution. In the 1930s, Vionnet was using godets, flared skirts, and halter and cowl necklines in dresses without fastenings in a feast of sensuality. Favored fabrics were crepe de chine, chiffon, satin, gaberdine, and silk, which were ordered in broader widths to accommodate Vionnet's draping requirements. She had to persuade manufacturers to weave for her in widths that were wider than standard.

Such was Vionnet's success that in 1925 Madeleine Vionnet Inc. opened on Fifth Avenue in New York, selling ready-made styles that could be fitted to the customer.

Vionnet was a designer who was more engaged with fashion as an industry than interested in its frivolity, and she instigated several improvements that benefited both its designers and workers. She ensured that her employees received benefits such as paid holidays

❝You must dress a body in fabric, not construct a dress.❞

MADELEINE VIONNET

Sybil, Marchioness of Cholmondeley, wearing a characteristically petaled Vionnet day dress. As the bias cut came to dominate fashion by the 1930s, the House of Vionnet claimed many high-profile clients looking for the magic of her sirenlike silhouette. Leading actresses—Garbo, Dietrich and Hepburn among them—all dressed *chez* Vionnet.

and maternity leave, child day care, a dining hall, and a house doctor and dentist, all of which were by no means standard provision.

Vionnet was also very concerned with the copyright of couture designs and, after closing her house in 1939, she advised other couturiers, passing on her experience and skills.

The Stylish Thirties

Introduction

After 1929, things weren't quite as "fast" as they had been in the previous decade. Women's fashion returned to the spirit of allure and feminine curves were once again reinstated. The financial crash resulted in a significant rise in domestic dressmaking, mending, and altering after the heady consumerism of the "roaring twenties." Fabrics such as broadcloth started to be used for evening wear and the development of synthetics was precipitated, with the price of artificial silk stockings now being affordable to all.

Fashion and the flickering screen

If economy was more prevalent, it was the kind where women were determined to make a silk purse from a sow's ear. The predominant feeling in fashion was for luxury—glamor was the word on every girl's lips. Escapist visits to the movies ensured that glamor turned heads during the stylish thirties. The fantastical lives of the screen sirens incorporated many wardrobe changes every day, and of a quality that previously only haute couture clients enjoyed.

As well as endorsing fashion, Hollywood movies often demystified the fashion system, poking fun at the ridiculous extremes and the social divide, as in *Roberta*, a 1935 movie based in a Paris model

house or *modiste*. This resulted in a feeling of accessibility to a wider fashion awareness. Movie audiences were regularly seeing a standard of design that they felt should be theirs—from Ginger Rogers's sequins to the square-shouldered "business suits" in James Cagney's gangster flicks.

The dichotomy of the era was that depression was calling for a halt to consumerism, whereas technological developments were speeding things up. By 1936, Kodak had released Kodachrome onto the market, the first color photographic film, which changed editorial publications forever. American *Vogue* was behind a push to establish a domestic fashion industry after the Wall Street Crash had left the country in need of revenue from areas that had previously had no import restrictions.

The scandal of the decade was the English king who abdicated from his throne for the love of an American divorcee. The Duke and Duchess of Windsor, denied constitutional duties, dedicated their life together to style. Living between Paris and New York, Wallis's wardrobe represented a roll call of couturiers of the day, and she draped her coat-hanger figure with a celebrated severe artfulness, while Edward influenced men's fashion with classic Savile Row tailoring and gaudier sportswear.

The influence of the flourishing surrealist movement in the 1930s was to offer creative freedom to designers, such as Elsa Schiaparelli. The ideas adopted by its founder, André Breton, encouraged artists to explore the unexpected. Photographer Man Ray entitled a picture in 1933 "Beautiful as the chance encounter of a sewing machine and an umbrella upon the dissection table," a line taken by Breton to illustrate his ideas. It encapsulates the starting point for Schiaparelli's witty surrealist designs.

For a moment, prewar, the 20th century seemed to bring the continents closer. Travel became an obsession, with ocean-liner voyages between Europe and the United States depicted on film and their art deco interiors reproduced in design. This echoed the luxurious stance of thirties fashion. International high society was still the bastion of haute couture, but fashion designers and buyers found it necessary more and more to cross the Atlantic on a regular basis to sustain their businesses in an industry that was becoming increasingly global. Air travel became the next novelty, with Amelia Earhart the first woman to fly long distances, and fashion answered with wardrobe possibilities.

Growing political tensions in Europe were to shatter the "fun 1930s" depicted in Hollywood. The coverage of the 1936 Berlin Olympics, which saw the infamous Jesse Owens wearing Adidas running shoes, revealed disquieting menace.

Facing the threat of Fascism after the takeover of the decadent Weimar Republic in Berlin, Paris threw elaborate costume balls. Nevertheless, on the eve of the fall of France, crisis meetings were held by the Syndicat de la Couture.

The Paris Suit 1930s

The embodiment of elegance

The monied few of the 1930s were an international crowd and their conscious display of wealth was undeterred by the depression. Indeed, for those movie stars whose careers depended on upholding a glamorous image, it was essential. For those others who hadn't lost their money in the crash, Paris couture separated them from the mass-marketed fashions available to other women. Elsa Schiaparelli's designs encapsulated the hard, stylized lines of exceptional cut. But for those who did not embrace surrealism, the pre-World War II couture industry still thrived despite developments in ready-to-wear, and there were plenty of designers delivering exquisite made-to-measure garments devoid of shock factor. Above all, it was the unmatched Paris tailoring that commanded continuing respect for couture.

ELEMENTS OF FASHION

- *afternoon cocktail suits*
- *small hats worn tilted over one eye*
- *veils*
- *gloves*
- *the matching ensemble*

▶ Woolen suit, Molyneux, 1930s

Dress codes for women of society still indicated that a well-cut suit was indispensable for formal day activities and English tailoring retained its reputation for excellence—tweeds were still essential for country pursuits for a certain class of woman. A former British army captain, Edward Molyneux had achieved the position of couturier in Paris after training with the House of Lucile, and during his career accomplished a fashion *entente cordiale* to match Creed and Worth. Dark or muted tones, such as claret and beige, were very popular for day suits and Molyneux led the way in understatement.

Lined suit edged with astrakhan, Jeanne Paquin, 1930s

Madame Paquin died in 1936, but the House of Paquin continued for another 20 years. Like Poiret, a stalwart of Parisian chic, Paquin welcomed the globalization of fashion, sending her collections on tour in the United States with unrestricted entry for the price of a ticket. Paquin mixed practicality with creativity, ensuring that her designs were wearable. Fur trim was very popular during this period and sable, chinchilla, mink, Persian lamb, and silver fox were often used to add gravitas to tailored ensembles.

"A woman can never be too rich or too thin."

WALLIS SIMPSON

Double-breasted woolen suit, Chanel, 1933

Chanel's simple approach worked well with the severe tailoring used for the day suits of the 1930s. Her preferred color match, navy and white, is softened with a typical floppy bow tied at the neck, a favorite styling technique of hers since the 1920s, but widely used in the 1930s as even tailoring sought to feminize the look. The school-girl collar demonstrates how she adapted classic detailing from everyday life.

Very tailored—
with
Soft Necklines

Models—
AUGUSTABERNARD

Tailored suits, Augustabernard, 1932

These ensembles from the couturier Augustabernard show the thirties longer calf-length skirt for day wear and are a less severe interpretation of the Paris look. The outfit on the right is a tailored afternoon dress with jacket, which was an alternative to the suit. Some suits came with a blouse attached to the skirt to create a dress when the jacket was removed.

The Siren Dress 1932

The allure of the silver screen

All the Hollywood studios had their own costume designers: Travis Banton and Edith Head at Paramount; Orry-Kelly at Warners, and Adrian at MGM. These individuals were greatly influential in translating the idea of fashion into glamor—a concept that turned the wheels of the movie industry during the depression when audiences lived vicariously through the stars several times a week. The American writer and critic Margaret Thorp explained glamor at the time as "sex appeal plus luxury, plus elegance, plus romance." It was the job of the costume department to transform actresses from real women into goddesses, often having to find solutions to less-than-perfect figures with special corsetry, padding, and other visual tricks.

"We, the couturiers, can no longer live without the cinema any more than the cinema can live without us. We corroborate each other's instinct."

LUCIEN LELONG

▷ **Joan Crawford in *Letty Lynton*, organdy dress, Adrian, 1932**
Adrian's white confection for Joan Crawford in Clarence Brown's *Letty Lynton* had been conceived with huge ruffled sleeves to disguise the star's broad shoulders. The dress was greatly influential—copied in the same year by the department store Macy's, and over 500,000 were bought across the United States. By the late 1930s, studio designers had their own retail collections and pattern companies made versions of screen fashions to sew at home.

Lili Damita, photographed by Baron de Meyer, 1933

Adolph de Meyer was the first photographer appointed to the *Vogue* staff in 1913. In this picture, taken after De Meyer had moved back to Europe to become the *Harper's Bazaar* photographer in Paris, the French actress Lili Damita is wearing an organdy gown by couturier Maggy Rouff, which nods to Adrian's *Letty Lynton* dress. Damita had signed to MGM in 1928 and married Errol Flynn in 1935.

Bare-back evening dress, Jean Patou, 1934

The silhouette of the early 1930s was tall and slender with broad shoulders and slim hips. Skirts had dropped again and the waist had returned to its natural position. The new focal interest—and the new erogenous zone—was the back and this illustration was originally captioned as "giving the impression of nudity, despite the panel and the flippers."

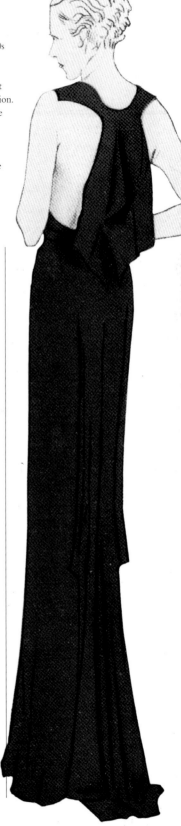

Evening dress, chiffon with iridescent sequins, Chanel, 1932

Chanel's approach to the siren dress in the 1930s was typically elegant and understated, but her masterly simplicity was not the Hollywood studios' fantastical interpretation of glamor. For her, a sequinned sheath was not to be tampered with. Her contract with MGM was short-lived, partly due to her opposition to superfluous embellishment at a time when the public had a need for escapism.

ELEMENTS OF FASHION

- capelets or boleros over backless dresses
- short, curled hairstyles
- fashion parades in movies, such as Roberta; Vogues of 1938; Mannequin; Artists and Models
- period costume as in The Barretts of Wimpole Street (1933) reintroduced elements of romanticism
- Irene Dunne's 1890s leg-of-mutton sleeves in Cimarron (1931) influenced broad shoulders

Beaded pleated sheath dress, Jean Patou, 1937

The sun-ray pleating on the skirt of Patou's beaded gold sheath is a reference to a signature art deco motif that was perpetuated by Hollywood glamor. The fabric flares out from pleats cut on the bias. From the interior of the luxury liner SS *Normandie* to cocktail bars in the movies, the sun-ray pattern signified a stylized perception of the high life.

CHRONOLOGICAL CATWALK
The Thirties Female

Top-to-toe polished glamor

The example of on-screen Hollywood glamor reinforced the importance of meticulous grooming for the thirties woman from makeup to a pedicure, made necessary by the fashion for open-toed sandals. In a 1937 short movie, the actress Constance Bennett demonstrated her skincare routine in order to "help" ladies who might have been confused about such vital matters, exclaiming that "the only time we're not on parade is the time we spend in front of our dressing tables."

Siren silhouette
The thirties female reached goddesslike proportions, achieved through rigorous calisthenics and dietetic regimes. Waists may have risen back to midpoint, but fashion served to accentuate the length of the legs in long sinuous folds of skirts and pants. It was an illustrator's dream, with the angular, dramatically emphasized shoulders, tiny waist, and slender hips of a fashion drawing come to life.

Backless
The siren silhouette offered a sensual surprise when seen from the back. Dresses began to be designed as if they were meant to be viewed from behind. A brown back was very desirable and, partly due to stills of movie beauties by Californian pools, swimsuits became more of a fashion item and elements of their design came to influence day and evening wear.

Halter neckline
The halter neckline was very popular as it eliminated the need for spoiling the back detail with straps, leaving an uninterrupted area of skin to expose to the sun by day and display by night. The cowl neckline was a softer alternative to the throat-clutching neckline. All three elements were popularized by Vionnet as a result of her development of the sleek bias cut.

Wide shoulders
Broadening the shoulders by padding or some visual device was taken to extreme lengths. Schiaparelli's pagoda shoulder was just one of many techniques. Butterfly sleeves, shoulder flares, and pleated sleeve caps also helped to achieve the "coat-hanger silhouette." The line was also elongated by starting the dress at the throat and finishing just above the ankle for day and at floor length for night.

Flared skirt
Lengths had dropped but skirts were molded to the body by means of the bias cut, so for the first time the shape of a woman's behind could clearly be seen. Adding to the titillation was a glimpse of suntanned leg, because narrow skirts were often split to facilitate walking or flared out from below the knee by means of pleating or triangular-shaped inserts called godets.

Brown and backless, vacation attire, 1934
In the 1930s women's fashions were generally neat and feminine for day and sweepingly glamorous for night, but summer leisurewear often bridged the gap, as designers found ways of smartly showing off the contemporary tanned and toned figure, illustrated here in 1934 resort wear from Fortnum & Mason and Victor Stiebel in Britain.

The Wide Pants 1930s

Elegance takes over from boyishness

After the 1920s, pants for women gradually moved from their sportswear functionality to leisure wear, but it was not until the mid-decade that they were acceptable for everyday casual wear. Movies, such as *The Philadelphia Story*, starring Katharine Hepburn, showed the carefree possibilities of pants, and American designers, including Elizabeth Hawes, championed the emancipatory benefits of pants for women. Hepburn herself, a keen sportswoman, wore pants as a matter of course. Gradually, fashion shifted from elegant draped pajamas for idle beach life to Butterick and Vogue patterns for pants for women with get-up-and-go.

Informal print fabric, 1930s
Nautical motifs were popular for the beach pajama when fashion took a literal view of resort wear. Fun prints were often specifically designed for the wide-leg pants either for beach- or leisure wear at home, setting the style apart from more formal attire.

Woolen pajamas, Jean Patou, 1931
Pants were worn as casual or as functional wear in the 1930s, but it was mostly at the beach that they were an essential item. Since Chanel had adapted bell-bottomed sailor's pants in the 1920s, the wide-legged beach pajama had become a seaside staple, often keeping the marine theme in the design with front button detailing. They were worn over a swimsuit or with a sun top such as this one by Jean Patou.

"I dress for the image. Not for myself, not for the public, not for fashion, not for men."

MARLENE DIETRICH

▼ Summer beachwear, 1932

The beach pajama, as seen on the 1932 cover of the Summer *Tatler* edition, was a cheerful vacation outfit, paired with a jaunty short jacket and a wide-brimmed sunhat, as opposed to the tiny perched town hats. The confident wide-legged stance of one girl, with her head thrown back and a mischievous grin, and the nonchalant cigarette of the other reflect the informal, independent image of the thirties pants-wearing woman.

▼ Pajama suit, 1930

This illustration features two slightly more dressed styles of pajamas. The Maggy Rouff on the left is a Russian-style orange-and-black crepe de chine outfit. During the 1930s, the international set was awash with Russian émigrés and their influence was apparent. This suit could have doubled for an "at home," as informal evening or lounge wear was called. The Lenief costume on the right incorporates striped swimwear as a blouse.

Marlene Dietrich, 1933 ▲

The characters of the Hollywood stars had much influence on dress reform during the silver-screen era. Marlene Dietrich was only too aware of the captivatingly incongruous sexual allure that cross-dressing gave her. In 1930, Greta Garbo caused headlines when she was spotted walking down Hollywood Boulevard wearing pants and her incognito uniform was soon adapted by costume designer Adrian into an iconic image.

ELEMENTS OF FASHION

- *pleated shorts covered by a wrapover skirt*
- *masculine braid detailing and cuffs*
- *wedge-shaped heels*
- *sunglasses*
- *a tan*

American Innovation 1934–1939

The rise of the American designer

After the Wall Street crash, a 90 percent import duty placed on original Paris couture caused U.S. buyers to opt for duty-free toiles, supplied with making-up instructions. At the same time, the American fashion industry began to promote its own. New York stores commissioned ready-to-wear collections from the U.S. designers Elizabeth Hawes and Muriel King in 1933 and *Vogue* brought out its first all-American issue in 1938. U.S. fashion gained more independence when designers such as Hawes, who had worked in Paris, returned home to set up their own brand of design. Key to its being taken seriously were Charles James and Mainbocher, both of whom would make respected contributions to couture history— James's quilted jacket introduced a new dimension to design.

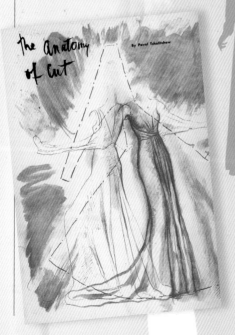

Evening dress, Charles James, 1934 ◄
A James gown drawn by Pavel Tchelitchew to illustrate "The Anatomy of Cut." James was fascinated by mass production, and after working in London and Paris, returned to New York, where the fashion market was changing from the Paris system. He established partnerships with various manufacturers but found it impossible to compromise the complexity of his cut and workmanship for a cheaper market.

"Pneumatic" quilted jacket, Charles James, 1935–1937 ▲
On seeing James's down-stuffed satin jacket, Salvador Dalí called it "the first soft sculpture." James's work is, however, more architectural than sculptural. Obsessed with perfecting his techniques, he constantly redesigned his work throughout his career, and created an artform through mathematical precision. He was one of the first designers to incorporate the new zipper fastener.

"To be well turned out, a woman should turn her thoughts in."

MAINBOCHER

ELEMENTS OF FASHION

- *severe elegance and a longer line*
- *retail collections by Hollywood studio designers*
- *diet fads, including the Hay diet, slimming soap, and diet pills*
- *Lilly Dache hats*
- *permed hair*

Wedding dress for Wallis Simpson, Mainbocher, 1937

American Wallis Simpson remained loyal to her country fellows when choosing the gown for her controversial marriage to the Duke of Windsor in 1937. Main Rousseau Bocher was originally from Chicago but had become Editor of French *Vogue* after serving in Europe in the Great War. In 1930, he became the first American to open a couture salon in Paris and the first journalist ever to do so.

Corset, Mainbocher, 1939

Mainbocher understood the couture tradition of refined style achieved with elegance of cut, and managed innovation in his less-is-more way, introducing the strapless evening dress. A forerunner of the postwar New Look was his 1939 corseted collection. His sculptural foundation garment was photographed by Horst and manufactured by the Warner Corset Company, which financed his prewar move back to the United States.

Evening dress, Valentina, ca. 1934

Russian-born Valentina brought a sense of drama to American fashion. After fleeing the Russian Revolution via Paris, Valentina moved to New York in 1922 and immediately stood out with the singular sense of style that she applied to her dressmaking. Like James, she favored the architectural exploration of design, which was a development of the bias cut, and coming from a theater background, designed stage costumes that influenced her fashion design.

CHRONOLOGICAL CATWALK
The Thirties Male

Top hat and tails

While the depression resulted in widespread poverty on both sides of the Atlantic, fashion for men as well as women reflected an aspirational desire for affluence. On-screen the gangster suit was an exaggerated version of the business suit. Although fortunes foundered for some, for the most part the social elite continued to live a charmed life and the fabled white-tie-and-tails look became a mainstay of the musical comedy.

Top hat

With the popularity of musical movies such as the 1935 *Top Hat* with Fred Astaire, the "topper" saw an evening wear revival in the luxurious nightspots that existed for most people only on the screen, while Marlene Dietrich used the top hat as a symbol of cabaret decadence.

White tie

The white tie is only worn after dark, or after the cocktail hour. This was integral to the structure of the fantasy world that represented the aspirational escapism of thirties entertainment. Noël Coward wrote the revue *Tonight at 8:30* as a singing and dancing showcase for Gertrude Lawrence and himself. It ran in London and New York, while Astaire simultaneously immortalized the "affluent toff" look on screen.

Tailcoat

The evening attire of top hat, white tie, and tails was sometimes known as the "soup and fish suit" because it was worn to formal dinners where two courses were served before the entree. The outfit was immortalized in Irving Berlin's song, "Puttin' on the Ritz," celebrating an invitation to a high-class party.

Patent leather shoes

The patent leather court shoe, or opera slipper for dancing, had its origins in Regency evening court dress. By the 1930s, the bow-fronted slip-on had gone out of fashion and lace-ups were worn at all times with white tie and tails, or "full dress." The shininess served to highlight the nimble footwork of the thirties hoofers.

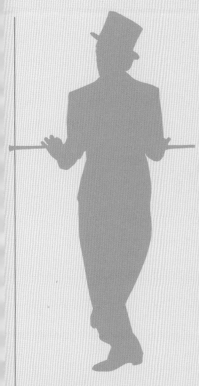

Elegant silhouette
Although Noël Coward conjured up an image of an elegant cocktail-sipping wit in smoking jacket, and the white-tie-and-tails image was redolent of the art deco musical, the shape of thirties menswear tailoring was gradually altering in silhouette. The drape cut, a V-shaped double-breasted jacket, instigated by Frederick Scholte of Savile Row, was developing into the distinctive broad-chested look of the time.

Noël Coward and Gertrude Lawrence in *Tonight at 8:30*, 1936
The personification of nonchalant elegance, Noël Coward was a thirties example of an individual not born to greatness using the vehicle of stardom to become part of a society that valued wit, charm, and celluloid shine. Coward's comedies, often partnered by Gertrude Lawrence, were huge hits during the depression.

Elsa Schiaparelli 1890–1973

The eccentric but practical Elsa Schiaparelli was born in Rome to a wealthy and aristocratic family—her father was dean of the university. According to her autobiography, *My Shocking Life*, in which she flits between using the first and third person when talking about herself, she had far more adventures than the average Italian girl at that time. After living in London, marrying, and moving to New York, Schiaparelli befriended Gaby Picabia, wife of the Dada artist Francis Picabia, who ran a boutique selling French fashion. Schiap, as she was called by everyone, worked for Gaby Picabia, meeting other artists, such as Man Ray and Marcel Duchamp.

Abandoned by her husband, Count Wilhelm de Wente de Kerlor, for Isadora Duncan, in 1920 she moved with her daughter to Paris, single and penniless. She became friends with Paul Poiret, who gave her clothes, and through him began to appreciate fashion. Schiap's first idea for a business plan was a black knitted sweater with a white trompe l'œil bow. She had to fulfill an order for 40 of these from New York and gathered together a group of Armenian knitters. Her first private customer was Anita Loos, author of *Gentlemen Prefer Blondes*, and soon every woman in the Ritz was wearing one.

Born
Rome, 1890

Manifesto
To break the mold with wearable eccentricities.

Schiaparelli's daughter Gogo was diagnosed with infantile paralysis and, in order to pay for her operations and schools, Schiaparelli had to rely on her wit, creativity, and good sense. She professed to have no business acumen, although this could be contested in view of the fact that, by 1930, she had more than 2,000 employees and 26 workrooms.

In 1935, Schiaparelli opened one of the first couture boutiques after moving to the Place Vendôme. Pour Le Sport sold the first divided skirts for tennis players. It soon became Pour Le Sport, Pour La Ville, and Pour Le Soir.

Her business expanded for a while to England, where, shocked by the English nobility's attitude to money, she introduced an ingenious points plan for payment. Horrified by the Fascist hold on her native Italy, she decamped to Paris, where her innovative designs were devised with the silhouette that shaped the decade's look—small waist, wide shoulders, and long, straight skirt.

Schiaparelli searched for novelty and humor in everything and embraced the trend for double meaning that the surrealists had introduced. The shoe hat that she produced from a sketch by Dalí became as iconic as his lobster telephone. Dalí designed many fabrics for her, including the suggestively phallic "Lobster" dress, but she was also responsible for many fashion innovations of her own. Her first main collection used brightly colored zipper fasteners as functional decoration but nearly ruined her, because duty laws prevented zippers from being imported to the United States—a ruling that Schiaparelli saw repealed. Ever resourceful, when materials were scarce at the beginning of the war, the designer used dog-leash chains and clips. She also transformed the use of Viyella, a fabric that had previously only been used for the nursery, much as Chanel had done with jersey.

The antithesis and rival of Chanel, although both designers championed simplicity in their own way, Schiap, like Coco, had her own perfume. The bottle was inspired by the shape of Mae West's tailor's dummy—Schiap had made costumes for the star for the movie *Every Day's a Holiday* (1937). The launch of her perfume, named Shocking, with its eponymous pink color, inspired by a pink Cartier diamond owned by her friend Daisy Fellowes, made her world famous in her time.

Schiaparelli left for New York for a lecture tour of the United States when France was invaded by the Nazis and she remained there until 1945. She reopened in Paris, but the "New Look"

"A dress cannot just hang like a painting on a wall, or like a book remain intact and live a long and sheltered life."

ELSA SCHIAPARELLI

was not for her, and the business continued only until 1954, when she closed her doors and retired to Tunisia.

Schiaparelli had charm and an innate sense for publicity, and her friends wore her designs in all the important places. Her relationship with the artistic community was mutually rewarding and afforded her innovative design as well as column inches.

Schiaparelli's Dalí-print "Lobster" dress was worn by Wallis Simpson when she was officially photographed by Cecil Beaton shortly before her third marriage. His images of the future Duchess of Windsor wearing this dress did much to raise the profile of its designer, once dubbed by Chanel "that Italian artist who makes clothes."

The Surrealist Dress 1936–1939

Surrealist couture

The 1930s were marked by a collaboration between surrealist artists and fashion designers. This was not simply each creative seeking a new medium, as in the influence of art on fashion at the turn of the 20th century, but a fascination with one another. Surrealist artists were interested in exploring the unconscious with reference to the ideologies of Karl Marx and Sigmund Freud and did not limit their ideas to painting, but expressed notions of the unlimited possibilities of the imagination in everyday objects using photography, furniture, and clothing. Surrealist fashion was not just confined to Schiaparelli's couture creations but reached a wider audience through fashion shoots and artwork.

"Ceci n'est pas une pipe."

RENÉ MAGRITTE, *THE TREACHERY OF IMAGES,* CA. 1928–29

ELEMENTS OF FASHION

- *Dali's diving suit*
- *Dali's moustache*
- *Schiaparelli's buttons shaped as peanuts, acrobats, lollipops*
- *aspirin necklaces*
- *the newspaper print*

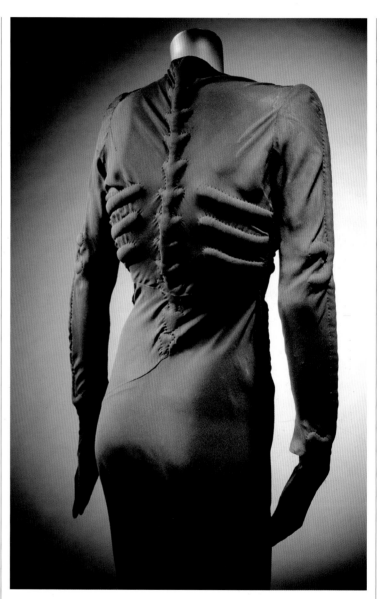

"Skeleton" dress, Schiaparelli/Dalí, 1938
From her first designs for trompe l'œil sweaters, Elsa Schiaparelli sought to make fashion amusing, in a way that was in tune with surrealist thinking. Her collaboration with Salvador Dalí produced her lamb-cutlet hat and desk suit, as well as this skeleton dress for the Circus collection. Made from black silk crepe, it uses the trapunto quilting method to create the spine and ribs.

Harper's Bazaar cover, April 1938

Surrealism was often applied to fashion in editorial layouts and illustration during the years suffused with its idiosyncratic imagery. In 1936, there were surrealist art exhibitions in both London and New York, and in 1938 Marcel Duchamp curated an international exhibition at the Paris Gallerie des Beaux-Arts. Man Ray and Lee Miller both contributed to avant-garde photography and movies, while Cocteau directed movies such as *La Belle et La Bête* and *Orphée*.

"Tears" evening dress, Schiaparelli/Dalí, 1938

Schiaparelli's collaborations with artists also led to a darker interpretation of the "amusing." Flayed flesh was a recurring motif in Salvador Dalí's art and the "Tears" dress Schiaparelli created uses a Dalí print that shows torn flesh and a veil with appliquéd tears. The fabric used for Dalí's print was marocain, a kind of ribbed crêpe, but Schiaparelli was also well known for experimenting with new textiles. For example, she worked with Charles Colcombet, a French textile manufacturer who offered developments in synthetic fabrics including acrylic, cellophane, and various derivatives of rayon.

"Profile" evening coat, Schiaparelli/Cocteau, 1937

A collaboration between Schiaparelli and artist Jean Cocteau resulted in a jacket and a coat embroidered by Lesage, the Parisian couture embroidery house. The jacket incorporates a woman whose long blonde hair trails down one sleeve and whose arm encircles the waist. The coat, shown above, has two profiles face-to-face, creating the simultaneous illusion of a vase for the roses that bedeck the shoulders.

The Effect
of War

Introduction

Fashion history would have been very different without the enforced austerity of World War II. Clues to a romantic, corseted, full-skirted look were already evident in the late 1930s—paralleled by the number of period dramas put out by Hollywood, which culminated in *Gone With the Wind*.

War prompted a *volte-face*; fashion was besieged by propaganda and in 1942 *Vogue* proclaimed in London that "Dressiness is *démodé*." Dresses in sparse lines were made up in fabrics printed with slogans, such as "Dig for Victory" and the actress Vivien Leigh caused a sensation in her "66 coupons" blouse, a garment reflecting the need to ration during austere times.

Utility prompted advances in utilitarian styles not seen since World War I. The shortage of nylon stockings, seen as such a liberator when commercially launched by DuPont in the United States in 1937, and the demands of becoming part of the labor force, made younger women embrace pants which were previously strictly confined to leisure wear.

Fashion flies the flag

British women became starved of fashion, but the Incorporated Society of London Fashion Designers, employed at home to design severe governmental lines, produced frivolous gowns for export in the early war years. As part of the initiative to assist the war effort, "Buy British" stores were set up in the United States and the still-rich States-side clientele was urged to do its bit for Europe after the fall of France rendered buying from Paris impossible.

Not only did war give American designers the chance to show their abilities in the absence of Paris fashion, but the spread of boogie-woogie and swing resulted in one of the first music and fashion cross references. Dance music fashion took a rebellious stance—the zoot suit contravened fabric restrictions —but the stylish uniform as worn on screen by the morale-boosting Andrews Sisters became a global association with boogie-woogie.

Ultimately, as the war became global, American designers initiated a clean-lined sports or casual look. For the first time, inspiration was insular and Mexican-style dresses, Davy Crockett fringing, and Civil War memorabilia became U.S. fashion motifs.

During the liberation celebrations in Paris, Lee Miller, the surrealist turned photojournalist, reported on the flamboyance of Parisian girls. Nations still under rationing were shocked and in 1944 the first couture collections since 1940 were held, with a return to simplicity. In a bid to reconnect with U.S. buyers, GIs were invited to view the showings.

The British and U.S. fashion industries were now in a strong position, helped by the repatriation of Paris couturiers Molyneux and Mainbocher, and mass-marketing had been further developed due to uniform production. Haute couture rallied and a group of designers produced the Théâtre de la Mode in 1945, a collection of dolls dressed in miniatures, that was shown in Europe and the United States.

Couture may not have been finished, but change was in the air. In January 1947 a press report told the British public of the U.S. "teenage" phenomenon.

Haute couture's response to Nazi occupation revealed just how integral fashion is to the French national identity. While the British and U.S. fashion industries were involved in the war effort, Parisian women used dress as a form of defiance and simply refused to present themselves as downtrodden. Fashion for women in other countries was subject to heavy restrictions, but in France creativity flourished under oppression.

The Utility Suit 1940s

Rationing

In 1941, clothing was rationed in Britain, which meant that clothes were agonized over and bought to last. *Vogue* ran articles on "Your One and Only Dress," and fashion became bound to necessity and duty. Silk was banned from civilian use and American soldiers became a source of nylon stockings. Women were once again needed as part of the workforce in Britain, but by December 1941, the National Service Act (No. 2) had been passed so that for the first time women could be called up. Designers rallied to the cause of patriotism, and military detailing on civilian clothing contributed to a sense of unity. Many wedding photographs from the era show brides and grooms in uniform or wearing boxy suits made on Utility lines.

Women's work, poster, 1941

Propaganda material tended to glamorize the role of women in the war, focusing not only on the heroic aspect, but on the smart uniformed line. Women's services included the Land Army, Auxiliary Territorial Service, Women's Auxiliary Air Force, and the Women's Royal Naval Service. The added bonus was that the impossible-to-obtain stockings were provided as part of the uniform in the WRENS.

Gas-mask bag, 1940–1942

H. Wald & Co. converted a necessity into a high-end accessory with this tan reptile-skin gas-mask bag. The company was known for its handmade and painted satin purses, called Waldybags, which became so popular with GIs as gifts to send home to their girlfriends that they became known as "sweethearts' purses." Wald merged with Rayne, bag and shoemakers to Queen Elizabeth II, in the 1950s.

ELEMENTS OF FASHION

- *checks pieced together, cut straight and on the bias*

- *wraparound coats or capes to minimize button use*

- *the siren suit, an air-raid jumpsuit*

- *the kangaroo cloak with hood and large pockets*

- *handknits*

WOMEN OF BRITAIN
COME INTO
THE FACTORIES
ASK AT ANY EMPLOYMENT EXCHANGE FOR ADVICE AND FULL DETAILS

Utility suit, Victor Stiebel, 1942

In 1942, the Board of Trade commissioned the Incorporated Society of London Fashion Designers to design a range of utility clothing. Led by Captain Molyneux, the team included Norman Hartnell, Digby Morton, Hardy Amies, Victor Stiebel, Bianca Mosca, and Peter Russell. Under the CC41 Utility label, 32 designs were mass-produced from four basic outlines of a coat, suit, dress, and a blouse, which had to minimize materials and labor.

> **"It's time to pull our socks up —after we darn them."**
>
> MAKE–DO AND MEND PROPAGANDA, 1943

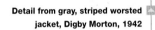

Detail from gray, striped worsted jacket, Digby Morton, 1942

Textiles became strictly controlled and not only was the Utility plan limited in yardage as most uniforms were also made from wool, but trimmings and buttons were measured and counted. British *Vogue* was relied on by the Board of Trade for making austerity chic, and fashion was given a responsibility to be economical, which made the cut of a Utility suit very spare.

Wartime work wear, book cover, 1941

Female factory and munitions workers wore overalls and boiler suits with their hair bound up in turbans. Hairstyles were the last vestige of glamor that women clung to and hair was kept shoulder-length and curled. Some factories installed in-house salons to discourage absence for hair appointments.

"Make-do and Mend" propaganda, 1943

This campaign was launched by Britain's Ministry of Information because fabric production was reserved for uniforms, etc. It showed women how to darn or reknit, how to make a skirt from a pair of pants and underwear from household linen, although most women preferred parachute silk.

Go through your wardrobe

Make-do and Mend

Hardy Amies 1909–2003

Born in London in 1909, Edwin Hardy Amies' mother was a seamstress and *vendeuse* at the court dressmaker, Mme. Durrant. At the age of 18, Amies was sent to work in France and Germany to improve his languages and so fulfill his ambition to be a journalist. Instead, he returned to Britain in 1930 and, after writing a description of a dress worn by his partner to a dance, he was appointed in 1933 to replace Digby Morton as designer to Lachasse, the subsidiary couture company of his mother's employers. The novice Amies had to learn in situ, but by 1935, then at the age of 26, he was appointed managing director and designer.

At the outbreak of the war, Amies' knowledge of French and German found him placed in the Intelligence Corps, but when the government decided to promote trade and export in fashion in 1941, he was given leave to take part in a joint collection with the other leading London designers, which was to be sent to South America. This led to the establishment of the Incorporated Society of London

Born
London, 1909

Manifesto
To support British fashion.

Fashion Designers, and in 1942 the Civilian Clothing Order resulted in the Utility plan.

Posted to Belgium, where he became head of espionage, Amies used the names of fashion accessories as codewords, although he fell foul of the authorities when he arranged a post-D-Day *Vogue* photoshoot in Brussels.

After Amies was demobbed in 1945, he set up his own couture house in a bombed-out building in Savile Row. The waiver of austerity regulations and larger quotas of cloth from the Board of Trade, in an effort to boost the export market, allowed the designer to move toward his desire to refeminize fashion. His designs showed that his creativity was progressing along similar lines to Christian Dior's, with a soft shoulder line and greater volume in the skirt, and when Dior launched his Corolle line in 1947, Amies' riposte was the British answer to the New Look.

Amies made many trips to the United States to secure orders for his curvaceous tailoring in wool and tweed. His wearable designs became a favorite of Princess Elizabeth and after her coronation he was awarded a royal warrant. It is as Dressmaker to the Queen that Amies is often remembered because she continued to wear his lavish ball-gowns until 1990, when he relinquished

ff The best-dressed woman is one whose clothes wouldn't look too strange in the country. JJ

HARDY AMIES

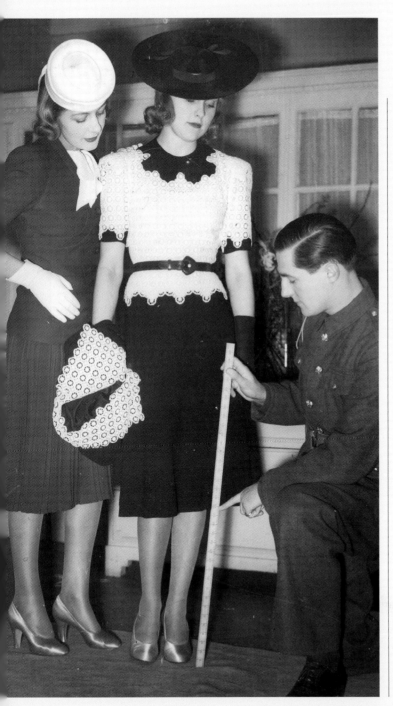

Hardy Amies showed ingenuity in conquering the restrictions of the Utility fabric limitations, and the precise tailoring signature that he had begun while working for Lachasse developed out of necessity.

the warrant to make way for younger designers. The dress he designed for the official portrait for the Queen's Silver Jubilee in 1977 was "immortalized" on a thousand cookie tins.

In 1950, the Hardy Amies ready-to-wear boutique was opened and in 1961 he entered the menswear ready-to-wear market with a contract with Hepworths, becoming the first womenswear couturier to design for men and the first designer to stage menswear fashion shows.

With the demise of women's made-to-measure in Britain, Amies became known as a menswear designer, publishing *The ABC of Men's Fashion* in 1963 after the success of his column in *Esquire* magazine, which spelled out his dress code for men. His house also undertook corporate commissions after designing for the winning 1966 English World Cup soccer team, ranging from the 1972 British Olympic squad to the London Stock Exchange, although his 1968 costumes for Stanley Kubrick's *2001: A Space Odyssey* were somewhat more futuristic although staying true to his tailoring mastery.

Hardy Amies remained at the company helm until his retirement in 2001, aged 92.

CHRONOLOGICAL CATWALK
The Wartime Female

Regulation regimes

Fashion magazines in Britain and the United States attempted to glamorize the slim pickings that rationing granted the wardrobe of the stylish woman. Only in Paris, where couturiers fronted by Lucien Lelong had negotiated exemption from rationing and brazenly wasted their occupiers' resources, was there fabric to make free with. London and New York editors were obliged to censure the wastefulness of the French and advocate the sparse, coordinated look of their own designers working under regulations.

Utility silhouette
The wartime silhouette was an interpretation of the Schiaparelli line, adapted for minimal use of materials. The outline was severe, with padded square shoulders, a boxy jacket, and a skirt that finished just under the knee. The bias cut was still utilized, not to cling, but to make a little cloth go a long way.

Hat
Hats were not rationed in Britain, although elastic was difficult to obtain, so designs had to stay on. Wide-brimmed styles often aped men's hats in shape. Wartime austerity meant that womenswear borrowed the idea of understatement and restraint from menswear, with a masculine smartness. The high-crowned thirties shape was still popular, often with one side of the brim upturned to give an angle.

Turban
A requirement of health and safety in the factories, the turban became a style that defined the look of the war years. It concealed unkempt hair that working women no longer had time to dress, kept the head warm, and could be fashioned from scraps of fabric to match an outfit. The snood was an alternative to the turban and both styles inspired shapes for more expensive hats.

Short skirt
Skirt lengths had been raised due to shortages during the war and shorts and culottes had become common for bicycling because of the requisitioning of cars and lack of fuel. There was constant concern over the lack of nylon stockings and if no gifts of nylons from GIs were forthcoming, girls had to wear ankle socks or resort to drawing fake stockings on.

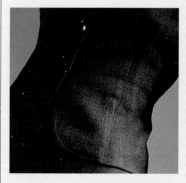

Nipped waist
The nipped-in waist was a continuation of the thirties line. The peplum had started to appear before the war but now that fabric had to be conserved, such flamboyance was tamed. Anything less than minimalist, conservative dressing was seen as vulgar, inappropriate, and unpatriotic. The nipped waist served to save the short jacket from being too masculine.

Man-made fabric

The scarcity of silk and of petroleum-based synthetics, such as nylon, led to further fabric research and the wood pulp-base viscose and rayon were used instead. In the United States, a 1942 propaganda movie, *Hemp for Victory*, was produced to promote crop expansion for hemp fiber for uniforms and rope. Textile design was also advanced as bright florals relieved the severe cut.

Fashion in London, 1944

Trimming under the Utility plan was so taboo that there was virtually no difference between a high-fashion model and its mass-marketed version. By 1944, coupons issued for rationing had dropped from 66 to 36. The 1946 exhibition, "Britain Can Make It," held to promote British production, was dubbed "Britain Can't Have It" by the public on realizing that the goods on show were only for export.

The Paris Hat 1940–1944

Occupation and the effect on couture

After the fall of Paris, French women literally wore their hearts on their heads, developing a style that laughed in the face of Nazi occupation with huge, elaborate hats that they wore with dignity. After the war it was suggested that couturiers had created their designs to make their German women customers look ridiculous. There was a feeling that some sense of control could be maintained, albeit in a small way, if they could dictate fashion. Clothing was even used as a subversive device with scarves printed with maps of France employed by Allied parachutists and bags made with false bases in which to hide Resistance leaflets.

"La Femme Chic," Fath, 1943
Jacques Fath had opened a modest salon in 1937 and was recognized as a talented designer, anticipating the New Look, in 1939, when he was conscripted. He was taken prisoner of war in 1940 and on his release he reopened his salon in Paris, producing clothes for those who could afford them during Paris' occupation. This outfit illustrates the "fashion of defiance" that Schiaparelli noted.

Outfit by Lucien Lelong, 1940
Lelong, as President of the Chambre Syndicale de la Couture Parisienne, persuaded the Nazis not to move the Paris fashion industry to Berlin to commandeer it as German. He kept French couture active during the war, although designers were criticized because their only clients were German. After the Liberation, Lelong undertook a mission to the United States to invite buyers back.

Red and white woven straw hat, Madame Suzy, ca. 1939
In the 1920s Madame Suzy had become a leading milliner who was known for exoticism and her use of color. As the occupation took hold, French women had to resort to recycling raffia, newspaper, worn-out upholstery, even wood shavings and old car tires to use as materials to fashion their extraordinary hats.

"[The silhouette] denoted a Paris ... trampled but still possessed of a sense of humor and intent on putting up a front that skirted on the edge of ridicule."

ELSA SCHIAPARELLI

Coat, muff, and hat, Nina Ricci, 1943
The house of Nina Ricci, opened in 1932 by Maria Ricci when she was 50 years old with her son Robert, was one of the 90 couture houses that stayed open during the war. Cut off from Britain and the United States, French fashion developed to extremes that overcame shortages in defiance of the German occupation— towering turbans became a fixture on the streets of Paris.

Winged hat, Madame Suzy, 1940
Madame Suzy continued to design for the American market during the war. In France, Paulette created wool-jersey turbans for girls who had to bicycle due to the wartime gas shortages. Reboux, the most famous of the Paris milliners, started by Caroline Reboux in 1870, was run by Madame Lucienne, and was a destination and meeting place for those wanting to be in a fashionable atmosphere during the occupation.

ELEMENTS OF FASHION

- hats concocted of flowers, beads, ribbons, and feathers
- Bettina, mannequin/socialite and figurehead for French fashion
- garish colors to contrast the "souris grises" (German women)
- huge skirts and sleeves from the 12 couture houses granted rationing exemption
- accessories with patriotic motifs

The Popover Dress 1940–1946

American Ready-to-wear

The isolation of Paris during the Occupation meant that the United States was pushed to produce entirely original designs for the first time. Ready-to-wear had been developed by such designers as Elizabeth Hawes and Hattie Carnegie and was more in tune with the American market. Carnegie took inspiration from haute couture but translated it into smart American conventionality, while younger designers were schooled in her sparse execution and moved away from Paris to a look that chimed with the sensibilities of their countrywomen. Fabric restrictions prompted a survey that resulted in sizing standardization for the first time, which proved indispensable to a ready-to-wear fashion industry.

> **"[My] inspiration was always America, its freedom, its casualness, its good health. Clothes can say all that."**
>
> CLAIRE MCCARDELL

Popover dress, Claire McCardell, 1942
Claire McCardell was one of the designers who revolutionized American design, marking its territory in the ready-to-wear market. Creating the "Monastic" tent dress in 1938 secured her a job with Hattie Carnegie before designing under her own name in 1940. She persuaded Capezio to manufacture a soled ballet pump; and in 1942 her wraparound Popover dress became a best seller and remained in production for 20 years.

The all-American beauty, Rita Hayworth, 1946
Key elements of the emerging American look in the 1940s were youth, simplicity, and independence. Pin-ups, such as Rita Hayworth and Betty Grable, became favorites of the forces, but were also all-American beauty ideals. Swimwear, sportswear, and functionality inspired bare midriffs, shorts, and the shirtwaist dress, while Valentina introduced the ballerina skirt inspired by Russian ballet. Dungaree dresses came from farming overalls.

Bonnie Cashin designs for *Laura*, 1944
From the lead established by Hattie Carnegie, Bonnie Cashin's designs avoided extravagance and were as uncomplicated as McCardell's in their functionality. From designing sportswear in 1937, Cashin moved to 20th Century Fox in Hollywood in 1943, creating the wardrobe for over thirty movies. In 1949, she set up on her own in New York, and became known for loose-fitting layers in leather, suede, canvas, poplin, and mohair.

Sleeveless jacket, Norman Norell, 1945
Norman Norell worked as a costume designer at Paramount before also joining Hattie Carnegie, with whom he worked until 1941. Norell's simple and sophisticated signature was very much in the Carnegie vein, and part of the "American Look." During the war, he introduced sequinned sheaths using unrationed sequins, and the evening shirtdress, and continued his success with his 1945 sleeveless jacket.

WPB dresses, mid-1940s
In 1942, the American War Production Board issued Regulation L85, which limited fabric use. Width, length, and trim restrictions lasted until 1946 and affected the cut of clothing. Designers responded to this in ingenious ways and all dress patterns were adapted to minimize the amount of cloth required. Contrast cutting, an economy measure to use remnants that otherwise would have been discarded, became very popular.

ELEMENTS OF FASHION

- *print and patchwork pioneer dresses*
- *plaid lumberjack shirts*
- *comic book-inspired superhero hoods, stockings and belts*
- *velvet corselet belts on ballerina skirts*
- *hairstyles with artificial flowers*

CHRONOLOGICAL CATWALK
The Wartime Male

In and out of uniform

At the outbreak of World War II, there were only nine khaki manufacturers in Britain and many enlisted men had to wear their uniforms from World War I. By 1940, the number had increased to one thousand. In 1946, the first American army-surplus stores opened and a stalwart street style started due to a demand for clothing in a time of need.

▶ The broad-shouldered silhouette

To a Britain living on wartime rations, and a starving Europe, the American and Canadian servicemen who arrived after 1942, when the war became global, were representative of a race of giants, shining with health. The fit of their uniforms revealed broad chests and even broader shoulders. Their squared off crew cuts emphasized their solid physiques and seemed far more modern than the Brylcreemed styles worn by the RAF.

▶ Tailor-made tunic

The superiority of the cut and cloth of U.S. uniforms over their European counterparts was evident, but was exacerbated by the fact that officers often had their uniforms tailor-made. The glamorization of the American serviceman was completed with the appearance of the uniformed Glen Miller, the jazz musician and big-band leader who featured in a number of Hollywood swing musicals.

▶ Tone-on-tone shirt and tie

The U.S. Marine officer's uniform came in two tones: a pink-beige, called "pinks," and a brown-olive, called "chocolates," which could be mixed and matched. The tone-on-tone shirt and tie, always worn with the tie tucked into the shirt, had its legacy—it was to resurface in pop culture trends in the 1980s. The U.S. Navy introduced a new type of undergarment—the T-shirt.

▶ The power of the uniform, 1942

The insouciance of the American-style icon, already so familiar from the movie screen, was transformed into flesh when the country entered the war. The females of Europe were bowled over by the uniforms that seemed to enhance their wearers' sexual mystique. The popularity of U.S. service-men led their detractors to coin the phrase "overpaid, oversexed, and over here."

Single-breasted suit , 1939

This "single-breasted country lounge model of nubby wool tweed" was advertised as "midway between the strictly business suit and active sports togs" in the United States in 1939. By the mid-1940s, production in the country and Britain was limited due to the demand for uniforms. The British soldier was issued with a "demob" suit at the end of the war—a mass-produced set of civvies in inferior fabric.

The civvy silhouette

Civilian suits in the United States were subject to just as many restrictions as those in Europe, with the result that the silhouette of wartime menswear was pared down, with sloping shoulders and narrower pants than those of the preceding two decades. The majority of men spent so much time in uniform, which in turn monopolized clothing production, that developments in men's fashion were limited during this time of austerity.

The fedora

Film noir replaced the gangster movie in the 1940s and the style was epitomized by the fedora hat, accessorized with a cigarette, as seen in Humphrey Bogart's roles. Bogart went on to inspire a generation to hunch their shoulders in a trench coat. The tough fedora look translated to Britain when Richard Attenborough starred in *Brighton Rock*.

Wool blend

Germany was first to introduce fabric restrictions with a coupon system similar to the British rationing plan. By 1942, the U.S. War Production Board had decreed that wool in suits had to be reduced by 26 per cent. In France, double-breasting, cuffs, pleats, darts, and yokes were all banned. Both the British Utility suit and the American Victory suit were produced from a wool/synthetic blend.

Swing Style 1942–1946

Boogie-woogie, big band, and swing

Once American troops began mobilization, dance crazes spread with them. Boogie-woogie, big band, and swing became the soundtrack of the war and young GIs brought a touch of glamor and exuberance to Europe. Swing style became an integral part of forties fashion, and the distinctive zoot suits that the musicians wore, with high-waisted, wide, pegged-leg pants and a long jacket with wide lapels and wider padded shoulders, influenced the shape of men's suits during that time. The zoot suit was a conscious display of daring to be different, and for some, it was a highly contentious symbol of the racial situation in the country at the time.

> ## "A killer-diller coat with a drape shape, reet pleats, and shoulders padded like a lunatic's cell."

MALCOLM X

Zoot suit, replica of 1943 design
Musician Cab Calloway spawned the drape fashion in the Harlem jazz clubs in the 1930s. Adopted by African-, Latino-, Filipino-, and Italian-Americans, it became a badge of identity and subsequently one of the first youth tribe or street fashions, while in France the Zazous had a similar scene. The Zoot Suit Riots of 1943 in Los Angeles were a result of tensions between the U.S. Marines and the Hispanic community, whom they saw as unpatriotic.

At Last on the Screen! The Musical Comedy Sensation!

CABIN IN THE SKY

Starring
★ ETHEL WATERS ★ Eddie "ROCHESTER" Anderso
(Famed Torch Singer) (Funnier Than Ever)
★ LENA HORNE
(Gorgeous Song-Bird)
with ★ LOUIS ARMSTRONG ★ REX INGRAM ★ DUKE ELLINGTON AND HIS ORCHESTR
★ THE HALL JOHNSON CHOIR
A Metro-Goldwyn-Mayer Picture

Jazz and swing on the screen, poster, 1943
Cabin in the Sky, an adaptation of the story of Faust, opened on Broadway in 1940 and was made into a movie in 1943. The production broke new ground with its all-black cast, and the fact that MGM released the movie, starring Lena Horne, to a country where movie theaters were subject to racial segregation on- and off-screen was an indication of how important jazz and swing had become to the American national consciousness.

Sammy Davis Jr., 1944
Pre-Rat Pack, Sammy Davis Jr. performed with his father in the Will Mastin Trio vaudeville act. Although his father and Mastin are more conservatively dressed, Davis Jr. is seen here as a jazz-style ambassador in full zoot regalia, which demonstrates the look of the generation. He had served in the U.S. Army, where he had been moved to the entertainment corps after experiencing racism—a problem for him even after he achieved fame.

ELEMENTS OF FASHION

• *suspenders*

• *zoot hats—felt fedoras or tandos with brims of at least 2¾ inches (7cm)*

• *brightly colored or boldly patterned fabrics*

• *wide patterned ties or bow ties*

• *long watch chains*

• *two-tone spectator shoes*

Zoot suiters dancing, 1943
The creation of the zoot suit has been accredited to numerous people, one of them being Harold Fox, a big-band trumpeter and clothier in Chicago. A fashion born out of a music subculture, zoots were the correct wear for dancing to jazz and swing, and the baggy-suit look spread to regulars of dance clubs regardless of background, albeit in a diluted way.

Andrews Sisters
With their string of hits, including "Boogie Woogie Bugle Boy," the Andrews Sisters continuously entertained the forces during the war, often wearing military uniform as they did in the 1941 comedy *Buck Privates* with Abbott and Costello. As in Europe, uniform became a fashion influence and it was deemed patriotic to design using military detailing. The uniforms for the navy WAVES became style items themselves, designed as they were by Mainbocher.

The
New Look

Introduction

The Paris collections of 1947 heralded what came to be called "the Golden age of couture." The worldwide fashion system had already started to change as the 1939–1945 war had affected population demographics and production. Nevertheless, the mania caused by Dior's debut proved that fashion's potential to capture the imagination had never gone away—and neither had the demand for a "new" dress.

The Chambre Syndicale in Paris breathed a sigh of relief when the haute couture industry that had bravely scraped through the war could once more resurrect itself and regain the status of being a source of national pride and revenue.

The French were not the only nation intent on using fashion design and production as a way of boosting their postwar crippled economy. The 1951 Festival of Britain was held on London's South Bank to celebrate Britain's advancement in technology, culture, art, and design of which fashion and accessories were a part—some of the modernist work such as the textiles of Lucienne Day were seen as revolutionary accomplishments in the field of industrial design.

A whiff of change

Less ravaged by war and with a head start on the European designers, the American fashion system seemed fresh. Young custom designers, including Norman Norell, James Galanos, Pauline Trigère, and Anne Klein, grasped the potential of ready-to-wear and the American Look was now firmly established.

The "LBD" had been the brainchild of Chanel in the 1920s, but the timeless piece was made iconic by Givenchy's design for Audrey Hepburn. The relationship began in 1953 with *Sabrina* and the wardrobe collaborations came to be emblematic of fifties chic, sophisticated dressing. While *Breakfast at Tiffany's* opened in 1961, Hepburn's dress is redolent of this era.

The rise of the Italian designers in the 1950s, including Pucci, Roberto Capucci, and Simonetta, was due to the established Italian couture industry (Ente Italiano Moda), which had been formally set up in 1935 by Mussolini to keep Italian fashion domestic. In 1951, Giovanni Georgini was employed by American department stores to showcase Italian fashion, and the Palazzo Pitti runway shows were started in Florence. Meanwhile Rome became the capital of "la Dolce Vita" and a movie and fashion center.

The American and Italian influence resulted in a gradual deformalization of fashion. The elegant and mature fifties woman was introduced to an element of fun, and—for the first time—youth had an influence on the market. *Vogue* adopted teen-speak and in 1959 Pierre Cardin presented the first prêt-à-porter collection from a member of the Chambre Syndicale.

Meanwhile, in London, Mary Quant in Chelsea and Bill Green and John Stephen in Carnaby Street were offering a radical taste of things to come.

Although a master couturier, what really cemented Christian Dior's legacy was an innate understanding of the psychology of fashion. To present your audience with the new, the practically unattainable —to fulfill a desire to have something once more to covet—is what sustains the fashion industry and why Dior's New Look made fashion history.

After years of making do and mending, the fifties obsession with new and neat was not just a whim of fashion. Matching ensembles were deemed essential, with mandatory coordinating accessories. Cosmetics, beauty products, and leisure time all became accessible, and the memory of these as unattainable luxuries spurred the vogue for meticulously finished grooming at all times.

Dior's New Look 1947

Couture reestablishes Paris with the Corolle line

During the war, the mass conception of luxury was a new coat, chosen carefully to last. On February 12, 1947, the hardships did not change, but the imagination did. Christian Dior launched the Corolle line—his first own-name collection—and the world gasped at his audacity. It was immediately dubbed the New Look. Without doubt, with his *coup de foudre* of 16 yards (15m) of fabric for a day dress and 27 yards (25m) for an evening dress, Dior reinstated Paris as fashion capital after the war. American buyers may have viewed imports as unpatriotic, but when Carmel Snow, Editor of *Harper's Bazaar*, heralded the New Look from the front row, it was a prophecy that buyers, designers, manufacturers, governments, and women would eventually concede that the shape indicated a healing of a war-weary world.

Detail of suit with corseted waist, Lachasse, 1948

Although Dior had his detractors and had deliberately provoked reaction, he was aware of a collective desire for a return to femininity. The tiny waist, as seen here on a 1948 Lachasse suit from London, became a fixture of the 1950s, although other designers, particularly Balenciaga, Balmain, and Fath, had already shown early versions of this silhouette before World War II had interrupted the progression of fashion.

ELEMENTS OF FASHION

- hemlines dropped by 9 in (23 cm)
- percale linings
- bustier bodices
- wasp waistlines
- heavy, close-weave fabrics
- abundant detailing

New Look bar suit, Christian Dior, 1947

Dior's bar suit exemplified the Corolle-line silhouette, and was not only one of the collection's most popular models but one of the most copied. Despite this, the New Look became contentious, perceived as a class statement after the democratization of war. The fact that fabrics, such as silk, were being used so extravagantly was incendiary. In Montmartre, mannequins wearing the outfits for a *Vogue* photo shoot were pelted with fruit by market stallholders.

Berlei corseted girdle, late 1940s

Dior's models had built-in *guepières*, or "waspies"— a waist corset. Not only did the return to corsetry provoke a militant voice of protest from women's organizations in the U.S. and from female Members of Parliament in London, who spoke against the retrogressive effect on emancipation, but corsetry had been banned under rationing, so opinion was divided between economy and forbidden pleasures.

"Have you heard about the New Look? You pad your hips and squeeze your waist ... it creates class feeling in a way no sables could."

NANCY MITFORD
LETTERS, LATE 1940S

Couture design for shantung silk dress, Stiebel, 1950s

Dior had created a moment when fashion had wider impact. While the British Government was dismayed at the furor surrounding the collection, a secret showing was arranged for Princess Margaret as a glamorous image was seen as essential for the role of the two princesses as upkeepers of the nation's morale. At the end of rationing in 1949, British designers revelled in the extra yardage—as this Victor Stiebel design demonstrates.

Hardy Amies skirt suit, 1947

Hardy Amies also showed signs of answering women's longing for softer, fuller lines and cleverly worked the hourglass Winterhalter shape for British women still under rationing. Dior's New Look became essential wear and made-to-measure manufacturers had little choice but to follow his lead, although the demands of women still active in the workforce in Britain also required that the line was modified for reasons of practicality.

Christian Dior 1905–1957

Christian Dior is the designer whose fortunes are most intertwined with the fashion history of the 1950s; although his timely achievement with the Corolle line overshadowed the rest of his career, Dior continued to develop and innovate as a couturier until his untimely death in 1957.

Dior was born into a family of agri-chemical manufacturers in Granville, France, in 1905. Although drawn to art, he studied political science at the behest of his family, but consequently opened an art gallery with a friend in Paris, which failed when his father lost his money in the depression.

In 1935, Dior began to sell sketches to fashion houses and in 1938 he worked as assistant designer to Robert Piguet. In 1942, after serving in the army before the fall of Paris, Dior was employed by Lucien Lelong, where he worked with Pierre Balmain until 1946, when fabric magnate Marcel Boussac offered to back a couture house with Dior at the helm. In returning to the prewar emerging silhouette of a long, full skirt, Dior not only answered a desire for femininity but used yards of Boussac's product.

❝My dream is to save women from nature.❞

CHRISTIAN DIOR

Born
Granville, France, 1905

Manifesto
To refeminize fashion.

The 1947 collection made Christian Dior a household name worldwide and brought him as much criticism as accolades. The French government, however, could not have been more pleased, as his New Look reestablished Paris as the fashion capital and saved the important haute couture industry. The government showed the collection in French embassies worldwide, with the result that it was bought by royal families and international figures in the public eye, including Eva Perón. It was said to be fury at Dior's success and the reinstatement of the corset that spurred Coco Chanel to reopen in 1954 with her unstructured suits.

For Dior, the instant success meant a rapid expansion, with extra staff taken on to complete the orders. For other couturiers, the fact that Paris fashion was now the subject of so much attention brought them more custom. The flourishing houses of Fath and Balmain took advantage of the ready-to-wear system that had expanded in Europe and the United States from wartime supply and demand, and modified their designs for that market.

Boussac installed a business manager, Jacques Rouet, at Maison Dior who conducted licensing agreements. Creatively, Dior now had to follow on from the headline smash of the New

Look, and each season had to have a new surprise and as much impact.

Dior always named his collections, and 1948's Envol (meaning flight) showed a new line of skirts worn with jackets that scooped up at the back as if winged, and collars that stood up. In the ensuing years, Dior honed the skirt to a straight line—another fifties classic—and used horseshoe collars, coolie hats, the Princess line, and the cardigan jacket, all of which became women's-wear staples of the era.

In 1953, Dior's experiments with line, cut, and the waist resulted in the barrel-shaped coats and jackets with shorter skirts, which were in direct conjunction to the sculptural designs of Balenciaga and Givenchy. The H-line showed in 1954, which recreated the Tudor cut and flattened the bust that had kickstarted fifties conical bras and sweater styles in 1947. Then followed the A- and Y-lines (named because the cut resembled the shape of the letters), and the use of Orientalism, which resulted in a craze for cheongsam-cut cocktail wear, was again inspirational.

Christian Dior's career ended with his death after his 1957 Spindle line, but the House of Dior had grown into a huge concern comprising couture, ready-to-wear, jewelry, accessories, furs, and perfume. The combination of

Jacques Rouet's business acumen and Dior's understanding of fashion had resulted in some sound judgments including a ready-to-wear boutique on Fifth Avenue in New York, and a percentage payment from the stocking manufacturer holding the Dior licence, which instigated a royalty payment system instead of a one-time fee. Dior's short reign had proved that, postwar, the *grandes maisons* still had relevance within the fashion system.

Each Dior creation was named, as revealed in Paul Gallico's 1958 novel *Mrs. 'Arris Goes to Paris,* in which a London charlady buys herself a dress called Temptation. This model, Zémire, part of the Dior H-line collection, was inspired by the classic riding habit. The ensemble here was a private commission and, being made in an innovative man-made fabric, was extremely expensive. It was sold by Susan Small, the company that made ready-to-wear versions of couture originals for Harrods under licence.

The Floral Day Dress 1950s

The best-selling summer dress

The word "corolle" is a botanical term used to describe the opening of a flower, so it is apt that the silhouette that Christian Dior developed for his 1947 collection that came to be known as the "New Look" should have been adopted for one of the most recognizable fashions of the 1950s—the floral dress. After the war, the job market had to be reclaimed for the returning male workforce, and women were encouraged to reprise their traditional roles as homemakers. Fifties fashion became doll-like in its ultrafemininity and a fondness for splashy, *bayadère*-style, horizontally printed florals, taffeta, satin, bows, and trimmings predominated.

Gray cotton printed with pink and white flowers, Horrockses, 1953
In 1952, Dior began using floral prints by Ascher of London and professed himself inspired by fabric design to create dresses. This stimulated a huge popularity for floral prints in the 1950s, which crossed the whole fashion system. While designers were branching into the ready-to-wear market and the sale of *Vogue* patterns for home sewing was at a premium, Horrockses were known for using couture styling on their designs.

Horrockses Fashions *in Fine Cotton*

THE QUEEN, MARCH 2, 1949

Illustrations for Horrockses, ca. 1950
Horrockses' fashions were synonymous with full-skirted bright floral dresses in Britain in the 1950s. A ready-to-wear company with a high production rate, the dresses still maintained a certain cachet. Horrockses designs were placed at the high end of the market with a relatively expensive price tag, and their reputation for quality was such that it was not at all unusual to see the Queen wearing one of their dresses.

ELEMENTS OF FASHION

- short, curled hairstyles or chignons
- costume jewelry made from synthetics
- matching nail polish and lipstick
- round-necked cardigans
- stockings

"Let us be frank about it. Most of our people have never had it so good."

PRIME MINISTER HAROLD MACMILLAN,
SPEECH TO BRITISH CONSERVATIVES, 1957

Pink floral day dress, 1955
Bright florals on fresh cotton also had an ingénue appeal—a sign of carefree times after the hardships of the war. The burgeoning teen market made the fashions its own, worn with flat pumps and a ponytail. American department stores opened teen departments, inviting popular high school girls to serve on fashion boards as teenage consultants and to model for in-store fashion shows.

Floral-print dress fabric, Horrockses, 1955
Horrockses commissioned fabric design from commercial studios and well-known artists, such as Edouardo Paolozzi and Graham Sutherland, as well as having an in-house design studio. The print was intended to work with the dress designs—this one is interspersed with contrasting horizontal stripes banded around the full skirt and as a bodice detail. Horrockses had modernized their factories after the war and produced a high-quality cotton specifically for their Fashions range.

American mother and daughter in florals, 1950s
The floral print had cross-generational appeal in the 1950s and mother-and-daughter styles could be bought or made at home. The fresh prettiness appealed to the American appetite for the wholesome Doris Day image, signifying as it did the rise of suburban respectability. This image was a key marketing tool in advertising of the era, playing on the importance placed on family values and the increased affluence of the ordinary household.

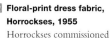

CHRONOLOGICAL CATWALK
The Fifties Female

The power of advertising

Perfect grooming was the sartorial aspiration of the fifties woman and beautifully tailored outfits fitted the thinking. Television broadcasting had been either suspended or severely limited in most countries during the war and, once reestablished during the 1950s, commercial television stations became widespread and advertisements presented women as being impeccably dressed at all times.

Pencil silhouette
Foundation garments were the unseen accessory of the fifties woman. Bras were padded and could lift and separate. Long-line, all-in-one corsets were worn to achieve the slimline silhouette required for the fifties pencil skirts. These came inset with panels of power net for two-way stretch, starting with a strapless push-up bra and finishing with garters to hold up the stockings that no lady was ever without.

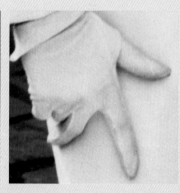

Gloves
No lady's outfit was complete without gloves, which must always be spotless. White or cream gloves came in cotton that could be easily washed and pattern companies issued patterns in a basic style that could be cut to suit in a coordinating color. Leather gloves were also essential for winter, particularly in a gauntlet style, and ruched nylon or satin elbow-length styles were worn in the evening.

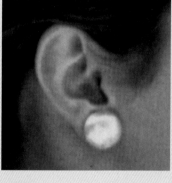

Earrings
Dior and Chanel made designer costume jewelry to complement their designs, while in Britain jewelry design was inspired by the Festival of Britain and was modernist in execution. The United States became a big producer of costume jewelry with brands, such as Miriam Haskell or Trifari, as worn by Mamie Eisenhower, interpreted in the mass market as cute animal or flower-shaped diamanté brooches.

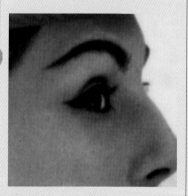

Eye makeup
The fashion mannequins of the 1950s were selected for their patrician air and thoroughbred features and the feline eye, made up with a swoop of eyeliner, topped with an elongated penciled eyebrow, lent an air of hauteur and mystique. Eyeglasses also underwent a makeover in the 1950s, with winged frames inset with diamanté, such as those worn by Marilyn Monroe in *How to Marry a Millionaire* (1953).

Lipstick
Color movies were integral to the development of cosmetics in the 1950s. In the early half of the decade, red was still the preferred shade, as it had been since the 1920s, but technology improved the texture. Companies experimented with adding titanium to produce a more subtle tone, which also resulted in a shimmering finish that inspired later paler pastel and frosted colors for the youth market.

▶ Quality suit fabric
The Utility clothing plan had played to its domestic strengths: tailoring and textiles. Postwar, the British government endeavored to recapture the interest of American buyers. Much of fifties suiting was made of wool, cotton, or linen mixes.

▶ The art of elegance, 1953
Accessories were an extremely important part of the fifties female's wardrobe and coordination was key. Whether the woman in question was demonstrating the wonders of new convenience foods in her kitchen in shirtwaist and apron, presiding over a picnic in gingham, or besuited for shopping in town, it was important to give an overall impression of finished elegance. This photograph by John French shows fifties models Anne Gunning and Fiona Campbell-Walter, both renowned for their sophistication as well as their beauty.

Cristóbal Balenciaga 1895–1972

Cristóbal Balenciaga's legacy to fashion was equally as important as that of his contemporary Christian Dior, but in his lifetime, although revered by the fashion cognoscenti, the Spanish designer shunned the limelight and publicity.

Born in the Basque fishing town of Guetaria, Balenciaga was the son of a seamstress. The rags-to-riches—possibly apocryphal—story of his youth, tells how, on seeing the Marquesa de Casa Torres, the boy remarked on her outfit. When she learned that he could sew, the marchioness gave him a suit by Drecoll to copy. She became Balenciaga's patron, revealing to him the world of couture, assisting his training, and helping to fund his first outlet in San Sebastián. Eventually, Balenciaga set himself up as a couturier, using his mother's name, Eisa, with branches in Madrid and Barcelona.

In 1937, civil war forced Balenciaga to leave Spain, and he opened in Paris. At first, his very Spanish signature in design, referencing Goya and Velásquez, was not appreciated, but a few saw

Born
Guetaria, Spain, 1895

Manifesto
To construct beauty.

talent in one of the only couturiers who could design, construct a toile, cut, and sew an entire garment. Among them, Carmel Snow, Editor of *Harper's Bazaar,* became Balenciaga's champion; while deeming his ideas still too raw, she recognized the potential.

World War II determined a further move for Balenciaga, and he returned to Madrid. After the war, amid the furor of Dior's Corolle line, he set about realizing his design ambition. His first suits, with their dramatic starkness that cut in and out again at the waist over a slim skirt, were similar to those of other designers and there was a unifying "Paris" fashion. As he moved into the 1950s, Balenciaga asserted his originality with his Barrel line, playing with the silhouette by broadening the shoulders and abolishing the waist.

In 1952, Balenciaga showed his unstructured suit with the back of the jacket hanging freely from a stand-up collar, which he had created for Carmel Snow to hide her short neck. In 1955, his first tunic dress made an appearance and by 1957 this developed into the sack dress, which has remained an influential design. By now, Balenciaga and Givenchy had more in common, moving from the tailored to the shapeless, a prerequisite to the next moment in fashion. Both designers

"Women did not have to be perfect or even beautiful to wear his clothes. His clothes made them beautiful."

TRIBUTE BY A LONG-STANDING CLIENT, 1972

This Empire-line evening cape is made from Balenciaga's favorite fabric, silk gazar, because of its weight, which allows for body and structure. The gazar was a result of a colloboration between Balenciaga and the Swiss textile manufacturer Abraham, to create a fabric that would satisfy Balenciaga's legendary perfectionism.

were able to carry off this shapelessness because of exquisite cut, so that the fabric fell perfectly. Balenciaga, in particular, understood proportion and balance and used huge or tiny hats to offset the main shape of the dress.

Balenciaga's sculptural work and perfect cut always retained an element of the Spanish, using a color palette of earth and blood tones. The man himself was upright, proud, and disdainful of publicity and the press. With Givenchy, Balenciaga moved back his press showings so that at times presentations happened weeks after other designers in Paris. While Dior met the press and buyers with charm and professionalism, Balenciaga refused to appear at his showings, and, unlike Dior's patrician youthful mannequins with their exaggerated walk, his models were women of a similar age to his clientele.

Balenciaga ignored the stipulations of the Chambre Syndicale and, in the spirit of Worth, refused to meet the requirements of the client, working on a dress until he alone was satisfied.

Eventually tiring of the rigors of fashion, Balenciaga retired in 1968 at the age of 74 and closed his houses in Paris, Barcelona, and Madrid. He died in 1972 in Javea, Spain.

The Sack Dress 1954–1960

Cutting-edge designs

No sooner had the New Look achieved world domination, becoming one of the fastest lines to experience the trickle-down effect to the main street, than couturiers began to tire of conforming to waist-centric design and turned the idea on its head. The sack dress, also known as the chemise line, began to appear in the mid-1950s with Balenciaga's I-shaped line and Dior's 1956 tunic dresses a predominant influence. The outcomes of experimentation resulted in seminal work from Balenciaga and Givenchy, but in London Mary Quant also adopted the shape for the youthful Chelsea art-student dresses in her 1955 boutique Bazaar.

▶ H-line embroidered satin evening dress, Dior, A/W collection, 1954–55
Christian Dior's 1954 H-line collection demonstrated an exploration into alternatives to the cinching of the waist and was extremely controversial at its launch when it was criticized by the press for its bust-flattening propensities, inspired by the Tudor cut. The line progressed to a slim-cut tunic suit and developed into a more tubular style, but all the models shared a molded, elongated shape, that became a classic cut of the era.

ELEMENTS OF FASHION

- *restrained volume*
- *pillbox hat*
- *spinnaker sail-back dresses*
- *assymetric stoles*
- *bracelet sleeves*

Sack dress in black wool, Balenciaga, 1957 ▲
The shape with which Balenciaga started to experiment in the 1950s was in direct contrast to the structured, waisted styles that dominated fashion. The "chemmy" was deceptively simple: in order to be flattering, the cut of the loose-fitting dress relied on precision. The line was all important because the elegance that is so resonant of the style of the era was still a factor.

Audrey Hepburn in Funny Face, 1957

The movie *Funny Face*, a gentle satire on the fashion industry, runs the gamut of fifties shapes, but it is Audrey Hepburn's first outfit in her role of the dowdy intellectual idealist working in a bookshop that epitomizes the sack shape, which later reprised after her transformation to model girl in a far more chic rendition shown here.

"Every girl on every page of *Quality* has grace, elegance, and pizzazz."

DICK AVERY, FASHION–PHOTOGRAPHER CHARACTER IN *FUNNY FACE*, 1957

Tiered lace and silk evening dress, Balenciaga, 1950s

Cristóbal Balenciaga often incorporated references to his Spanish homeland in his designs, as is apparent in this mantilla-inspired dress. The couturier was known for his restraint and innovation—a forerunner of the late-20th-century intellectual designers. This dress, with its exaggerated dropped waist and satin bows, is an elegant version of the late-1950s baby doll, which teenagers would claim in the 1960s.

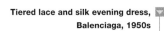

Princess-line satin evening dress, Givenchy, 1950s

Like Balenciaga, Hubert de Givenchy, who designed the costumes for *Funny Face,* was an experimentalist and developed the chemise line into a kite shape: wide at the top, dropping into a slim skirt, tapered below the knee. It was based on the hobble-skirt silhouette that Jacques Fath reintroduced in 1948, which became the pencil skirt of the 1950s. Givenchy's satin gown with matellasse brocade works the sack into the skirt, echoing the fabric massed at the neckline.

The Little Black Dress 1950s

Cocktail chic

Before Coco Chanel invented the Little Black Dress in the 1920s, black was reserved for mourning, but her design was so consummate in its simplicity that *Vogue* called it "Chanel's Ford," claiming it was the dress that every woman should have. However, in the 1950s, the "LBD" was reborn as the classic cocktail style. Cocktail dressing in shorter dresses created an hour of new wardrobe possibilities, but a woman walking into a party wearing a delightful confection of printed taffeta or a Chinese silk cheongsam with a fur stole or an embellished cardigan would immediately feel overdressed at the sight of another woman in a plain black shift, perhaps accessorized with diamonds, and definitely with a martini.

ELEMENTS OF FASHION

- *balloon or draped skirts*
- *tone-on-tone detailing*
- *gloves*
- *a Shady Lady cocktail*
- *Italian sunglasses (for the morning after the Shady Ladies)*

Sheath dress with yoke, sleeves and side volant, Mme. Grès, 1955

Even leisure time in the 1950s had rigid social codes and scheduling and it was the rise of the cocktail party, particularly when it became a part of suburban life, that made the "LBD" such an indispensable item. In contrast to the full-skirted crisp cottons or tailored wool of day wear, a little black dress in satin and tulle allowed a woman to express the inner *femme fatale*.

Tiered cocktail dress, Pierre Balmain, 1957

Like Dior's Corolle line, Balmain adopted a New Look silhouette in the 1950s with his long, bell-shaped skirts and pulled-in waists. A designer for the international set, Balmain, who studied architecture before beginning a career in fashion, was known for styles that were both elegant and fun, as seen in this design, which plays on the ballerina-style *mode* of the era.

"When a little black dress is right, there is nothing else to wear in its place."

WALLIS SIMPSON

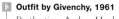

Outfit by Givenchy, 1961
By the time Audrey Hepburn starred as Holly Golightly in *Breakfast at Tiffany's* in 1961, the "LBD" was well-established, but Givenchy made the style fresher and younger, and in doing so created an iconic fashion moment. Hepburn's elfin looks and slight figure contrasted directly with the smoldering sexuality of Anita Ekberg in her gravity-defying black dress in Fellini's *La Dolce Vita* of the preceding year and anticipated a style to come.

Wrap dress in jersey, silk, and wool, Mme. Grès, 1957–1959
Madame Grès, who before the war had designed couture under the name Alix, was already known for her classically sculptural styles. Her pleated evening gowns are reminiscent of Greek statues, but in turning her hand to a little black dress in the 1950s, she used her favorite jersey to accentuate womanly curves in this wrap style, which predates another classic wardrobe staple.

Cover of *The Queen* magazine, 1954
The simple chic of the little black dress works well as the perfect backdrop to accessories, particularly for the feature hats worn for cocktail hour. *Vogue* had called the dress "a uniform for all women of taste" in the 1920s, but what had become apparent by the 1950s was that the "LBD" had developed a persona of its own—one of sexy, uncompromising glamor.

The Sunsuit 1950s

Sun, sea, and skin

Increased leisure time and bustling postwar resorts gave rise to a new wardrobe of vacation separates—from informal slacks to palazzo pajamas for the beach. Beachwear styles were big sellers both in the United States and Europe, but the newest fashions originated on the French Riviera, where the Union des Créateurs de la Mode Côte d'Azur held annual fashion shows in St. Tropez. It was here that in 1947 the bikini was unveiled, named after the atoll where the first nuclear testing took place. Despite the explosive reaction to the two-piece when Roger Vadim put Brigitte Bardot in one for *The Girl in the Bikini* in 1952, most women in the 1950s still opted to sun themselves in a variety of one-piece suits.

"[The French Riviera] is a sunny place for shady people."

W. SOMERSET MAUGHAM

▶ **Grace Kelly at Cannes in beachwear by Edith Head, 1954**
Alfred Hitchcock's *To Catch a Thief*, starring Grace Kelly and Cary Grant, was filmed in the South of France and won an Oscar for best costume. In this scene, designer Edith Head has channeled the Côte d'Azur beachwear elegance with matching turban and sunglasses. It was at the 1955 Cannes Film Festival, while promoting the Hitchcock movie, that Kelly met her future husband, Prince Rainier of Monaco.

Screenprinted rayon, British Celanese Ltd., 1951

This fabric, produced for a Festival of Britain project to combine science and design, was inspired by diagrams of crystal structures to show the arrangement of atoms. Rayon was woven with elastic fibers to create a two-way stretch. By the 1950s, other synthetics were being developed, such as polyester and acrylic, with quick-drying properties.

ELEMENTS OF FASHION

- *playful beach separates*
- *espadrilles with ankle ties*
- *mules*
- *brightly colored prints*
- *frilled or patterned bathing caps*
- *Italian sunglasses*

Swimsuit, printed satin with elastic, ca. 1950

Beachwear prints, often garish in the 1940s, became a more sophisticated niche market in the 1950s. In the United States, Hawaiian-Japanese-inspired prints were often used. In Europe, Emilio Pucci moved swimwear textiles on a generation when he began to design prints for Rose Marie Reid swimwear. Pucci's boutique, Emilio of Capri, soon expanded and his unlined clothing, which flowed with the body was perfect for poolside.

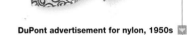

DuPont advertisement for nylon, 1950s

This manufacturer promised that its swimsuit would give the wearer a desirably *soignée* silhouette. DuPont had been experimenting with stretch fabrics for underwear and leisure wear to give a lighter touch and an element of control, which facilitated strapless designs without boning. Elasticated panels covered the midriff for stomach control. In 1959, the DuPont laboratories discovered spandex, which revolutionized swimwear.

Printed cotton sunsuit, Federica, 1958

The somewhat daring bikini was not such a common sight as the one-piece swimsuits on the beaches or poolside in the 1950s. More modest options included the bloomer swimsuit with little puffed legs or the skirted suit, like this example, photographed for *Vanity Fair* by John French. Playsuits were jumpsuits ending in flared shorts, or midriff-baring bikini tops with shorts or skirted bloomers. Toweling wraps in matching print often completed the outfit.

The Stiletto 1950s

The Italians whittle a heel into an icon

If the New Look, with its dictatorial inner structure, was the fashion revolution that heralded the 1950s, then the stiletto was its footwear equivalent. In 1952, the stiletto heel became the new shoe of the season. The spiked style was offered simultaneously in the collections of Italian shoemakers Ferragamo, Albanese of Rome, and Dal Co., and in Paris by Roger Vivier, and as with so many fashion innovations, its originator is unclear. The technology in each company's model was the same, with the inner structure of the spindly heel hiding a metal spigot embedded in plastic to support the wearer's weight.

Silk stiletto, Givenchy, 1955
Collaborations between couturiers and shoe designers produced footwear possibilities to match every model in a collection. Shoes with rapier heels and sparse, pointed toes were constructed in every conceivable material. This opportunity to accessorize was seized upon eagerly by the mass market, and leopard-skin, gold, brocade, and print stilettos became popular. Matching shoe and purse combinations were thought very chic, and heels made from lucite were produced to match lucite box-shaped purses.

Embroidered and studded stiletto, Dior/Vivier, 1958–1960
In 1953, Roger Vivier started to work for Christian Dior. Their decade-long collaboration coincided with the stiletto, rendering the spike heel synonymous with the memorable fifties silhouettes launched by the couturier. However, the shoes that won most attention at the time for Vivier were the gold kidskin pair studded with garnets that he made for Queen Elizabeth's coronation in 1953.

Embroidered stiletto, Rayne, 1955

Edward Rayne took over from his father as managing director of the shoe company by "Royal Appointment" in 1951 at the age of 28. He loved the Paris night life and used his social contacts to promote British design in the United States at a time when most buyers were visiting only France and Italy. In 1958, Rayne produced a series of porcelain heeled stilettos in collaboration with Wedgwood for a trade show in the United States.

Sophia Loren at Cannes, 1955

Beloved by starlets, the stiletto was the shoe for a glamorous icon, dangerous, sexy, and aggressive. Sophia Loren wore them as her Italian birthright. Jayne Mansfield owned over 200 pairs, and Marilyn Monroe supposedly carved a sliver from one of the heels of each of her pairs to facilitate her famous wiggle. Doctors warned women against the hazard of broken ankles, and the shoes were banned from many public places—all to no avail.

"Stiletto, I look at it more as an attitude as opposed to a high-heeled shoe."

LITA FORD

CHRONOLOGICAL CATWALK
The Fifties Male

Italian elegance

In 1952, the Rome-based company Brioni showed menswear on the catwalk for the first time at Palazzo Pitti in Florence. Seeking a market wider than the domestic, Italian men's fashion, with its tradition of quality from family-run businesses, was celebrated in trade shows. The influential Italian-American community quickly embraced the style, which translated particularly well to the movie screen.

Hairstyle
The brushed-back hair of the 1950s was allowed to grow a little longer at the front than in the 1940s, when most men had to conform to the service regulations. It is said that Elvis Presley had the idea for the longer, back-combed DA quiff when he saw the Italian haircut, worn by Tony Curtis, in which the crown and sides are short but longer curls fall on the forehead.

Sharp silhouette
The Italian-style silhouette was sharper, leaner, and altogether more European than the American sack cut that had dominated before the war and, postwar, had garnered influences from the zoot suit. The whittled-down line, narrow lapels, and spare detailing had begun to be influential in Britain where London's Soho was incubating a new modernist movement, known by the 1960s as the Mods.

Open-necked shirt
Italian suiting was generally worn with a white shirt and skinny black tie, but by the 1950s, casual wear for the young made the open-necked shirt more acceptable on the street. Newly developed for summer leisure wear were the ventilated fabric shirts. The open-weave merino mix resulted in a pliable fabric that kept its shape. In the United States Hawaiian shirts became ubiquitous, elevated from beachwear to President Truman's casual shirt of choice.

Jacket
The American cut remained wide-shouldered, high-waisted, and long in the 1950s, while Savile Row tailoring toyed with the neo-Edwardian influence and a new Dandyism for a while. In Italy, tailoring companies, such as Brioni, Canali, Kiton, and Caraceni, and Nino Cerruti (with his Hitman ready-to-wear line) were producing more streamlined, shorter jackets that didn't crease on the seat of a Vespa, with three buttons, rounder shoulders, and higher-cut armholes.

Slim-fit pants
Italian tailoring achieved a reputation for exercising elegance and taste over traditional menswear in the 1950s. The slim-cut pants lifted over the ankle when seated to reveal the narrow, thin-soled Italian leather shoes. In 1955, Bill Green opened Vince Man's Shop in Carnaby Street, London. He was followed by John Stephen in 1957, both selling young men's fashion with a distinctly Italian influence, translated into London style.

Quiet quality

The fifties Italian man about town favored a neutral look of pared–down elegance in his casual dress, matching similarly toned fabrics in choice of shirt, pants and accessories. The fabrics themselves were likewise understated but assuredly of quality.

Cheap, stylish chic, 1957

In 1946, Piaggio introduced the Vespa as a functional, cheap mode of transport. It received *gratis* promotion in 1952 when Audrey Hepburn perched behind Gregory Peck in *Roman Holiday;* sales of the scooter topped 100,000. The craze became the cool way to get around, as actors Edmund Purdom and Genevieve Page, caught on camera in Rome, 1957, demonstrated. The Vespa's modern lines complemented the modernist cut of Italian menswear launched on the international market in the 1950s.

The Blue Jean mid–late 1950s

Youth adopts its own uniform

Jeans in the 1950s were the preserve of nonconformists and teenagers. As rebellious *Catcher in the Rye* disaffection captured the teen imagination, denim jeans and jackets became the uniform of the young. Nothing belonged to the fifties teenager more than rock 'n' roll, and the forties bobby-soxer look developed into youth culture where fashion was inextricably linked to music. A love of Elvis manifested itself in poodle skirts and pedal pushers, but in an age when a tight-bodiced, crinoline-skirted silhouette could span three generations of one family, a teenage girl wanting to assert herself could be sure that a pair of jeans would distance her from her mother.

▶ **Levi 501s and leather boots, 1950s**
Serge de Nîmes, the hard-wearing fabric from the eponymous French town, was woven with a navy weft and Italian sailors from Genoa wore a similar hard-wearing navy fustian fabric. While the origins of denim jeans are firmly in the work wear of the European laborer, after Levi Strauss & Co.'s jeans grew in popularity post-Gold Rush, other brands, such as Wrangler and Lee Cooper, manufactured the classic pants and it became essential Western cowhand wear. Jeans aficionados recognize that Levi's made before 1971 have the label written in upper case and are extremely collectable.

Hollywood's Western style, Levi's, 1950s ◀
Marilyn Monroe, who in most of her movies was a vision of cantilevered satin and diamonds, showed her curves in a new light when she donned jeans to film *River of No Return* in 1954. She reprised this in John Huston's 1960 *The Misfits*, wearing Levi's Big Es.

James Dean, 1955

The original rebel without a cause, James Dean was the on-screen embodiment of the new generation gap. In Britain, the angry young man was making his own way and teddy boys formed gangs in neo-Edwardian drapes and brothel-creepers. Stateside, teens were greasers with leather jackets, DA quiffs, and motorcycles, and in Australia they were known as "bodgies." Dean, along with Marlon Brando, represented disaffected youth, influencing teens everywhere.

> ## "I wish I had invented blue jeans. They have expression, modesty, sex appeal, simplicity—all I hope for in my clothes."
>
> YVES SAINT LAURENT

Neal Cassady, 1955

The nonconformist attitude of Beat writers Neal Cassady (right), Jack Kerouac, and Allen Ginsberg, who made New York's Greenwich Village their base but the road their home, meant that jeans suited their lifestyle and sent out the right messages. The Beat Generation, known as Bohemian hedonists, rejected commercialism. The counterculture they created gave rise to the beatniks, attired in beards, sandals, and turtlenecks.

French youth worship, late 1950s/early 60s

Left-Bank existentialists were the European answer to the Beat Generation. Denim-clad youths sat and smoked while they listened to Jean-Paul Sartre at the Paris Café de Flore in St.-Germain. Brigitte Bardot morphed from groomed starlet to oozing sex appeal in beatnik mode with unbrushed bed hair, blue jeans, and a guitar.

ELEMENTS OF FASHION

- *Haynes T-shirts*
- *Converse Chuck Taylor All Star high-top baseball boots*
- *black "Perfecto" leather jackets*
- *lumberjack shirts*
- *black turtleneck sweaters*
- *Capezio ballet slippers*

Denim-clad silhouette

Jeans in the 1950s were straight cut or boot cut, Western style, high waisted, and worn pulled in with a belt. Boys teamed them with a T-shirt and a leather or denim jacket with the collar turned up. Girls wore jeans rolled above the ankle to give shape, with flat shoes and a masculine shirt with a turned-up collar or a Mexican peasant blouse. From now on, the shape of denims would tell the story of a decade.

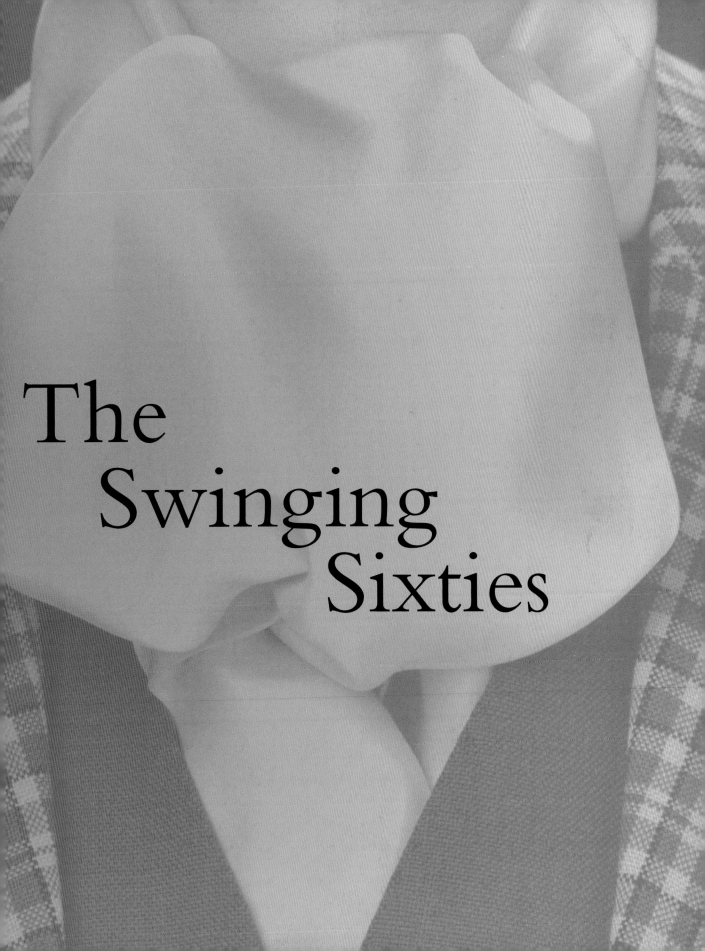

The Swinging
Sixties

Introduction

In a time of turbulence, flux, and social reorder, fashion in the 1960s reflected the fast-changing climate of the decade. For those who had found the teenagers of the 1950s a threat, their worst fears were realized. Young people became instrumental in commerce and culture; parental approval was not the priority that it had once been.

Historical events of the early 1960s were to have a massive impact. The Berlin Wall was erected in 1961, confirming in bricks and mortar the ominous impact of communism to the Western world. Space exploration became a preoccupation of the superpowers. In 1963, John F. Kennedy was assassinated and his wife Jacqueline refused to take off her pink Chanel suit stained with her assassinated husband's blood, wearing it for the swearing in of Lyndon Johnson.

The neat styles of Jackie Kennedy typified the look for most women during the early 1960s and even the juniper dresses of Mary Quant's beat continuation had a similar silhouette, but Bridget Riley's op art swirls and the Beatles' mop-topped collarless suits predicted real change as the decade progressed.

The Youthquake

In London, the 1960s did not so much settle in as were shaken up. Suddenly, all was liberation and revolution, with youth's rejection of the establishment. Carnaby Street and Chelsea flowered, with color spilling out from eccentrically named boutiques. The fashion experience of this generation had consisted of witnessing their parents shopping for watered-down interpretations of couture styles in department stores. Fashion was dusty, stiff, dull, and made by grown-ups. If the next generation wanted an alternative to jeans, they were going to have to make it themselves.

Nothing separated freaks and squares in the 1960s more than psychedelia. At first, swirls of color indicated that the wearer was "switched on" but they were soon adopted by more mainstream fashion and psychedelic print became ubiquitous. Meanwhile, the countercultural lifestyle was satirized in movies, such as *I Love You, Alice B. Toklas!* with Peter Sellers.

New York readily followed suit, Paris went hypermodern, and Italian ready-to-wear was biting at the heels of the Alta Moda. London, the core of the Youthquake, was swinging, or at least a small proportion of it was for a few minutes, and the availability of the Pill aided in establishing the sexual revolution and the miniskirt.

Travel, broadened horizons, a desire to shock, and expanded consciousnesses produced a melting pot of ideas, all of which were translated into display. Young men in England strutted in a rainbow of finery. Meanwhile in the United States, threatened with conscription, the countercultural generation embraced love, racial integration, and hand-painted denim, while the media tut-tutted over the lack of haircuts.

The idealism of the final years of the decade fell into the realm of fantasy and nostalgic longing, of which fashion's manifestation was a romantic fairy-tale mix of craft, color, pattern, and texture – gypsy clothes to wear to the mythical Avalon of King Arthur legends in refuge from the stark modernism of a world where, in 1969, man walked on the moon and the supersonic Concorde flew the Atlantic in less than four hours.

Modernity and antiquity were equally important to fashion and lifestyle in this decade. Youngsters seeking to be different mixed romantic vintage clothing with a forward-look way of living. A stylish few did not want to look the same as everyone else, picking over thrift stores and flea markets and pairing their finds with boutique pieces to create originality.

The Shift Dress early 1960s

Young simplicity

The early sixties shift dress was a development from the fifties sheath dress for the emerging younger market. Mary Quant's designs for Bazaar, although still relatively expensive and seen as rather elitist, inspired a wave of retail outlets for the young working woman and teenager. John Bates started designing the Jean Varon line in 1960, which sold through provincial U.K. department stores and was priced for a secretary's wage. In London, when the Temperance Seven jazz band opened the 21 Shop in Knightsbridge, lines formed around the block, and it wasn't long before Young Jaeger, Way In at Harrods and Miss Selfridge were in operation.

Sketch, Oleg Cassini, early 1960s

The sleeveless A-line dresses, box-jacketed suits, and pillbox hats that made up the First Lady's wardrobe during President Kennedy's tenure were immediately copied. Oleg Cassini, as her premier designer, worked with Jackie Kennedy to Americanize the simple but chic Paris couture styles that she preferred, cutting demure but youthful shifts in bright colors, matched with hats by Halston for Bergdorf Goodman.

Gingham shift worn by Pauline Stone, Barbara Hulanicki, 1964

In 1963, Stephen Fitz-Simon encouraged his fashion-illustrator wife, Palestinian-Polish Barbara Hulanicki, to start designing her own dresses. Lacking the capital to open their own store, the couple started Biba's Postal Boutique. The venture's business was slow until the *Daily Mirror*'s Fashion Editor, Felicity Green, published a full-page promotion of this dress with a keyhole back. The dress was given a moderate price tag and over 17,000 were sold.

PRINTED PATTERNS
BUTTERICK 3493 4/6

SIZE 12 BUST 32
METRIC 81cm

JEAN MUIR OF
Jane & Jane

MISSES
10 12 14 16 18

▲ **Coat and shift by Jean Muir, Butterick, 1964**
Jean Muir started her design career at Jaeger in 1956, then left to set up her own label, Jane & Jane in 1962. It was bought by Susan Small, the company that translated Paris couture styling for the British ready-to-wear market. This Jane & Jane Misses design for Butterick patterns shows a distinct Jackie Kennedy influence.

ELEMENTS OF FASHION

- *black stretch stockings*
- *bouffant hair set in a long bob with the ends curled*
- *juniper dresses*
- *the Twist*
- *gingham and flannel*

▼ **Lace shift ensemble, Kiki Byrne for the 21 Shop, 1961**
In 1961, Martin Moss, the managing director of London's Knightsbridge department store Woollands, was inspired by Mary Quant to open an in-store boutique for the youth market. His buyer, 22-year-old Vanessa Denza, looked to the Royal College of Art where, under Janey Ironside, a wealth of new talent was emerging. London's Royal College of Arts graduates stocked at the 21 Shop included Kiki Byrne, Foale & Tuffin, Ossie Clark, and Gerald McCann.

> ❝Snobbery has gone out of fashion, and in our shops you will find duchesses jostling with typists to buy the same dress.❞
>
> MARY QUANT

▲ **Wool shift dress with center pleat, Mary Quant, 1960**
Started in 1955, Bazaar was the forerunner for the youth market, but was set up on a small scale by Mary Quant's future husband Alexander Plunket-Greene and friend Archie McNair, with Quant as buyer and designer. Quant created drama from simplicity, using bright colors, such as the tomato red of this shift, often juxtaposed with black in a way that seemed excitingly fresh.

Mary Quant b. 1934

Mary Quant was born in London and the relationship between the designer and her home town has become one of historical significance.

Although interested in fashion, her teacher parents insisted that she study for an art-teacher's diploma at London's Goldsmith's University, and it was here that she met her future husband, Alexander Plunket-Greene. He was from a Bohemian Chelsea background and introduced Quant to an English eccentricity that she at once embraced, and the two of them mixed with the "Chelsea set" in a coffee bar owned by Archie McNair. Quant, Plunket-Greene, and McNair opened Bazaar on the King's Road in 1955, catering for the Bohemian artists, writers, students, and socialites of the area with the same antiparent philosophy of life as fun.

Quant's initial role was that of buyer, stocking the store with what she called a "bouillabaisse of clothes and accessories," and advertising the whole with her innovative window displays using mannequins modeled on a Shrimptonesque body with high cheekbones and chin-skimming bobs.

The expensive mannequins are a clue to the social placing of Bazaar in the second half of fifties London. Quant has likened the atmosphere of Bazaar to a "cocktail party" and certainly

Born
Blackheath, London, 1934

Manifesto
To address youth fashion.

the prices of the clothing would be affordable to only the priveleged clientele that shopped there—for example, sixteen and a half guineas for a juniper dress was a steep price tag.

Quant soon found that she preferred selling her own clothes to buying, making youthful shapes that she would wear herself, although her inexperience saw her buying fabric from Harrods. The popularity of her easy shapes meant that machinists could eventually be employed, leaving Quant to concentrate on design. A pair of "mad house" pajamas that she designed for herself for the store opening were featured in *Harper's Bazaar*, resulting in copies for the American market.

After opening a second Bazaar in Knightsbridge in 1957 and a selling trip to Paris, the fashion press took over the reporting of this youth phenomenon, which had previously been consigned to the social pages. Quant wore her own designs and epitomized the "dolly bird" image of London's young sixties girl, so it was no surprise that, with the help of Plunket-Greene's gift for publicity, Quant was credited with the invention of the miniskirt; in fact, this is a moot point. What she did do was make an emerging idea her preserve. Quant's interpretation of the mini was far from the

Mary Quant attributed her success partly to being in the right place at the right time. She was certainly at the center of a burgeoning influential scene and created the "Chelsea look." Among her associates were Jean Shrimpton and David Bailey, who started out as assistant to photographer John French.

architectural constructions of Paris, and used easy jersey T-shirt shapes in vibrant stripes and blocks of strong color that moved away from fifties pastels.

The influence of Bazaar was paramount to the emerging London fashion scene as a global authority on cool. In 1962, a licensing agreement was signed with J. C. Penney for clothing and underwear design, and the demand

for expansion was satisfied in 1963 with the founding of the Mary Quant Ginger Group Wholesale Clothing Design and Manufacture Company, which bought the Quant touch of youthful simplicity to the masses when most teen clothes were still only available in independent boutiques in London. That same year, Quant was recognized in the *Sunday Times* International Fashion Awards, while 1966 saw an OBE award from the Queen for Services to the Fashion Industry, the initiation of Quant's cosmetics range, and the instantly recognizable daisy logo that came to feature on licensed goods from bed linen to carpets on an international scale, including the Japanese market. This involvement lasted until her resignation from Mary Quant Ltd. in 2000, following a Japanese buyout.

In 1974, a retrospective entitled "Mary Quant's London" was the last exhibition of the London Museum before it became a part of the Museum of London, a formal recognition of the woman who had helped shape London's "swinging" moment.

❝Fashion is not frivolous. It is part of being alive today.❞

MARY QUANT

The Mini mid–1960s

Swinging starts

Mary Quant and John Bates in Britain and André Courrèges in Paris have all been proclaimed to be the "inventor of the miniskirt." What is generally accepted is that the mini became the symbol of the swinging sixties and, as *Time Magazine* proclaimed in its April 1966 cover story, nowhere was more swinging than London. In 1965, Paul Young secured a contract with the U.S. Puritan Fashion Corporation to mass-produce designs for youngsters, and a group of British models was taken on an American tour to showcase clothes by designers including Foale and Tuffin, Ossie Clark, Sylvia Ayton, and Zandra Rhodes.

Printed cotton mini, Ossie Clark and Celia Birtwell, 1968
Ossie Clark started designing for Alice Pollock's Chelsea boutique, Quorum, while still at the Royal College, in London, and his 1965 graduation collection was featured in *Vogue*. One of the stand-out features of his work was the print collaboration with his wife, Celia Birtwell. Her romantic, abstract textiles reproduced on Clark's favored moss crepe often worked with the cut of the designs to produce the impression of a custom-made finish.

Long sleeved purple suede minidress, Jean Muir, 1965
The minidress, with its overtones of a baby doll's wardrobe, freed women from the tightly corseted waists of the 1950s and dropped the erogenous zone from the bust to the legs, shockingly exposing the thighs. Jean Muir's first own label, Jane & Jane, was bought by Courtaulds in 1966, and the British designer set up her eponymous brand where she further developed her signature stitched and seamed style in jersey and suede.

Illustrations for mini, Mary Quant for Ginger Group, 1960s
By 1963, Mary Quant had become so successful that she opened another branch in Knightsbridge and formed the Ginger Group, which moved her output into mass production and started exporting to the United States. Together with John Bates's designs for Diana Rigg in the TV series *The Avengers*—which gave him exposure for Jean Varon—Quant moved the mini into the mainstream simply by supplying demand.

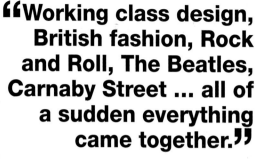

> **"Working class design, British fashion, Rock and Roll, The Beatles, Carnaby Street ... all of a sudden everything came together."**
>
> ROBERT ORBACH

Pop Art mini linen dress, Foale and Tuffin, 1966
RCA graduates like Ossie Clark and Celia Birtwell, Marion Foale, and Sally Tuffin produced minidresses and pant suits that were cut for the tiny frames of the sixties generation, often taking inspiration from modernist designs. This dress demonstrated the effect that pop art had on fashion in London and New York, an effect associated with artists such as Andy Warhol, Roy Lichtenstein, and Peter Blake, who took imagery from advertising and popular culture.

Striped A-line mini, Betsey Johnson for Youthquake, 1967
In 1965, New York joined the British boutique revolution when Paul Young opened Paraphernalia on Madison Avenue. Betsey Johnson, friend of Andy Warhol and wife of the Velvet Underground's John Cale, was appointed designer to the Youthquake label, making fun T-shirt dresses. The store also stocked young British designs from Quant, Clark, and others, mixed in with the Warhol-inspired Johnson disposable paper or transparent plastic dresses.

ELEMENTS OF FASHION

• bodysuits under transparent dresses

• color blocking

• hand-painted prints

• Sally Kirkland, fashion editor at Life Magazine

• Mary Quant collections for JC Penney

• Larry Aldrich dress fabric

179

CHRONOLOGICAL CATWALK
The Sixties Female

"The Face of '66"

Lesley Hornby of Neasden, north London, aka Twiggy, could not have been more different from the patrician fifties supermodel Barbara Goalen. First trumpeted in British popular newspaper the *Daily Express* as "the Face of '66," her popularity paved the way for models to project a personal look: the exotic Donyale Luna became the first black model to be internationally successful, while Prussian-born Veruschka presented herself as an artistic Bohemian.

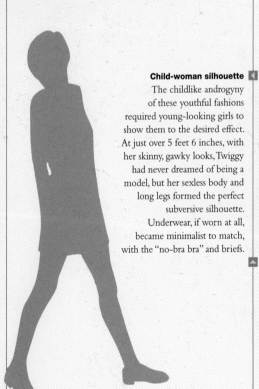

Child-woman silhouette

The childlike androgyny of these youthful fashions required young-looking girls to show them to the desired effect. At just over 5 feet 6 inches, with her skinny, gawky looks, Twiggy had never dreamed of being a model, but her sexless body and long legs formed the perfect subversive silhouette. Underwear, if worn at all, became minimalist to match, with the "no-bra bra" and briefs.

Hair

As much of an innovator as Mary Quant, Vidal Sassoon was the man who completed the sixties look with his geometric cuts. Quant herself sported Sassoon's "5 point" and he was also behind Mia Farrow's elfin crop for *Rosemary's Baby*. Sassoon's protégé, Leonard of Mayfair, cut Twiggy's hair. Photographed by Barry Lategan, the transformation earned Twiggy her title "The Face of '66."

Eye makeup

As the model-girl ideal moved from elegant lady to teenage waif, so did the makeup to fit that persona. Models did their own makeup and Twiggy's look evolved from her early mod style. She wore three pairs of false eyelashes over her own and then painted dolly lashes onto her skin, and blocked out her lips with pancake (foundation) so that her huge eyes became her main feature.

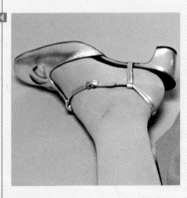

Shoes

In order to get the proportions of the new youthful look right, heels had to be lower. Shoes were dainty to refine the ankles—sling-backed or school-girlish Mary Janes in acid brights or metallic shades. The look was refined as the go-go boot became popular when *The Avengers*' heroine Honor Blackman wore them, and in 1966 Nancy Sinatra sang "These Boots are Made for Walking."

Baby-doll dress

The child-woman of the 1960s, who wanted to look as different as possible from her mother, adopted a Lolita style of dressing her waiflike figure, which gave out a message of life as a game. Dresses often featured oversized buttons, Christopher Robin collars, and little puffed sleeves, while the miniskirt hastened the production of pantyhose, which came colored, patterned, or in fancy stitches.

Twiggy, 1966

If Jean Shrimpton, with her naturalistic style, was one facet of the changing times of the 1960s, then Twiggy was the embodiment of the Youthquake generation. The Adel Rootstein "Twiggy" shop mannequin soon displayed the "Twiggy" range of clothing, while her face advertised everything from cars to breakfast cereal in Japan and the United States.

André Courrèges b. 1923

Born in Pau, France, in 1923, André Courrèges's early studies in civil engineering are an indication of the architectural influence in his work.

After serving as a pilot in the French Air Force in World War II, Courrèges went to Paris in 1945 and worked at the couture house of Jeanne LaFaurie. In 1950, he moved to Balenciaga, who would remain a friend and mentor, and where he learned the tailoring precision of the master while other couturiers relied on their atelier.

In 1961, the House of Courrèges was established, which he set up with his wife Coqueline, who had also worked at Balenciaga. He set about engaging his learned technical skills and his vision of modernism with the architectural application of Le Corbusier. One of the designer's first innovations was to replace the by now institutional LBD with the little white dress, thus heralding a new age of space awareness in fashion. At first Courrèges's collections mainly adhered to the dictates of haute couture, but with a simplicity that belied the cut. Gaining confidence, Courrèges started to use futuristic fabrics, including PVC and vinyl, and introduced to the couture client the innovations that were the preserve of the youth: hemlines above the knee; the pant suit; acid colors.

Born
Pau, France, 1923

Manifesto
To bring the future closer.

The year 1964 was marked by the Courrèges Moon Girl. The space-age white and silver collection with sheer chiffon tops and thigh-high skirts in geometric shapes with cutout portholes were central to the space-race fashion of the mid-1960s and delighted the renegade art world. Courrèges was careful to make his elected wardrobe wearable and comfortable for young women, with the construction of his tunic tops, matching pants, and little dresses allowing for freedom.

The flat, white boots that Courrèges designed to ensure not only ease of movement but correct proportions became adopted internationally as go-go, or kinky, boots and were integral to the dance steps of the mid-1960s.

After a brief hiatus of discontent following the pirating of his designs, Courrèges reopened in 1966, having devised a plan to beat the copyists at their own game: a tiered fashion system with three ranges priced and manufactured on a sliding scale: Couture Future, Prototype, and Hyperbole, which was intended as mass-marketed prêt-à-porter. With the

Courrèges often mixed white with color and this 1965 white worsted ensemble trimmed with blue spandex demonstrates how the designer modernized even the most traditional of couture outfits. As well as binding in color, he used signature circle welt seams around the armholes and over the ribs, and details picked out in topstitching.

"A woman is truly beautiful only when she is naked and she knows it."

ANDRÉ COURRÈGES

integration of ready-to-wear into the fashion system and the cultural changes in the second half of the 20th century, this became the model adopted by couture houses attempting to survive. An introduction of a Courrèges house scent cemented the name as a brand.

In 1967, the "second skin" all-over tights were launched—part of a wave of leotard-inspired clothing that interested designers at the time and an innovation that remains a cyclical fashion stalwart. In 1969, the ancient Egyptian look was given the Courrèges treatment with metallic geometric bobbed wigs, frosted lips, and "mummy" bands of sequined fabric interspersed with transparent silk.

Always interested in sportswear, and known for tennis separates, he designed a uniform for the 1972 Olympics with interchangeable pieces and in 1973 launched Courrèges Homme with a sporty, tailored silhouette. By the end of the decade, licensing diversifications including fine leather goods and beauty products had followed.

André Courrèges retired in 1996 and was succeeded by his wife, Coqueline. The Courrèges brand has become synonymous with technological research and advancement and has moved into furthering the development of the electric car, with which Courrèges was originally involved during the 1960s.

The Space-Age Outfit 1964–1969

Pushing the boundaries

With access to TV becoming much more widespread in the 1960s, fact and fiction merged when cosmonaut Yuri Gagarin became the first man to orbit the earth in 1961 and sci-fi no longer looked so far-fetched. Courrèges launched his house in Paris in that year and in 1964 revealed his Space Age collection, at the same time as the space race to land the first man on the moon. Artificiality influenced fashion and with the use of new materials, such as paper, plastic, and plexiglass, couture was becoming increasingly irrelevant. The sixties "life as art" stance translated into the Mylar and inflatables decorating London boutique interiors and the silver walls of Warhol's New York studio, The Factory, and appeared in the geometric shapes and space-age fabrics used for Courrèges' mini, John Bates' *Avengers* designs, and Betsey Johnson's ideas for Paraphernalia.

> **"Can one show oneself in the street dressed in creations designed for the year 2000?"**
>
> *VOGUE,* 1965

Disk dress, Paco Rabanne, 1967

Spanish-born Paco Rabanne initially studied architecture at the Beaux Arts in Paris, and became a freelance accessories designer, using his interest in pop art to create soft plastic sculptures. Rabanne was interested in modern materials and often used linked plastic to create dresses reminiscent of industrial design. This minidress is made of silvered plexiglass disks linked together with metal chains.

Cosmos cream tunic, Pierre Cardin, 1967
Pierre Cardin had worked in Paris couture since 1945. Always forward-looking (he was the first French designer to see Japan as a potential market in 1959), his Cosmos unisex collection dressed men and women as if they were about to embark upon a space odyssey, in matching unitards, zipped jumpsuits, tunics, and leggings. Cardin went on to open his own cultural center, the Espace Cardin, where he showed his collections and promoted new artistic talent.

Oliver Goldsmith eyewear, 1960s
Brothers Andrew Oliver and Ray Goldsmith were the third generation at the helm of the family eyewear firm that had first taken glasses into the fashion realm in the Britain in the 1930s. Andrew Oliver started designing in 1963, taking inspiration from popular culture and securing celebrity endorsement, making sunglasses for Audrey Hepburn in *Two for the Road* and *How to Steal a Million*.

ELEMENTS OF FASHION

- *goggles and visors*
- *Jeanloup Sieff's photographs of Donyale Luna in space-age fashion for* Nova Magazine
- *white with colored detailing*
- *2001: A Space Odyssey*
- *Pucci flight-attendant uniforms for Braniff Airlines with bubble helmets*
- *Marshall McLuhan's* The Gutenberg Galaxy

Space-age erotica, Jane Fonda as Barbarella, 1968
Roger Vadim, the French film director who first put Bardot in a bikini, directed his then-wife Jane Fonda for her title role in the erotic space drama *Barbarella*, adapted from the French comic books. The movie credits refer to Paco Rabanne as inspiration, and certainly Fonda in futuristic molded plastic bustiers and leather leotards recalls the futuristic leanings of sixties couture. In the movie's opening scene, Fonda undresses in "zero gravity," lying on a sheet of plexiglass to achieve the illusion.

Provocation 1964–1969

The topless sixties

The shock factor of 1960s fashion, once it had been through mod styling, visited outer space, and swung, was practically expected. Rudi Gernreich's topless swimsuit, which became known as the monokini, was an early example of sixties extremes and innovation in 1964. Breaking new ground, Gernreich was commissioned by Warner's to design a flesh-colored, stretch-nylon body stocking, which was to be the underpinning for many women wearing the revealing fashions of the era. Experimentalism by Paris couturiers was cross-pollinated with the "kinky" PVC styles of go-go dancers, the toyland vacancy of London's young "dolly bird," and the architectural lines of Le Corbusier to produce a kind of restrained madness.

> **"It may well be a bit much now. But, just wait. In a couple of years topless bikinis will be ... regarded as perfectly natural."**
>
> RUDI GERNREICH
> TELEVISION INTERVIEW, 1964

Topless swimsuit, Rudi Gernreich, 1964
The son of an Austrian hosiery manufacturer, Rudi Gernreich arrived in the United States with his family as a refugee in 1938. After art school, he worked as a dancer and dance-costume designer and it is this background that facilitated his initial swimwear designs without inner support. This culminated in the topless swimsuit, which came to be a signifier of the "permissive society."

ELEMENTS OF FASHION

- *a vacant stare*
- *15 minutes of fame*
- *Sally Jess bags*
- *Beth Levine stocking boots*
- *model Peggy Moffitt*
- *Rabanne and Cardin PVC premolded clothing*
- *Jean-Charles de Castelbajac's postcard coat*

"Variable Sheets," zipped panel mini, Stephen Willats, 1965
Polyvinyl chloride (PVC) was originally developed from experiments with oilcloth in 1844. In the 1960s, it became fashionable with the mods, dyed in bright colors and made into scooter coats. Shiny, wet-look PVC was among other novel textiles that were used by designers interested in the op art and pop art being produced to express clothing's artistic and sculptural possibilities.

Bunny suit in white sateen, Courrèges, 1969
As the couturier of the miniskirt and the instigator of the architectural space-age look, Courrèges felt that his designs were subject to plagiarism and sold his business to L'Oréal in 1965, only retaining a few select couture clients. Reopening a year later, he softened his geometric edges with catsuits and cutout dresses, although by 1969 his shock factor was more in tune with mainstream fashion.

Breastplate, cloak, and mini, Ungaro, 1969
Emanuel Ungaro, born in Provence to Italian parents, went to work in Paris at the age of 22 and joined Balenciaga after a tailoring apprenticeship. In 1961, Ungaro joined Courrèges, who had also been at Balenciaga, then went on to open his own house four years later. However, the collaboration that Ungaro enjoyed with textile designer Sonja Knapp created a tactile dimension to his work.

Psychedelic Prints 1964–1969

Lucy in the Sky with Diamonds

By the mid-1960s, the graphics of op art and the colors of pop art had been combined in an expression of a state of mind. Ken Kesey's bus full of Merry Pranksters set off on its tour across the United States in 1964, offering LSD to anyone willing to turn on, tune in, and trip out. The swirling colored patterns that decorated the bus became symbolic of a counter-culture revolution. Psychedelia slowly encroached upon Swinging London with the 1967 "14 Hour Technicolor Dream" at Alexandra Palace, where sharp mod suiting mixed with long hair and beads and naked girls were painted to match the lights.

**Corduroy suit,
Mr. Fish, 1967**
Michael Fish designed floral, ruffled shirts for Turnbull & Asser of Jermyn Street, in London, and became known for his flamboyant style, which won him work as a movie costumer, using Liberty prints for suits for Terence Stamp in *Modesty Blaise* in 1965. In 1966, he opened the Mr. Fish boutique on Clifford Street, selling wildly patterned suits, voile shirts, and his signature kipper ties.

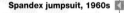

Spandex jumpsuit, 1960s
Rudi Gernreich and fellow designer Giorgio Sant'Angelo, also American-based, followed in the footsteps of Claire McCardell, experimenting with stretch and active wear. While Gernreich had developed McCardell's leotard into the body stocking, Sant'Angelo worked with DuPont to produce spandex-enhanced stretch bodysuits. These were the perfect uninterrupted base for the psychedelic print, and fashion's answer to body paint.

> **"For every visible hippy, barefoot, beflowered, beaded, there are a thousand invisible members of the turned-on underground."**
>
> TIMOTHY LEARY

"Flower Power," hippy in California, 1967

The 1967 Summer of Love, centered in California, was heralded by the June release of the Beatles' album *Sergeant Pepper* and summed up by Scott Mackenzie urging people to "be sure to wear flowers in your hair" if they were going to San Francisco. Thousands of young people, dubbed "hippies" by the media for their long hair and free way of dress, converged on Haight-Ashbury.

The Who, Woodstock, 1969

Although the Council of the Summer of Love in Haight-Ashbury had performed a "death of the hippy" ceremony in October 1967, the free-love period continued into the summer of 1969 for the Woodstock Festival, which brought the London and American music scene together in a melting pot of UFO, London, West Coast and East Coast sounds, looks, love and peace.

Paper dress, probably American, 1967

In 1966, the American Scott Paper Company produced a range of promotional paper A-line dresses in op art and paisley prints, and disposable fashion was realized. Betsey Johnson designed paper dresses for Paraphernalia and the speciality Waste Paper Boutique opened. Sylvia Ayton and Zandra Rhodes of the Fulham Road Clothes Shop in London sold their paper dresses through Miss Selfridge department stores, where the staff struggled to prevent customers from tearing the hems out of curiosity.

CHRONOLOGICAL CATWALK
The Sixties Male

Dedicated followers of fashion

By 1966, John Stephen owned His Clothes along with five other stores in London's Carnaby Street, which was at the time lined with menswear and unisex stores that precipitated the Peacock Revolution. Bill Green's Vince's Man's Shop was mainly for gay men and the bold colors and flamboyant finish spread into a mainstream campiness in men's fashion by mid-decade. In 1967, the Stones—devotees of ambiguous peacockery—made a promotional movie for their single "We Love You," with tongue-in-cheek reference to the persecuted dandy, based on the trial of Oscar Wilde.

The new dandy silhouette

The silhouette of the peacock male started as skinny in order to give justice to the hip-hugging, straight cut, and often vertically striped pants. Shirts were close-fitting, collars high, and the double-breasted long jackets that had evolved from the Edwardian style had sloping shoulders, which were frequently hidden by an overcoat or fur coat thrown over the shoulders.

Wide-brimmed hat

Boutiques, such as Granny Takes A Trip and Hung On You, where boyfriend and girlfriend could shop together, reinforced the unisex interchangeability of clothing. Mod fashion had rejected head wear as dangerous to the hairdo, but peacockery embraced a Wildean floppy brim, and Brian Jones's Garboesque elusive stare from under his perfectly cocked hat epitomizes the sixties dandy.

Savile Row stripes

Musicians such as the Rolling Stones, who had started out dressing in the Mod tradition, grew self-assured as their fame and fortunes rocketed. By mid-decade, tailors who had initially ignored the dictates of the young fashions had to take notice as that generation started to invade Savile Row: Tommy Nutter, Mr. Fish on Clifford Street, and Blades on Dover Street.

Cravat

Mr. Fish's kipper ties were the incarnation of adornment that set the peacock revolution apart from the restraint of their Mod forerunners. A Mod tie was skinny and black. Kippers, cravats, and scarves were worn with custom-made Deborah & Clare shirts from Knightsbridge, hand-made in every possible fabric and print—as long as it didn't match.

Fur

Fur had become linked with the Rolling Stones' wicked image in the public's mind after Marianne Faithfull had wandered into the drugs bust at Keith Richards' country house wearing nothing but a fur rug. Anita Pallenberg wore fur coats found on antique stalls as did her boyfriends—first Brian Jones, then Keith Richards—the touch of decadence chiming perfectly with their reputation for Dandyish hedonism.

Silk-jersey prints, 1960s
By the middle of the
1960s, when a new
fondness for decoration
and flamboyance was
pervading womenswear
and menswear alike,
Emilio Pucci's signature
kaleidoscopic swirls were
an inspiration for the
psychedelic revolution
in fashion, embraced by
peacockery and
counterculture.

The Rolling Stones, 1967
When the Rolling Stones
formed in the early 1960s,
they were sartorially in the
Beatles mold. By the time
their precocious manager,
Andrew Loog Oldham,
had fed the papers with
the headline "Would you
let your daughter go with
a Rolling Stone?," the
band had adopted the garb
of unfathomable youth that
the media had painted
them to be.

Yves Saint Laurent 1936–2008

The boy wonder who took over the mantle of head designer at the House of Dior at the age of 21, Yves Saint Laurent was not only born great but had greatness thrust upon him.

Born in Oran, Algeria, in 1936, to a middle-class French colonial family, Yves Saint Laurent came first in the International Wool Secretariat design contest in 1984 at the age of 18, and by attracting the interest of French *Vogue*, was employed as design assistant at Dior.

Following the sudden death of Christian Dior in 1957, Saint Laurent's first Trapeze collection for the house won acclaim, but his efforts to introduce the beat aesthetic into his Left Bank collection in 1960 appalled the respectable middle-aged Dior clients and the house took advantage of his call-up for the Algerian War to replace him with Marc Bohan.

Army life proved disastrous for the designer, who had already had his natural sensitivity sorely tested. Saint Laurent was discharged after suffering a breakdown and mental illness would dog him all his life.

Born
Oran, Algeria, 1936

Manifesto
The first haute couturier to design and produce a full prêt-à-porter collection.

Saint Laurent sued the House of Christian Dior for $40,000 and set up his own house with his business partner and lover, Pierre Bergé, in 1962.

In 1963, Saint Laurent revealed his affinity with the art movements of the time and unveiled his op art look, which had parallels with London fashion. The designer's first love had been theater costume, and a dual career in theater and movie design now blossomed with his little black dresses and suits for Claudia Cardinale and Capucine in *The Pink Panther*.

In 1965, this love found fulfillment when David Bailey took his then-wife Catherine Deneuve to meet the designer to order a dress for a London reception where she was to meet the Queen. Deneuve liked the dress so much that she asked Saint Laurent to make her wardrobe for the Luis Buñuel movie *Belle de Jour*.

Deneuve's character, the beautiful and bourgeoise Séverine, was perfectly suited to Saint Laurent's severely tailored ensembles, but her expensively chic and tasteful black PVC raincoat hinted at the dark side of the woman who becomes an afternoon prostitute. Saint Laurent had found inspiration for the military style of Séverine's outfits in the army and navy store on 42nd Street when he had gone to New York for the launch of

> **❝Chanel gave women freedom. Yves Saint Laurent gave them power.❞**

PIERRE BERGÉ

his "Y" perfume. He reworked the military styling on the uniforms to give Séverine a harsh, clinical respectability to such acclaim that this became a recurring motif in his work.

Saint Laurent's relationship with Deneuve became one of mutual appreciation and he used the 1969 Truffaut movie, *La Sirène du Mississippi*, to showcase the actress wearing his safari look, which imbued the iconic piece with an atmospheric sultriness. The designer surrounded himself with other women who became his associates and muses, among them Loulou de La Falaise and Betty Catroux.

In 1966, Saint Laurent and Bergé opened the Rive Gauche boutique selling the prêt-à-porter line. His fall/winter '66 collection featured Le Smoking suit, the tuxedo cut for a woman's shape that was fitted so painstakingly that the designer asserted the wearer should be able to travel comfortably in it. Sinuous and sexy, the suit was seen on Bianca Jagger, Lauren Bacall, and Liza Minelli, as well as the designer's acolytes, and was immortalized in a *film noiresque* photograph by Helmut Newton in 1975. A version of this classic has since been featured in every YSL collection by his successors: Alber Elbaz, Tom Ford, and Stefano Pilati.

The historic achievements of the "Sun King of Fashion" included his see-through looks of 1966, his Russian collection of 1976, and his Homage à Picasso of 1979, while color blocking juxtaposed with his favorite black became a signature.

In 1983, Diana Vreeland honored Saint Laurent with the first ever monographic retrospective at the Costume Institute at the New York Metropolitan Museum of Art for a living designer.

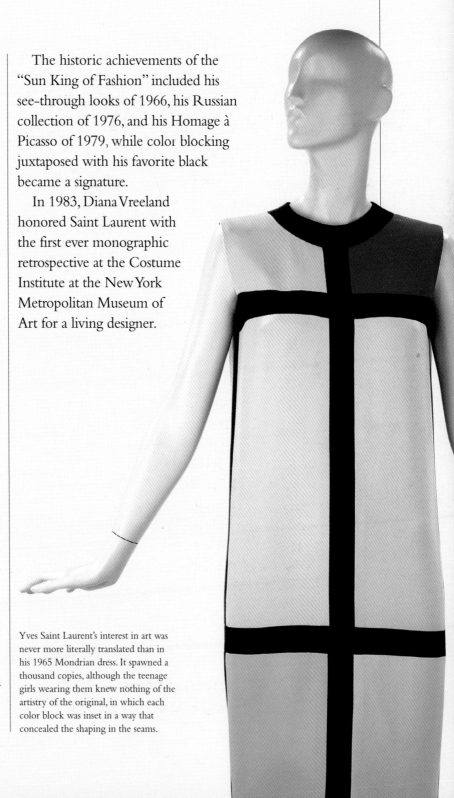

Yves Saint Laurent's interest in art was never more literally translated than in his 1965 Mondrian dress. It spawned a thousand copies, although the teenage girls wearing them knew nothing of the artistry of the original, in which each color block was inset in a way that concealed the shaping in the seams.

Unisex mid–late 1960s

His and hers

Sixties boutique culture revolved around a social scene where the people defined the look. Rules of fashion, retail, and comportment were all cheerfully broken by the movers and shakers, male and female. Male actors and pop stars began to be featured on the fashion pages of *Vogue,* and in 1966 Yves Saint Laurent launched his Rive Gauche prêt-à-porter with his pant suit designed for a woman's body. In London, Sally Tuffin and Marion Foale made their first hipster pant suit as an antiestablishment joke, but soon wearers of tailored pantsuits were being refused entry to every respectable public place in London, Paris, and New York.

COOL COUPLE . . . YOU TWO?
THEN WIN YOURSELVES A FORTNIGHT IN HAWAII

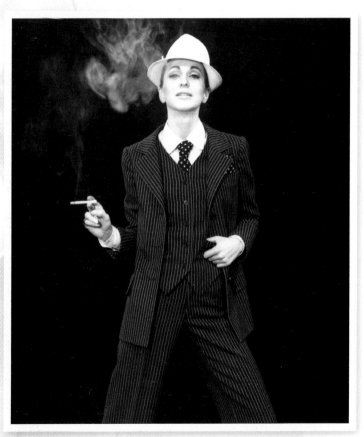

Three-piece suit, Yves Saint Laurent, 1967
When Yves Saint Laurent sent his first celebrated "le smoking" pantsuit for women out onto the catwalk, he made fashion history. Pants for girls had been at first daringly alternative, practical wear, then became a part of youth culture and a casual option, but never had high fashion taken the step to turn the pants into formal dress suitable for society lunches and elegant *soirées.*

Twiggy and Justin de Villeneuve, 1966
London Life magazine was an entertainment guide that incorporated *Tatler* but aimed to pick up on London's happening scene. In 1966, no couple was more happening than Twiggy and her manager Justin de Villeneuve. Twiggy's androgynous look was the perfect foil for sixties unisex tailoring, and the stylish de Villeneuve was the ideal partner for the his 'n' hers hip lifestyle.

ELEMENTS OF FASHION

- *Charlotte Rampling in Mary Quant pants in Georgy Girl*
- *designers Georgina Linhart, Janice Wainwright, Gina Fratini, Emanuelle Khan, James Galanos*
- *chisel-toe shoes and chelsea boots from Anello, Davide, and Honey; Queen and Town magazines*
- *1967 "Best of Britain" exhibition in Macy's, New York*
- *Habitat furniture and Countdown*

Three-piece wool suit, Tommy Nutter, 1966
In 1968, trained tailor Tommy Nutter opened on Savile Row with Cilla Black as a backer and Edward Sexton as partner. The two reinvented the Savile Row suit in fabrics such as colored velvets, suede, and denim with signature wide lapels. The idea of sixties fast fashion was taken back to custom-made tailoring, and Nutter made suits for all the in-crowd, including Mick and Bianca Jagger.

Twill pantsuit, Gerald McCann, 1966
RCA graduate Gerald McCann sold his designs everywhere, from a boutique in Raphael and Leonard's House of Beauty, to dealing wholesale with Woolland's 21 Shop. He was one of the most successful of the British designers to be sold through Paraphernalia in the United States, where his unisex tailoring was so popular that he secured deals with other American manufacturers, ultimately achieving recognition with his own label, which transcended the teenage market.

"I remember going to Turnbull & Asser and having a bright pink shirt made, then being asked to leave the Cavalry Club for wearing it ..."

DAVID MLINAVIC

Jane Birkin and Gervase, 1968
Jane Birkin was the young English "dolly bird" featured in the movie *Blow Up* in 1966, in which the central character, played by David Hemmings, is a photographer based on the unholy trinity of David Bailey, Brian Duffy, and Terence Donovan. In 1968, Birkin took her style to Paris, winning a part in *Slogan* opposite Serge Gainsbourg and the French adopted her, in place of Brigitte Bardot, as the girl who dared to sing "Je t'aime, moi non plus."

The Caftan 1966–1969

Eclecticism

The all-embracing diversity of counterculture fashion mingled old and new, East and West, color and texture to produce visions of kaleidoscopic antiestablishmentarianism. In the United States, frontier fashion with suede fringing and stetsons was adopted, while in Europe an afghan coat signified a rebellion against commercialism. The caftan, meanwhile, was worn not only by commune dwellers but became a garment that denoted a privileged, hedonistic existence, exemplified by Talitha Getty and millionaire husband Jean Paul on the roof of their Marrakesh palace, or by Mick Jagger and Marsha Hunt, hiding out in the south of France. Yves Saint Laurent and Halston both used the T shape in the 1960s, and Elizabeth Taylor had worn similar shapes from Pucci since the beginning of the decade.

Flowered caftan wearer at Woodstock, 1969
Another component of sixties magpie eclecticism was a draw to the ethnic. Spiritualism and the hippy trail to Morocco and India resulted in the adoption of the flowing traditional robes, eye-catching with their multicolored exotic prints, embroidery, and mirrors. It was the ultimate multipurpose, unisex garment and could even be fashioned, in festival times of need, from an Indian cotton bedspread.

ʺyou could wear anything you wanted, from a robe to a cape ... this new androgynous look made the straights particularly upset.ʺ

BARRY MILES, *HIPPIE*, 2004

Caftan worn by Fenella Fielding, Thea Porter, 1966

Thea Porter was born in Damascus, Syria. After her English family sent her to study French at London University, she studied painting in Beirut and then opened a store in London in the early 1960s selling antique Arabian and Turkish textiles. Its success spurred her to design her own range of ethnic-inspired clothing, making high-end ready-to-wear and custom-made, richly embellished velvet, chiffon, and silk caftans.

ELEMENTS OF FASHION

- *Maudie James and the Myers Twins photographed in Christopher Gibbs' apartment for* Vogue
- *Barbet Schroeder's 1969 movie* More
- *Jonvelle August 1969 gypsy shoot for* Nova *magazine*
- *Indian silver jewelry and bells around waist, wrists, and ankles*
- *cheesecloth and palmetto print*
- *beading*

Caftan dress, Zandra Rhodes, 1969

British Textile designer Zandra Rhodes had opened the Fulham Road Clothes Shop with her fellow RCA graduate Sylvia Ayton in 1967. In 1969, Rhodes produced her first solo collection and introduced what came to be her distinctive style—layers of filmy, hand-printed chiffons and silks in intricate patterns inspired by embroidery and knitting stitches —for which the caftan shape was an ideal silhouette.

Floral caftan, Philippe Venet, 1969

The comfortable shape of the caftan was appropriated into mainstream fashion and the ethnic overtures gradually died away by the 1970s. Philippe Venet had worked for Schiaparelli and Givenchy and this design owes more to haute couture than to Marrakesh.

Retro chic 1967–1969

Granny's attic dress

The atmospheric photography of Biba's catalogs and posters from the 1960s reveals the tendency toward "retrochic" that was developing. A nostalgic attempt to recreate the past, seen through contemporary eyes, in an interpretation that often resulted in pastiche, retrochic was a coming together of a cultural ransacking of granny's attic. While vintage was as yet unheard of, an interest in a different pace of life led to an examination of alternatives to mass production, and antiques markets were combed for hand-made treasures. Dramatizations of novels in TV and movies added period clothing into the mix; designers copied detailing, and boutiques, such as I Was Lord Kitchener's Valet, sold original guardsman tunics.

Portobello Road, London, late 1960s
The 1960s witnessed fashions develop from sources other than the dictatorship of haute couture. Secondhand clothes had always been the preserve of the underprivileged, but now Portobello market was being ransacked by people such as Jane Ormsby-Gore, who worked for *Vogue*, and whose husband Michael Rainey owned Hung On You. Anita Pallenberg, in *Performance*, wore her own mix of 1920s jackets and slips and boutique fashions.

Faye Dunaway in *Bonnie and Clyde*, 1967
The movie *Bonnie and Clyde*, starring Faye Dunaway and Warren Beatty, was greatly influential in fashion terms. Dunaway's look of beret, page-boy haircut, and sweater was interpreted through the eyes of the 1960s and helped to bring skirt lengths down to the mid-calf. The relationship between fashion and movie formed a strong bond during this period, with movie both reflecting and influencing fashion's exploration of other eras.

Monk's habit, Biba, 1969

The whimsical nostalgia of a period where contemporary musicians, such as the Incredible String Band and Pentangle, were dipping into traditional song uncovered an interest in the medieval and Renaissance periods. Early music instrumentalist David Munrow provided the soundtrack for TV's *Henry VIII* and Pasolini's movie *The Decameron* delivered an earthy reconstruction. Fashion was no less affected, taking the costumes of Franco Zeffirelli's *Romeo and Juliet* as inspiration.

"The King's Road is a wilderness of stoned harlequins."

CHRISTOPHER GIBBS
LONDON ANTIQUE DEALER

A
All wool pinafore dress, with a low V neck and cutaway back. A narrow bodice with a kick pleat at the front. Colours: Beige / brown herringbone tweed or black West of England wool. Price: £2·19·6

B
Huntsman's blouse in creamy white or black satin. Softly billowing sleeves gathered high on the shoulder and into buttoned cuffs. Price: £3·3·0

Jewellery see back page.

C
Riding mac with a military look, fastened with penny sized buttons high on the shoulder. To clean scrub like a riding mac. Colours: Clay or bitter chocolate. Price: £8·8·0

Shetland wool gloves see back page.

ELEMENTS OF FASHION

- *antique paste buckles and brooches*
- *Pre-Raphaelite curls*
- *Antonio Lopez medieval and art deco illustrations*
- *Renaissance slashed sleeves*
- *armholes cut high and tight in the medieval style*
- *Sarah Moon photography for Biba and Nova magazine*
- *Sonia Rykiel and Cacherel*
- *Serendipity, Granny Takes A Trip, and the Last Picture Frock boutiques*

Trench coast and hat, Biba, 1968

The introduction of the Biba mail-order catalog in 1968 was an extension of Hulanicki's policy that Biba clothing should be for everybody. Biba clothing was mass-produced, good design at prices that most girls could afford, but for many London was an unreachable dream. The catalog made the Biba aesthetic accessible to the provinces, introducing Hulanicki's vision of clothing that referenced the past with the eye of a costumier with a compulsion to use found objects.

From Glam to
New Romance

Introduction

The 1970s were a testament to the difficulty of pinning fashion down to a decade. The first half was, post-Woodstock, a continuation of what is generally regarded as late sixties fashion. The second half reveals a precipitation toward all that is considered to be the 1980s—a decade that left an indelible mark on the structure of the fashionable shape.

In fact, what the decade did bestow upon fashion was the confidence to continue a trend that had started in the 1960s: the establishment of groundbreaking ideas of how the system could work for younger people.

The boundaries of international fashion were becoming more relaxed as designers showed in other countries—Japanese designers introduced a new flavor to Paris fashion, just as the new prêt à porter system was officially established. The French had always seen fashion not just as a national source of pride, but of industry, and eventually shrugged the chip off their shoulder that was couture and paid attention to the successful American model. Karl Lagerfeld typified the new ready-to-wear outlook of Paris fashion. Employed by Chloë and Fendi, he didn't stop there, and at one point was said to be designing for 25 companies.

British fashion, which had had its hand in shaking up the 1960s, now made its first endeavors toward harnessing that talent and innovation into a viable industry since London's made-to-order designers had been usurped by youngsters emerging from fashion school.

The 20th century saw the rise of popular music and its effect on fashion. By the 1970s, the relationship was enjoying a "no holds barred" output of extremes. It was a moment for big egos and stack heels, and the platform shoe encapsulated the time of glitter and glam when fashion supplied a dressing-up box of sequins and feathers for Friday nights on the town.

The jet-set lifestyle

Ease of travel broadened the outlook of design in the 1970s. The international fashion pack —including Halston, Diane Von Furstenberg, Yves Saint Laurent, Ossie Clark, Anna Piaggi, and Antonio Lopez—mixed in a jet-set lifestyle with artists, musicians, creatives, actors, and models who were glamorous enough to reinvent themselves.

This fantasy world was central to fashion of the 1970s. For the beautiful people, the lifestyle revolved around hedonism and escapism. For the rest, recession and unrest made dreaming of satin glam or pastoral romanticism a welcome alternative. Fashion became inextricably linked with the music industry as the power of the image became all-important for the rock star.

In London, this was to be subverted by two characters who made a lasting contribution to fashion, although whether this was all part of the master plan or by default it is difficult to ascertain even in hindsight. The rumor was that the Sex Pistols couldn't play. In actual fact, they did know the chords and, likewise, Vivienne Westwood became a proficient technician.

Fashion via the underground was practically establishment by the 1980s, with club wear an overriding influence. The backlash to this was a return to the classics. The American designers Calvin Klein and Ralph Lauren and Italian Giorgio Armani took a fresh look at … the blazer.

Vivienne Westwood, with her partner in provocation Malcolm McLaren, bridged the gap between the 1970s and 80s with their rude explosion of punk. An irregular palpitation on fashion's heart monitor, punk was an extreme example of the kind of shake-up that fashion requires periodically.

The Maxi Dress 1969–1975

Romantic fantasy

After the Youthquake phenomenon, the second wave of notable designers to graduate from under Janey Ironside's nurturing breeding ground of talent at London's Royal College of Art encapsulated a romanticism that was in the air. This expression of fantasy, which had started with retromania in the 1960s, was present in fashion elsewhere—the colorful creations of Ottavio and Rosita Missoni and Roberto Cavalli in Italy corresponded with the wearable works of art being produced in London by Ossie Clark, Bill Gibb, Thea Porter, and Zandra Rhodes in the early 1970s. Designers were collaborating with textile specialists and experimenting with a *bricolage* of different crafts gathered together in a single garment.

Circular, high-yoked maxi coat, Zandra Rhodes, 1971
This screen-printed felt coat designed by Zandra Rhodes demonstrates the lack of distinction between fashion and costume for some designers of this era. The circular coat is pieced together from panels of two of Rhodes's textiles, "knitted circle" and "diamonds and roses," as if displaying her art in a fairy-tale garment. The coat was created as a stage costume for Irene Worth in *Tiny Alice* at the Aldwych Theatre, London.

Butterfly-winged shoe, Chelsea Cobbler, 1971
Accessories designers used their medium as a three-dimensional conduit for their imaginations. Chelsea Cobbler, started in 1967 by Richard Smith and Mandy Wilkins, made distinctive and original shoes in brightly colored leathers and paved the way for a generation of innovative footwear designers, such as Manolo Blahnik. Pablo and Delia, London-based Argentinian clothing and jewelry designers, also used leather with feathers, beads, felt, and suede to create their fantastical folk-art pieces that complemented the maxi dress.

ELEMENTS OF FASHION

- *Dior 1969 gypsy look*
- *Collier Campbell prints*
- *Thea Cadabra shoes*
- *Bill Gibb's fantasy dresses for Twiggy for The Boyfriend premiere*
- *Sue Rangeley quilting*
- *Roberto Cavalli leather patchwork*
- *Jacqmar silks by Zandra Rhodes, Veronica Marsh, and Althea McNish*
- *December 1973 Deborah Turbeville shoot for Nova*
- *Jessica McClintock at Gunne Sax*

Luxury knitwear, Missoni, 1975

On meeting the Missonis in 1969, Diana Vreeland said, "Who said that only colors exist? There are also tones." Rosita Missoni had started to experiment with stitches that could translate the colors and geometric patterns of her husband Tai's watercolors. The distinctive Missoni tonal look is achieved by immersing only parts of the yarn in the dye. This became the signature basis for glamorous mix-and-match knits de luxe, creating flowing lines reminiscent of the Renaissance.

"Look for the woman in the dress. If there is no woman, there is no dress."

COCO CHANEL

Liberty print dress, Bill Gibb, 1972

Designers had rediscovered Liberty prints in the 1960s, when Nigel Waymouth used Tana Lawn for his shirts for Granny Takes A Trip. Bill Gibb, who won a scholarship to the RCA in 1966, distinctively pieced together pattern and print in a single dress in medieval shapes for the Baccarat label. For his debut solo collection in 1972, Gibb produced a plethora of hand-printed leather, embroidery, knit, appliqué, and beading from a gathering of talented craftspeople.

Jazz Age Revival 1970–1977

Glamor and nostalgia

From the belle epoque retro chic of her tiny Abingdon Road store, Barbara Hulanicki had a different vision for the huge department store that had been Derry and Tom's on Kensington High Street and became Big Biba in 1971. This store was a folly of art deco, an ocean liner moored in west London. Hulanicki captured the seventies craze for the cocktail world of the thirties with shards of the twenties and a little forties craziness thrown in. The interior of the store was built like a series of Hollywood sets in the style of the original deco exterior, which was ideal for a time when fashion seemed determined to replicate the silver screen.

Velvet jacket and jersey skirt, Geoffrey Beene, 1974
This Geoffrey Beene suit is representative of the alternative to the floaty bias-cut Ossie Clark chiffon and crepes and Biba glamorous satin day-wear reinterpretation of the twenties and thirties look. Tweed tailoring came to be a particular New York favorite, with both Ralph Lauren and Calvin Klein using this for womenswear. Ralph Lauren famously went on to design Diane Keaton's tweed masculine baggy tailoring for *Annie Hall* in 1977.

Twiggy in Biba store, Kensington, 1971
The Rainbow Room in the Big Biba store was a social center of the London party scene, where the New York Dolls played as if they were a glam-rock cabaret on the *Queen Mary*. The interiors, designed by the young partnership of Whitmore-Thomas, were often used as locations for fashion shoots as well as advertising for the store itself.

"I like nostalgia, there is nothing bad about looking back at the past with fondness, but I also like to think about the future."

ELIO FIORUCCI

▼ Mia Farrow as Daisy, *The Great Gatsby*, 1974

After *Bonnie and Clyde*, a run of movies set in the 1920s and 30s continued the mutual back-scratching relationship with fashion. Twiggy starred in *The Boyfriend* in 1970 as a stylized mid-century flapper, and Ralph Lauren's wardrobe for Robert Redford in *The Great Gatsby* in 1974 resulted in Oxford bags and tweed caps in menswear, while Mia Farrow's wardrobe by costume designer Theoni V. Aldredge was adapted for a line that sold exclusively at Bloomingdale's.

▲ Guy Laroche, 1974

This Guy Laroche outfit for the prêt-à-porter Paris 1974 collections reinvents Bertie Wooster chic with heathery tweed plus fours, matching stockings, and striped golfing knitwear in seventies muted tones of soft pinks and plums. Nostalgic androgyny worked both ways, with womenswear adopting *Radclyffe Hall* chic as much as T-Rex's Marc Bolan emulated satiny, feather-boa'd vampishness.

ELEMENTS OF FASHION

- *Manolo Blahnik corespondent shoes*
- *Jean-Charles Brosseau cloche hats*
- *Antiquarius antiques market*
- *Brideshead Revisited; Bugsy Malone*
- *Butler & Wilson deco jewelry*

Ossie Clark 1942–1996

Born Raymond Clark in 1942, the youngest of seven, the nickname "Ossie" derived from the Clark family's wartime evacuation to Oswaldtwistle, Lancashire, England. As a boy Ossie drew and made clothing for dolls and his family, and trained in building at technical school from the age of 13, which opened his eyes to architectural design. He also attended Warrington Art School on Saturday mornings and was accepted into Manchester Regional Art College at the age of 16 in 1958.

Clark soon became part of the college's in-crowd, and was introduced to Celia Birtwell, who was studying textiles at Salford College. Clark was destined to leave the postwar provinciality of Manchester behind him and, while socially gregarious, he worked hard and was sent to Paris for couture work experience several times.

In 1961, Clark won a scholarship to the Royal College of Art in London and studied fashion under Janey Ironside, the tutor responsible for a coterie of exciting and talented young graduates who achieved success in the 1960s.

Born
Liverpool, 1942

Manifesto
To instil glamor with cut and print.

Celia Birtwell had also arrived in London and the two worked together for the first time on a paper dress design for Molly Parkin, Fashion Editor of *Nova* magazine. Clark had also developed a relationship with artist David Hockney and took a trip with him to the United States in the summer of 1964, which proved inspirational, introducing him to a world that he had formerly only experienced on the screen. His souvenir was a roll of pop art print fabric that was incorporated into his final collection for the RCA. One dress in the show was decorated with flashing lightbulbs and was featured in the media. He graduated with oustanding marks and the collection was photographed by David Bailey for *Vogue*.

Alice Pollock, who had opened her store Quorum in Kensington in 1964, had also spotted Clark's talent and thought that his style would complement the dresses she made. Pollock commissioned Birtwell, by now living with Clark, to design prints for the collections, and the creative partnership of skillful cutting and design using thirties couture technique and the art deco and botanical-inspired prints in unexpected colors was born. Clark and Birtwell, depicted in David Hockney's painting "Mr. and Mrs. Clark and Percy,"

❝Ossie Clark's name evokes a familiar pantheon of imagery—prettiness and privilege, spun-sugar rebellion ... a fog of incense, rose-colored spectacles.❞

ELIZABETH YOUNG, *NEW STATESMAN*, 1999

married in 1969 and had two children but separated due to Clark's hedonistic lifestyle and sexual orientation.

Quorum moved to Radnor Walk in Chelsea in 1966 and became central to the social scene that was a coming together of fashion, music, art, and personality. A roll of snakeskin found by Ossie became hot pants and jackets, one suit shared by Anita Pallenberg and Marianne Faithfull. Fashion shows were a happening of whirlwind printed crepes on dancing models, but ultimately Quorum was greatly in debt and was taken over by Radley Fashions.

Clark began designing the "Ossie Clark for Radley" line, a lower price, mass-marketed "diffusion," distributed to retailers worldwide. He was also invited to design a collection for distribution in France by the manufacturer Mendes, but failed to commit to the project. A lack of commitment was to become a recurring theme and Clark's career waxed and waned in later years, his romantic vision not being in step with the 1980s; he is remembered as a significant shaper of the times during the 1960s and 70s.

In 1999, the Warrington Museum & Art Gallery in Cheshire mounted the first Ossie Clark retrospective, which was followed by the Victoria & Albert monographic show in London in 2003.

Ossie Clark cut his faultlessly tailored designs in wool, tweed, suede, and leather, but it is his moss crepe and chiffon pieces in Celia Birtwell prints that are instantly recognizable. The romantic dresses, both shaped and flowing, work with the prints to reveal Clark's innate understanding of how clothing should work three-dimensionally.

Back to the Earth 1969–1979

Folk craft

During the 1970s, there was huge popularity for evening classes and books on craft as the sixties "cult of doing your own thing" grew into an interest of embellishment and of making and creating at home. Whether it was a heightened interest in ecology and back-to-nature ethics due to the oil crisis, or—in Britain at least—born out of a need to simply fill the hours during power shortages and when the three-day week was introduced—home baking, weaving, knitting, patchwork, and embroidery became widespread hobbies.

Folk style,
Joni Mitchell, 1970
Joni Mitchell, the dulcimer-playing folk warbler of the Laurel Canyon community, exemplified the naturalistic alternative lifestyle of a generation of people who went back to the land. In the United States and Europe, a rural idyllic lifestyle was seen as paradise and required natural fabrics, hand-tooled ornaments, and crafted clothing that was believed to be imbued with meaning and worth.

Summer print dress,
James Wedge 1970–1971
James Wedge, who began with unisex pantsuits and miniskirts for Countdown on the King's Road in London, had, by 1970, tapped into the flowing romanticism of the times with a prophetic use of patchworked prints that indicated a treasuring, nurturing zeitgeist instead of the disposable society of the mid-1960s. Even Yves Saint Laurent was translating patchwork into luxury.

Victorian-style dress and mob cap, Laura Ashley, 1974

Laura Ashley cornered the market in pastoral nostalgic printed cottons in the 1970s, running her small company from Powys in Wales, where her husband Bernard devised a flat-screen printing process that had been inspired by a display of traditional crafts in the V&A. By 1975, Laura Ashley had a turnover of £5 million a year, five stores in Britain, one in Paris, and international department-store concessions in the United States and Japan.

> **"What you make as a designer is an expression of yourself. I love music and painting and I prefer life in the country."**
>
> LAURA ASHLEY

ELEMENTS OF FASHION

- *Katharine Ross's clothing in* Butch Cassidy and the Sundance Kid

- *The* Little House on the Prairie *look styled by the Gunne Sax label also provided a sweet, romantic naturalism from the pioneer frontier*

- *ethnic blending and peasant styles*

- *Peruvian knits*

- *Navajo silver jewelry*

- *Clothkits printed do-it-yourself fashion*

- *clogs*

Coat by Zoë Hunt for Kaffe Fassett, 1979

Kaffe Fassett, who began knitting on trips to the Scottish highlands with his then-partner Bill Gibb, honed his skills in applied arts throughout the 1970s to become an artisanal designer championing the hand-made and working with knitting, crochet, quilting, ceramics, and paint in the colors of nature inspired by his travels.

Glam, Glitter & Pop 1970–1976

Platforms and stage costume

British writer and director Mike Leigh's 1976 television production, *Nuts in May* captures the pastoral whimsy of the 1970s versus urban glam rock, represented wonderfully in a five-inch red platform shoe protruding from a tent in a soggy country field. Glam rock was the manifestation of a glittering pastiche of excess that made it okay for construction workers and miners to feather their hair and wear frosted eye shadow. This had its roots in the modernism of Tommy Robert's boutique Mr. Freedom, which updated fifties Americana comic-book art in satin and lace, and the high-rise expressionism of the art rock of Roxy Music.

David Bowie wearing Kansai Yamamoto, 1973
Kansai Yamamoto first showed his signature mix of kabuki and pop graphics in London in 1971, with the designer conducting onstage as though for an orchestra. This resulted in Yamamoto designing David Bowie's stage outfits for his Ziggy Stardust and Aladdin Sane shows. Bowie had become interested in forms of performance art and the leotard knits became part of the singer's androgynous stage persona.

Brian Eno, pants, Claire McNicoll, mid-1970s
This suit designed for Roxy Music's Brian Eno by Claire McNicoll was typical of the style one-upmanship strutted onstage between the keyboard player and the singer, Bryan Ferry. The band's stylist, Anthony Price, who designed for Stirling Cooper and the boutique Che Guevara, was responsible for the iconic cover images for the first five albums, including Jerry Hall as a siren, and Amanda Lear in a black leather sheath leading a panther.

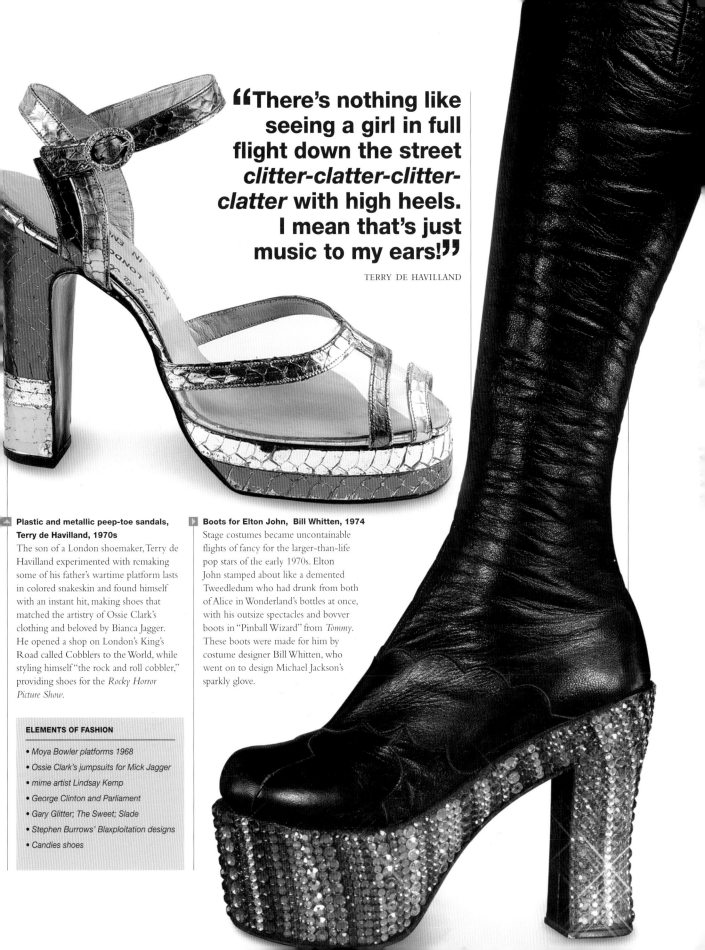

> **"There's nothing like seeing a girl in full flight down the street *clitter-clatter-clitter-clatter* with high heels. I mean that's just music to my ears!"**
>
> TERRY DE HAVILLAND

Plastic and metallic peep-toe sandals, Terry de Havilland, 1970s

The son of a London shoemaker, Terry de Havilland experimented with remaking some of his father's wartime platform lasts in colored snakeskin and found himself with an instant hit, making shoes that matched the artistry of Ossie Clark's clothing and beloved by Bianca Jagger. He opened a shop on London's King's Road called Cobblers to the World, while styling himself "the rock and roll cobbler," providing shoes for the *Rocky Horror Picture Show.*

ELEMENTS OF FASHION

- *Moya Bowler platforms 1968*
- *Ossie Clark's jumpsuits for Mick Jagger*
- *mime artist Lindsay Kemp*
- *George Clinton and Parliament*
- *Gary Glitter; The Sweet; Slade*
- *Stephen Burrows' Blaxploitation designs*
- *Candies shoes*

Boots for Elton John, Bill Whitten, 1974

Stage costumes became uncontainable flights of fancy for the larger-than-life pop stars of the early 1970s. Elton John stamped about like a demented Tweedledum who had drunk from both of Alice in Wonderland's bottles at once, with his outsize spectacles and bovver boots in "Pinball Wizard" from *Tommy.* These boots were made for him by costume designer Bill Whitten, who went on to design Michael Jackson's sparkly glove.

Flares 1969–1974

Widening the gap

Denim had grown up with the baby-boom generation and by the 1970s was fully integrated into the everyday wardrobe, from blaxploitation mojo to safari-suit smart-casual. The freaks and the heads had sewn inserts into the outer seams of their jeans to create flares and now the denim companies were following suit and creating whole ensembles from hats to shoes with accompanying accessories. By the end of the decade, the demand was so great that the denim companies were looking for alternative ways to produce jeans more cheaply and turning once again to sweatshop labor instead of factories.

Olympiad—Lee presents the "European Fit" that's snugger around the hips, narrower through the thighs and wider at the flares in these 100% sloan sateen cotton jeans (about $16) and matching jacket (about $20). Wide array of colors including Biscuit, Faded Green, Loden, Brown, Camel and Faded Blue create a perfect complement to the Lee Floral Shirt (about $14) with its dusky tones of Rust, Green and Brown. The Lee Company, 640 Fifth Avenue, N.Y., N.Y. 10019. (212) 765-4215. **Lee** A company of VF corporation

LEVI'S FLARES

Levi's advert, 1969
Levi Strauss & Co. had ridden the wave of the reinvention of denim from work wear to fashion fabric. In 1964, a pair of its jeans had been acquired for the permanent collections of the Smithsonian Institution in Washington, D.C. Levi's, known for their quality, became synonymous with the American Dream. The company declared that it regularly received letters from behind the Iron Curtain begging for a pair of Levi's.

Lee advert, 1970s
Levi Strauss & Co. was not alone in a market that had outgrown the confines of leisure wear. Falmer, Wrangler, and Lee were among the companies that were looking further than the blue-jeaned cowboy image of Western brands. By the end of the decade, with movies such as *The Electric Horseman* (1979), this look was again fashionable and Robert Redford's double denim look was key.

Abba, 1974

The 1970s was an era tainted with the memory of bad taste during a time when fashion was innovative, sexual, and expressive. The Swedish band Abba, loved by so many for their perfect pop tunes, were an example of how you can take two couples out of suburbia, give them a taste of stardom, and their own costume designer, but, clearly, you cannot take suburbia out of the couples.

Miss Mouse "bags," 1972

In fashion terms, the early seventies pants followed the shape of the high-waisted, wide-legged leisure pajama of the 1930s. The bow print was a signature of the Miss Mouse label, sold through department stores across the Britain. Designed by Rae Spencer-Cullen, part of the London arty crowd that included Zandra Rhodes, the clothing was cut using thirties and forties leisure wear silhouettes, such as these "bags."

> **"Blue jeans are the most beautiful things since the gondola."**
>
> DIANA VREELAND

ELEMENTS OF FASHION

- *Huggy Bear in* Starsky and Hutch
- *Blue Jeans magazine*
- *Brut and Denim aftershave*
- *the feather cut*
- *iron-on patches*

The New Prêt-à-Porter 1970s

Left Bank style

Since the 1960s, when Brigitte Bardot had petulantly declared that "couture was for grannies," Paris designers had started building up a ready-to-wear fashion industry that was more in tune with the younger clothing systems of the United States and Britain. Yves Saint Laurent had opened his Rive Gauche boutique and Didier Grumbach—who would go on to be President of the French Fashion Federation—teamed with Andrée Putman in 1971 to form the prêt-à-porter collective, Créateurs et Industriels, which would host Jean-Charles de Castelbajac's first solo collections. In 1973, the Prêt-à-Porter Paris fashion week was launched, which showed twice yearly on a similar seasonal schedule to the couture collections.

▶ **Layered dress, Kenzo, 1978**
Kenzo Takada was one of the first of a group of Japanese designers who started showing their labels in Paris in the 1970s, imbuing the French fashion industry with a wider cosmopolitanism. Kenzo opened his store, Jungle Jap, in Paris in 1970 and like Kansai Yamamoto, mixed Oriental influences such as *kabuki* with his interpretation of Western modernism, resulting in layered cottons, tunics, smocks, and baggy pants often in mixed kimono prints.

Evening dress, Halston, 1975
American designer Roy Halston Frowick is significant as being central to the international beautiful people, dubbed "Jetsetters," who flitted between Paris, London, and New York and included Paloma Picasso, Bianca Jagger, Andy Warhol, and Yves Saint Laurent. The Paris and New York set met when Andy Warhol's superstars filmed *L'Amour* in Karl Lagerfeld's Paris apartment in 1971. His long, flowing dresses—or copies of them—were much a part of the disco scene during the mid-1970s.

"Le prêt-à-porter est une réalité, la haute couture est l'élément essentiel de l'image."

DIDIER GRUMBACH

Emmanuelle Khanh, 1976–1977
Emmanuelle Khanh and her husband Quasar, also a designer, were part of the ready-to-wear movement of French designers in the 1970s determined to shake up the couture establishment. Khanh's collection was stocked in fellow designer Sonia Rykiel's boutique Laura. Grace Jones, the singer and model working in Paris, became something of a French institution during her collaboration with creative director Jean-Paul Goude.

ELEMENTS OF FASHION

- Popy Moreni; Elisabeth de Senneville; Agnès B
- Issey Miyake and Kansai Yamamoto 7-foot (2-meter) frieze in Nova, April 1972
- Chantal Thomas's Ter et Bantine boutique
- Daniel Hechter unisex sportswear
- French Elle prêt-à-porter reports
- Andy Warhol's Interview magazine
- Mr. Chow's Knightsbridge restaurant
- Jean-Claude Vannier music for Yves Saint Laurent

Bat-wing-sleeved dress and hat, Jean Muir, 1971
There was a severity and seriousness to Jean Muir's design that set her apart from many of her British "Youthquake" contemporaries. By the 1970s, her label had gained worldwide respect for its precision cut in soft, flowing fabrics with its signature seaming. Muir herself placed great emphasis on the worth of technical training, which had much in common with the Parisian aesthetic.

The Jersey Dress 1970–1979

Slink sculptures

The December 1972 issue of *Nova* magazine carried a fashion spread shot by the French photographer Guy Bourdin, in which the models struck statuesque prewar poses in slinky jersey columns. This captured elegance was subverted in typical seventies style by the positioning of live mice on the floor of the studio chased by a cat, while the models struggled to retain composure. Nostalgic glamor in the 1970s was injected with an element of humor. John Bates so exaggerated the backless thirties-style evening dress in 1973 that it was impossible to wear panties. In 1977, Halston led Bianca Jagger, Godiva-like, into New York's Studio 54 wearing his jersey dress and riding a white horse.

❝I design for the woman who loves being a woman.❞

DIANE VON FURSTENBERG

Frilled rayon-jersey evening cloak, Yuki, 1977
London fashion had its own Japanese influence with Yuki, who had already had a prestigious freelance fashion career in the United States and France. Yuki launched his solo collection in London in 1972, which was exclusive to Harvey Nichols and went on to win Yardley Designer of the Year in 1976. He was known for timeless sculpted, flowing jersey garments after the classical style of Madame Grès.

ELEMENTS OF FASHION

- *New York designer Scott Barrie's harem knickerbockers*
- *Joan Collins in Bill Gibb Qiana fabric in* The Stud
- *Bill Gibb's fashion show on the inaugural flight of the London–Paris Airbus*
- *Luchino Visconti's* The Damned
- *model Amanda Lear*
- *Italian designer Nanni Strada's pelle dress, 1973*

Knitted rayon-jersey dress, Yuki, late 1970s
Designers using jersey in the 1970s were happy to experiment with synthetics, including rayon and viscose, to explore the draping qualities. In 1968, DuPont had developed Qiana, a nylon jersey that was used by high fashion designers such as Bill Gibb and Yuki as well as manufacturers for the mass market. DuPont, along with many textile companies at this time, teamed up with designers to promote Qiana in editorial advertising.

Silk-jersey range, Diane von Furstenberg, 1976
Brussels-born Diane Halfin married Prince Egon von Furstenberg in 1968, and moved to the United States. She had worked for Ferretti, an Italian textile manufacturer, designing tunics and shirtwaists in printed silk jersey. In 1972, she opened her own business in New York, producing her celebrated, much-copied wrap dress that followed the natural curves of a woman with an easy-to-wear sexiness.

Matte jersey halter dress, Geoffrey Beene, 1975
Geoffrey Beene had studied at the Ecole de Chambre Syndicale de la Haute Couture Parisienne before working in ready-to-wear in the United States and started his own label in 1963, introducing the sporty Beenebag line in 1969. In 1972, Beene started to experiment with a modern style of draping jersey, making matte jersey a signature fabric and rejecting the traditional classic pattern construction of his early career.

CHRONOLOGICAL CATWALK
The Seventies Female

Volume and layers

The beginnings of the oversized look attributed to the 1980s had their origins in the experiments with scale and balance of the mid-1970s. Smocks and tunics billowed from yokes and dropped to mid-calf and sleeves became huge with rolled cuffs. Full-length coats had sweeping, capelike qualities, layered over peasant blouses and culottes.

▶ Double skirt

The tweedy layered look that lasted from the 1970s to the 80s, was derived from the peasant collections of Yves Saint Laurent and the *Annie Hall* baggy menswear of Ralph Lauren. A double skirt, with the split overskirt in large contrasting plaid, gave just the right amount of rusticity to urban fashions plus a nod to "le style anglais"— the peculiar Parisian interpretation of the English country look.

▶ Prêt-à-porter for French *Elle* magazine

The weekly *Elle* magazine was a faster fashion source than *Vogue* in the 1970s, and still only published in France. The title set precedents in European fashion magazines at the time when they used a black model—Beverly Johnson—on the cover, after Johnson's ground-breaking U.S. *Vogue* cover in 1974. It was a first for Paris fashion.

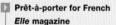

Unstructured silhouette ◀

Shoulders were still soft and unstructured in 1979 and skirts full and flowing. The relaxed country wool check skirts and pinafores were to prove so popular that the trickle-down effect lasted well into the early 1980s, being championed by such mid-range brands in Britain as Jeff Banks' Warehouse company, which launched its innovative Bymail catalog, moving mail order into a new phase.

Layered top

The contrasting layers of cashmere, topped with a casually tied scarf, and with legs hidden by tights and boots and hands by gloves, all belie a superbly toned late-seventies body and give the message of being sufficiently in control to wear seemingly shapeless layers. The casual sporty look of the time often centered around the coatdress and the jumpsuit.

Voluminous coat

Not since wartime uniforms and safety wear did women don so many layers that seemingly would have hidden the female form. Theorists observed the manifestation of women's liberation in fashion, which had been rejected in the 1950s after women had returned to the home from the workplace. By the end of the 1970s, Claude Montana and Thierry Mugler were beginning to show signs of power dressing.

Beret

Popularized by Faye Dunaway in the 1967 movie *Bonnie and Clyde*, the thirties aesthetic had carried the beret through the 1970s. This romantic rebel image had been helped by the Black Panthers, Che Guevara, and the MI-carbine-wielding heiress Patty Hearst in the revolutionary-minded 1970s.

The Drainpipe 1970s

From antifashion to mainstream

In the second half of the decade, pant legs began to be cut straight. This was exacerbated by a creeping in of a fifties kitsch revival. Starting as subversive antifashion, Malcolm McLaren and Vivienne Westwood's first World's End store, Let It Rock, was selling vintage fifties drapes. Roxy Music's Bryan Ferry sported an impeccable DA, while Antony Price dressed Kari Ann as a Vargas pin-up girl for the cover of their first album. Movies, such as the 1973 *That'll Be the Day,* starring David Essex and Ringo Starr, and the 1971 *The Last Picture Show* with Cybill Shepherd, captured the aesthetic for the big screen.

> **"Antony could go from a polka-dot fifties look, to lamé to faux leopard skin."**
>
> JULIET MANN, REFERRING TO ANTONY PRICE, IN MICHAEL BRACEWELL, *RE-MAKE/REMODEL*, 2007

▶ *Grease* **is the word, 1978**

The 1978 movie *Grease* had tuned into the seventies interest in the 1950s and transformed the era into a smash-hit mainstream musical that saw lines around the block. The 30-year old Olivia Newton John squeezed into tight-fitting spandex pants, and a hip-swiveling John Travolta bore little relation to fifties teenagers, but that didn't stop the audiences dancing in the aisles.

ELEMENTS OF FASHION

- spray-on satin by Wonder Workshop worn with spike heels
- straight-cut denim or canvas worn with Adidas, Kickers, or Converse
- satin baseball jackets
- halter-neck tops, fluffy mohair sweaters, Disney prints, and skin-tight T-shirts
- Paris vintage jukebox look sold at Les Messageries

"Brothel creepers," 1970
Mr. Freedom, started by Tommy Roberts and Trevor Myles in 1970 on London's Kensington Church Street, was a celebration of kitsch, using fifties American comic books and pop art as references. Mr. Freedom "brothel creepers" found an unlikely airing on the cover of hushed singer-songwriter Nick Drake's album *Bryter Later*. Myles went on to open Paradise Garage, which imported vintage American fifties clothing, including Levi's 501s.

Heather Favell, 1979
The interpretation of the straight-leg, skinny pants as a fifties style was typical of the nature of seventies fashion, which borrowed references and imagery from popular culture and turned them into an imaginary movie narrative. Fashion shoots dressed models in satin disco outfits and posed them in fifties diners. Even *Penthouse* had a fifties cheerleader making out with a greaser in the back of a Chevy, wearing saddle shoes and ankle socks.

Brutus, 1970s
Brutus Jeans, founded by the teenage Freedman brothers in 1966, stood their ground in the Brtitish denim market against the American giants throughout the 1970s. After the 1974 advertisement, "Put My Jeans On" sung by David Dundas, the single went on to be a worldwide one-hit wonder. Brutus Jeans had concessions in stores in every provincial town and advertised in local papers, becoming the number one soccer-crowd brand.

The Leotard 1975–1985

Synthetic stretch

Disco, the dance craze that helped to shape the stylistic memory of the 1970s, had lasting results on active- and sportswear. The seventies disco aesthetic was body conscious, which suited the Halston minimalism. Disco was about erotic display and "posing" and the interiors of discotheques with uplit dance floors and glitter balls lent a surreal quality to the atmosphere. Dancers lost in music wore shimmering spandex that reflected the lights and got the wearer noticed. Moving into the 1980s, aerobics classes introduced figure-hugging dance wear to the keep-fit studio. Pineapple Dance Studio, which was opened by Debbie Moore in 1979, was ransacked for fashion-forward spandex.

Leotard, Sheilagh Brown/Quorum, 1970s
Not since the body stockings and catsuits of the 1960s had the body been subjected to a covering that left so little to the imagination. The seventies disco leotard had more in common with swimwear, in shiny synthetic stretch fabrics, although often worn with tights and high-heeled sandals or boots for a night out and always accessorized with a flashing smile—these were good times.

Disco queen, 1977
The sex, drugs, and disco nightclub Studio 54 was opened in New York in 1977 by Steve Rubell and Ian Schrager and became a mecca for dancing queens eager to breathe the same dry ice as Bianca Jagger, Jerry Hall, Andy Warhol, and Liza Minelli. The venue was a fashion fest of the beautiful people, with a door policy that was as sadistic as the interior was hedonistic.

Leotard with crazy cut sleeve and one shoulder by Sheilagh Brown for Quorum £20. Wedge sandals from Russell & Bromley, £19.99. Inset Glossy blue bikini by Baltrik, £9-60. Bangles from Butler & Wilson. Dior sunglasses.

> **"It's the place where my prediction from the sixties finally came true: 'In the future everyone will be famous for 15 minutes'."**
>
> ANDY WARHOL, REFERRING TO STUDIO 54 NIGHTCLUB

Grace Jones wearing Azzedine Alaïa, 1985
Grace Jones, a 54 regular in New York, became the muse of Paris-based Tunisian-born Azzedine Alaïa during the 1980s. The distinctive spandex dresses with their laced-up sides that the private clients of Alaïa were wearing began to garner attention in the late 1970s. The "King of Cling" launched his own collections, first showing at Bergdorf-Goodman in New York in 1982.

ELEMENTS OF FASHION

• *Norma Kamali OMO bodysuit range*

• *Brooke Shields's Shogren leotards*

• *Harri Peccinotti's blue plastic swimsuit shoot in Nova, May 1974*

• *model Jerry Hall*

• *Norma Kamali sweatshirt fabric rah-rah skirt, 1981*

• *Legs and Co.*

• *roller disco*

Fiorucci advertisement, 1980s
"Halston, Gucci, Fiorucci" went the Sister Sledge anthem to seventies dance-floor action. Before the song made the Fiorucci label a household name, it was the Italian interpretation of colorful satin kitsch, which incorporated dancewear into the look using glittery spandex, stretch denim, spray-on hot pants, and leotard shapes. Staff of the Fiorucci New York store looked as if they had rolled into work straight from Studio 54.

CHRONOLOGICAL CATWALK
The Eighties Male

The power suit

On-screen tailoring frequently charts the changing shape of menswear. The 1976 movie *All the President's Men* shows Robert Redford and Dustin Hoffman in perfect examples of the wide-cut, stiff flannels of the later years of the decade, but an emerging influence was to produce the loosened-up suit of 1980, exemplified by a louche Richard Gere in *American Gigolo*, the movie that made Giorgio Armani a household name.

Suave silhouette
The theme of style was so central to *American Gigolo* that each scene was shot to display the suits to best advantage. At one point, an exasperated Gere was heard to say, "Who's acting in this scene, me or the jacket?" This sums up the eighties contrivance for effect. *American Psycho* —Bret Easton Ellis' power suit thriller—celebrates the grooming ritual that prepares central character Bateman's killer image.

Collar and tie
The wide collars and ties of the late 1960s and 70s had begun to look like a parody of a tired era. Toward the end of the 1970s, Giorgio Armani championed a return to understated elegance, albeit in a relaxed way—for the first time, it was acceptable to appear a little creased.

Shoulder
Armani's tailoring typified the Italian look of the 1980s. Put together with minimal interfacing and lining, the jacket was shrugged on and began to be worn with the sleeves rolled up in later years, over a T-shirt, à la Crocket and Tubbs in *Miami Vice*, the reverse of the structured Wall Street power suit.

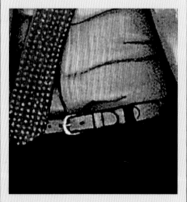

Belt
During the 1980s, designer accessories became as important as the designer suit for the style- and status-conscious man. Italian leather was particularly prized and a Gucci belt—preferably with the distinctive equestrian motif worn visibly— was key. This trade on name likewise spurred the designer-fragrance boom and a branded aftershave was the powerful smell of success.

Hair
The men's grooming-product market was developed in a major way in this period. Styling gel became available, which facilitated the artfully tousled locks of the male model. In suburban bathrooms everywhere, youths experimented with L'Oréal Studio Line to arrange their wedges and flicks. Designer stubble was also deemed suitable to go with the unstructured designer suit.

Studied insouciance

In 1977, Giorgio Armani was a stylist working for *L'Uomo Vogue* after working as a cutter for menswear manufacturer Nino Cerruti. Armani had launched his own men's collection in 1975 and two years later the menswear bible featured his relaxed, unstructured costume, which translated the suit into casual wear. By 1980, he was the ideal designer to dress Richard Gere's character in *American Gigolo*.

He's the highest paid lover in Beverly Hills.

He leaves women feeling more alive than they've ever felt before.

Except one.

American Gigolo

Vivienne Westwood b. 1941

Vivienne Isabel Swire was born in Tintwistle, Derbyshire in 1941, and her family moved to Harrow when she was 17. Vivienne studied at Harrow Art School but took up teacher training after a term, having decided that it was impossible for a working-class girl to make a living as an artist. She married Derek Westwood, a Hoover factory apprentice in 1961, and gave birth to a son, Benjamin, in 1963. The only clue to her future career lay in the jewelry that she made and sold from a stall in Portobello market in London.

On meeting the uber-confident, Svengali-like Malcolm McLaren, Westwood left to live with him in a rented apartment in London and had another son, Joseph Corré, the future proprietor of underwear store Agent Provocateur in 1967. When McLaren decided to open a boutique, Let It Rock, on the premises of the former Granny Takes A Trip boutique on the King's Road, Westwood matched McLaren's chutzpah with her realization of the outrageous vision.

Westwood's partnership with McLaren meant that their combined efforts were as much fueled by music and popular culture as fashion. Their ventures attempted to use their creative skills in as many ways as possible— McLaren's Sex Pistols showcasing

Born
Tintwistle, Derbyshire, 1941

Manifesto
To use shock tactics and tailoring.

Westwood's designs and, in turn, Westwood creating a memorable image for the punk band. When punk became commercialized, the two presented their first catwalk show, the swash-bucklingly glamorous Pirates collection in 1981—as much taken from, as inspiring, the new romantic club movement. "Buffalo Gals" in 1982, which was their first Paris show, was also the name of McLaren's chart hit.

Although now showing on the catwalk, the collections were still seen as street fashion in Britain and only featured in magazines such as *The Face* and *I-D*. In Italy, Westwood was taken seriously, resulting in a deal with an Italian backer, Carlo D'Amario. Money difficulties in Britain after opening another London store, Nostalgia of Mud, in 1983, led her to move to Italy after parting company from McClaren. D'Amario negotiated a deal with Armani for backing, production, and marketing.

Having cut her teeth on cult fashion, the designer's self-taught tailoring skills were to be a major part of her solo

> **"Fashion is very important. It is life-enhancing and, like anything that gives pleasure, it is worth doing well."**
>
> VIVIENNE WESTWOOD

label. She became fascinated with history and her research led her to produce the mini-crini collection of 1986, which mixed the 19th century with pop prints and introduced her rocking-horse platform shoes, which became a club-wear staple. Westwood interpreted historical manipulations of the female form and focused on the hips and breasts with padding and corsetry. Her version of sexualized fashion was to free curvy women from the tyranny of spandex in the decade to come and to give others curves where they had none.

In 1986, Westwood moved back to London and became interested in traditional British skills and fabrics. Her 1987 Harris Tweed collection had hunting, shooting, and fishing elements, which were also to become signatures, although typically subverted. Tartan was not to escape Westwood's eccentricity and the 1993 Anglomania collection saw her creating her own plaid, named MacAndreas, after her third husband and collaborator, Andreas Kronthaler.

Vivienne Westwood has become an unlikely doyenne of the establishment, having been British Designer of the Year in 1990 and 1991, awarded an OBE by the queen in 1992 and made a Dame in 2006. Her company is a stalwart of British fashion, and probably the most globally successful, along with Paul Smith, being composed of the semi-couture Gold Label, the ready-to-wear Red Label, menswear, and the jeans diffusion Anglomania.

These 1993 blue platform shoes in a stamped animal pattern caused a media furor when model Naomi Campbell fell off them during the Westwood catwalk show. The shoes came to represent the excesses of the fashion world and prompted much debate. They are among the most-viewed objects in London's Victoria & Albert Museum.

Bondage 1976–1985

"Oh Bondage, Up Yours!"

After renting the back of Trevor Myles's Paradise Garage for Let It Rock, Malcolm McLaren and Vivienne Westwood reopened as Too Fast To Live, Too Young To Die. In 1973, they opened Sex. The boutique became the hangout for the Bromley contingent, a group of disaffected youth, including Siouxsie Sioux, Billy Idol, and Sid Vicious, who were bound together by their hatred of hippies. This backlash had been preempted by Tommy Roberts when he opened City Lights Studio in Covent Garden after the demise of Mr. Freedom. Decorated in black with chains and scaffolding, City Lights captured the imagination of a young Rei Kawabuko, who established the Japanese Comme des Garçons label.

ELEMENTS OF FASHION

- *homoerotic Tom of Finland prints*
- *zippers, D rings and rubber hosing*
- *muslin panel-embellished T-shirts*
- *the queen's nose pierced with a safety pin*
- *anarchy*
- *Alex Michon and Krystyna Kolowska paramilitary look for The Clash*
- *The Buzzcocks in Manchester*

"I'm not trying to do something different, I'm trying to do the same thing but in a different way."

VIVIENNE WESTWOOD

Debbie Harry in Patti Smith T-shirt, 1977

New York punks, while no less nihilistic, favored more intellectualism and less spitting. The Max's Kansas City look was dyed chopped hair and a wasted monochromatic figure. Patti Smith inspired androgynous suiting, as worn in the cover photograph for her album *Horses*, shot by her lover Robert Mapplethorpe. Debbie Harry, whose group Blondie straddled the line between new wave and pop, injected sex appeal into the image.

Conceptual Chic collection, Zandra Rhodes, 1977

While Westwood was producing clothing for McLaren's
protégés, The Sex Pistols, and Sebastian Conran roped
in his brother Jasper for design help for The Clash, Zandra
Rhodes was gearing the attitude into high fashion. Mixing
the street fashion and slashed Elizabethan clothing in the
Victoria & Albert Museum, Rhodes's 1977 Conceptual Chic
collection featured pearled safety pins and ripped silk jersey.

**Adam Ant, "Prince
Charming" costume, 1981**

Adam Ant acted in Derek
Jarman's punk movie, *Jubilee.*
Experimenting with a more
idealized heroic image,
which was Westwood's
Pirates collection, McLaren
poached Ant's band to form
Bow Bow Wow, but Adam
and the (new) Ants went
on to chart success with
a new image formed
from the burgeoning new
romantic movement for
which the Pirate collection
had been seminal.

Westwood and punks, 1977

Vivienne Westwood's stock for the Sex
store, designed for the Seditionaries label,
moved the drainpipe into bondage
territory with her black and tartan suits,
which became part of punk rock uniform.
Westwood took the concept of the fetish
wear that they also sold and inspiration
from the style of Jordan, the shop's
manager, pictured on the left, and
incorporated it into clothes of the street.

The Buffalo Suit 1980–1985

Lookin' good in a Buffalo Stance

By the 1980s, street style and fashion were not only converging, they were overlapping, fissioning into subcultures, and coexisting. Stylists working for new magazines, *The Face, I-D,* and *Arena* were dipping in and out of youth identities from different cultures and borrowing inspiration from each. Ray Petri was the uberstylist who started the look that had a lasting influence on menswear. Together with fellow stylist Judy Blame, photographers Mark leBon and Jean-Baptist Mondino, and designer Jean-Paul Gaultier, Petri took inspiration from Jamaican ragamuffins, punks, and new romantics among other disparate ingredients and took the word "Buffalo" from Bob Marley's "Buffalo Soldier" single, McLaren's "Buffalo Gals," and Westwood's Buffalo collection to define the image.

Malcolm McLaren and rappers in Buffalo collection, Westwood, 1983

Malcolm McLaren released his album *Duck Rock* in 1983, which featured the single "Buffalo Gals." Fashion and music went hand in hand in his collaboration with Vivienne Westwood, and an oversized, unstructured collection also took that name. The track featured New York scratch DJs who mixed influences from Africa and the Americas. Neneh Cherry, who was later influenced by Ray Petri, released *Buffalo Stance* in 1988.

ELEMENTS OF FASHION

- *the Kamen brothers, models and singers*

- *eight-year-old Felix Howard on the cover of The Face*

- *Jean-Paul Gaultier skirts for men*

- *Frankie say ... Relax*

- *boxing*

- *white dreads*

- *Annie Lennox in suiting and leather eye mask*

- *Tama Janowitz Slaves of New York*

"Buffalo was androgynous in many ways ... women weren't women and men weren't men ... no one had done it before."

MITZI LORENZ

Madonna, styled by Maripol, 1983
Madonna's torn leggings, lace, and rubber-bangles look was the work of stylist Maripol—they were both members of the same Manhattan group of fashion, art, and music people as Blondie, artists Keith Haring and Jean-Michel Basquiat, photographer Steven Meisel, and designer Steven Sprouse. Sprouse designed for Debbie Harry and Madonna with his distinctive neon graffiti style that saw a resurgence in Marc Jacobs's Louis Vuitton collection of 2001.

Katharine Hamnett meets Mrs. Thatcher, 1984
Oversized streetwear as advocated by Ray Petri, who restructured clothing if he could not get the shape he wanted and used tough, stylized black-and-white imagery, had its influence on mainstream fashion. In 1984, Katharine Hamnett's "Choose Life" slogan T-shirts were worn by Wham!, copied by Paul Morley for his Frankie Goes to Hollywood "Relax" versions, and endlessly cited after Hamnett wore her own message shirt to meet the British Prime Minister Mrs. Thatcher.

Culture Club, 1983
Culture Club, whose protagonist Boy George emerged from the Blitz Kids' "Cult With No Name" which morphed into new romanticism, was an early eighties band which mixed New Wave, Soul and Reggae. George often wore clothing from the Boy London label, which became the clubwear label of the mid-decade. Boy George heralded the last bastion of shock—the eighties "gender-bending" when befuddled parents asked, "Is that a girl or a boy?"

1985
2020

Retro &
Revolution

Introduction

Time seemed to move faster by the end of the 20th century. An escalation of technological progress and improved communication facilitated instant exchanges and constant development. Fashion has always been a balance of innovation and reinterpretation, but, by the 1990s, post-modernist futurism vied for attention alongside a reevaluation of clothing from previous decades.

The advent of MTV in the 1980s cemented the link between fashion and music as the music video became as important as the record. Club culture also pulled together the two strains of street fashion and high fashion as the inventiveness of nightlife dressing became influential.

In 1985, Australian designer Leigh Bowery began the London club Taboo, which was central to the alternative fashion scene. Bowery had showed his collections "off schedule" during London Fashion Week and now showcased weekly at Taboo. He influenced a generation of designers, including Alexander McQueen and Gareth Pugh. He was also costume designer for the conceptual dancer Michael Clark, and his designs focused on distorting body shapes into fantastical sculptural effect.

In 1989, another nightclub, Kinky Gerlinky, opened in London, run by Gerlinde and Michael Kostiff, owners of the boutique World. That same year party promoter Susanne Bartsch started the Love Ball in New York. The drag ball scene was subsumed by supermodel glamor.

This image with its redolence of twenties art deco painter Tamara de Lempicka's work and outsize seventies-style glasses is indicative of the vintage mix-and-match that became part of fashion's rag-picker style from the 1990s. Stylists, photographers, and designers dipped in and out of fashion history and its wealth of references.

The media party

Contrary to the glamorous artificiality of the Versace and Mugler moment was the grunge movement in the United States, which, channeled by the young designer Marc Jacobs, coincided with a realism epitomized by *Paper Magazine* in New York and *Dazed and Confused* in London.

The media created Cool Britannia in the mid-1990s, claiming that under Prime Minister Tony Blair London was again swinging to Britpop. The radar turned to London Fashion Week for youthful talent, and established designers Patrick Cox and Paul Smith traded on the Brit image.

"Future vintage"

While London designers were being employed to revamp tired Paris fashion houses, it was the appointment of American Tom Ford to Gucci in Italy that heralded the status-obsessed turn of the century. Boutique hotels, designer denim, and concept stores, such as 10 Corso Como in Milan and Colette in Paris, were all products of the gilded lifestyle of the time.

The Dover Street Market concept store opened in London by Rei Kawabuko of Comme des Garçons featured a concession of Cameron Silver's Decades, a high-end LA vintage store used by the American celebrity stylist Rachel Zoe for her A-list clients. Vintage as a commodity was a money spinner at the start of the 21st century. In 2010—the same year in which the ardent celebrant of futurism Alexander McQueen died—the British Fashion Council announced a "Future Vintage" show at the vintage clothing festival in southern England to feature the promising talent that the Fashion Council predicted would come to be prized in future decades.

The rise of Prada during the 1990s was to establish the Italian label as one of the most enduring and influential of the period that spanned the turn of the 21st century. Miuccia Prada understood the prevalent feeling for vintage and continuously reinterpreted past styles in her updated, minimalist way. Her prowess as a fashion designer is understanding that modernity in fashion can come from different sources.

Power Dressing 1980s

The yuppie years

The 1980s were destined to be a decade of female authority. Helmut Newton's photo shoot for Paris *Vogue* in 1981, entitled "Sie Kommen (Naked and Dressed)," set the scene when he depicted four models advancing purposefully in chic, tailored separates while on the opposite page he showed the same women in identical stride wearing only stilettos. Clothed, they are women who mean business; naked, they exude amazonian sexuality. As Melanie Griffiths in the romantic comedy *Working Girl* (1988) put it, power dressing meant "A head for business and a bod for sin." Armani advertising, aimed at the new "yuppie" breed of female workforce, showed models clutching international newspapers, and fashion layouts brought the Wall Street aesthetic to magazines in a cross-pollination of glamor and high finance.

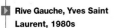

Rive Gauche, Yves Saint Laurent, 1980s

During the 1980s, Yves Saint Laurent's reputation preceded him as the man who had instigated Paris ready-to-wear as a viable alternative to couture. The strong Rive Gauche branding, together with the graphic linear approach of this advertisement, sums up the aspirational quality of eighties dressing.

Wool day dress, Donna Karan, mid-1980s

Donna Karan's dictum in the 1980s was to simplify the female working wardrobe. She devised a series of sportswear-inspired separates that conveyed a message of calm authority. Based around the much-copied body suit, her line was in the McCardell tradition of American dressing. The look culminated with her 1992 advertising campaign "In Women We Trust," shot by Peter Lindbergh, which depicted a woman being sworn in as President.

"People buy and people sell and I am a master at both!"

ALEXIS COLBY,
CHARACTER IN *DYNASTY*

Joan Collins in *Dynasty*, skirt suit, Nolan Miller, 1986
The entrance of Joan Collins as the superbitch Alexis Colby in the second series of *Dynasty* revived the ratings of the soap that was secondary to *Dallas*. The extravagant costumes of the female leads were designed by Nolan Miller, who created 25–30 glamorous outfits each week. The look exemplified the power shoulder, and the clothes became such a draw that a made-to-order *Dynasty* collection was available.

Double-breasted silk crepe jacket, Armani, 1980s
Italian quality received much attention for its background in tailoring in luxury fabrics. Backed by Italy's largest textile manufacturer, GFT, Giorgio Armani was heralded in the United States for his take on the working woman's wardrobe which feminized the masculine dominion— 1982 saw him on the cover of *Time*. Gianfranco Ferre's fortunes were also forwarded by appreciation from the Americans, while family-run manufacturers MaxMara and Alberta Ferretti made the move into ready-to-wear.

Jacket and skirt, ready-to-wear collection, Thierry Mugler, 1989
German designer Thierry Mugler, who first showed his eponymous line in Paris in 1973, numbers superheroes and fetish wear among his inspirations. His was some of the sexiest power dressing of the 1980s when he developed his signature structured suits, which owed much to couture traditions. The jackets are molded, padded, and seamed in such a way that the body is reshaped into an hourglass with a tiny waist.

ELEMENTS OF FASHION

- *ladies who lunch*
- *Trump Tower*
- *Microsoft*
- *Ralph Lauren, Giorgio Armani, Donna Karan*
- *Salvatore Ferragamo shoes*

The Japanese Label 1980s–1990s

Intellectual chic and the art of zen

Since Japan opened to foreign trade in the 19th century, with the wave of japonisme that coincided with the Paris International Exhibition in 1867, Western dress had gradually started to be adopted. By the 1980s, the Japanese designers showing in Paris had turned that on its head. Kenzo's cultural mix and the conceptual ideas of clothing and fashion introduced by Issey Miyake, and later by Rei Kawakubo, for Comme des Garçons, and Yohji Yamamoto, promoted an intellectualism in eighties design. Their cutting-edge ideas also appealed to a generation of style-obsessed consumers and the Japanese label became the height of designer chic.

"Many people will say ... clothes should be worn; but I think people can look at them in public, like seeing a film."

ISSEY MIYAKE

Lace sweater and cotton jersey skirt, Comme des Garçons, 1982
The press paired Yamamoto's and Rei Kawakubo's Comme des Garçons first Paris shows as "post-nuclear chic." The black, seemingly ragged clothing apparently encapsulated the zenlike Japanese idea of the beauty of conscious poverty and the power of the incomplete. Kawakubo has gone on to present her idea of wearable art with an uncompromising aesthetic, using padding to question the relationship between body and outfit.

▶ **Sleeveless dress, Yohji Yamamoto, 1988–1989**
The year 1981 was the year of the Japanese deconstructionalists, when both Yohji Yamamoto and Comme des Garçons first showed in Paris. The conception of fashion in Paris, which seemed to be set in stone, namely, the desire for the new with a focus on a particular erogenous zone, was challenged. Yamamoto's work seemed shockingly shapeless and sexless to Western eyes, but his attempt to present the wearer as an intelligent, independent human being was applauded.

**"Pleats Please," Issey Miyake,
F/W collection, 1990**

Issey Miyake started to experiment with pleating techniques in the late 1980s, resulting in his "Pleats Please" line. The presewn garments are twisted and heat pressed so that the pleats lie in various directions, which the polyester fabric "memorizes." Although Japanese designers are often associated with working in different shades of black, Miyake, like Kawakubo, has a bold, considered use of color, as did Yamamoto.

ELEMENTS OF FASHION

• *bonded fabric*

• *architectural sensibilities*

• *the philosophical writings of Jacques Derrida*

• *personal interpretation of clothing that could be worn in different ways*

• *Miyake's A-POC: ready-to-cut tubes of fabric*

• *a Filofax*

Grace Jones in ruffled dress, Issey Miyake, 1994

Issey Miyake studied art in Japan and fashion in Paris before working for Guy Laroche, Givenchy, and Geoffrey Beene. After establishing his design studio in Tokyo in 1970, he presented a collection in Paris in 1973, which introduced his concept of "A Piece of Cloth." This is inspired by the Japanese notion of clothing being a flat garment, which differs with each wearer's "*ma*," or space between body and cloth.

The Westwood Corset 1985

The new romantics

In a decade of conspicuous consumption, eighties romantic historicism first came from delving into the dressing-up box of club culture with the posturing new romantics, and segued into the 1990s with a baroque, oversized, overstated decorative slant. Club dance wear, the ripped tights, ballet tutus, and rah-rah skirts worn by Madonna and Bananarama in turn sparked new shapes in skirts that came from the historical research of designers, such as Vivienne Westwood, who launched her Mini-Crini collection in 1985. The museum and art-gallery obsession showed not only in her work, but likewise in that of Karl Lagerfeld for Chanel, Gianfranco Ferre, Franco Moschino, and Christian Lacroix. The sumptuousness of Romeo Gigli and the avant-garde of early John Galliano echoed Derek Jarman's movie *Caravaggio*.

▶ **Corseted dress, Westwood, 1996**
Whether focusing on the cheeky bosoms and full skirts aspect of history, or the robelike cocoon coat of Romeo Gigli, the opulence of the historical reinterpretation of the 1980s and 90s lent itself to ornamentation and embellishment. It was luxurious costume that recalled the lavish courts of Europe, parodying the days of sumptuary laws.

▶ **Corsets, Vivienne Westwood, 1990**
Vivienne Westwood's "Portrait" collection, which used photographic prints of François Boucher's *Shepherd Watching a Sleeping Shepherdess*, was inspired by 18th-century paintings held in the Wallace Collection in London. Westwood studied the Victoria & Albert Museum archive and referenced literature from that time. The pushed-up bust of the late 1980s was due in part to her use of the corset, a trend that lasted throughout the 1990s.

**Smocking dress fabric in silk and viscose,
Nigel Atkinson for Romeo Gigli, 1990**

The sensibilities of the designs of Romeo Gigli were
far more ethereal than the brashness of Westwood and
Lacroix, but had historical derivation. Gigli's designs also
took inspiration from the baroque and the Byzantine,
often embellishing rich fabrics with gold embroidery
and tassels. This "Edelweiss Smocking" fabric, a heat-
treated silk and viscose mix, was created in 1990
exclusively for Gigli by Nigel Atkinson, who specializes
in textured, innovative textiles.

"It's Lacroix, Sweetie."

ABSOLUTELY FABULOUS CATCHPHRASE

Evening dress, Christian Lacroix, 1989–1990

Christian Lacroix opened
his couture house in 1987,
after working for Jean
Patou, and launched his
prêt-à-porter line in 1988,
declaring that his best
customers were New York
drag queens. Lacroix takes
inspiration from the
opulent 18th-century
aesthetic of Madame de
Pompadour, introduced
to him by his art-loving
Dandy grandfather. He
mixes ornamentation and
color in fun shapes taken
from history, such as the
puff-ball skirt. This one
incorporates gauze sleeves
on a jeweled velvet corset.

ELEMENTS OF FASHION

• *Dangerous Liaisons and
Amadeus*

• *photographer Paolo Roversi*

• *'"Neobaroque" L'Uomo Vogue,
April 1988*

• *Gaultier underwear as
outerwear*

• *Galliano appointed to Givenchy*

Silk damask jacket, Scott Crolla, 1988

Former art student Scott Crolla launched the Crolla
label with his partner, fellow artist Georgina Godley, in
1981. Brocade was a signature as the historical leanings of
the clothing centered it in the male Dandy dressing-up
style of the eighties, born of the new romantic club
movement. Damask, straight-cut jackets and brocade
pants were worn with ruffled shirts, and velvet slippers
with white silk stockings.

CHRONOLOGICAL CATWALK
The Nineties Male

The rap scene
The New York hip-hop group the Wu-Tang Clan was formed in 1992 by three cousins. Each of its members goes by a pseudonym, such as Method Man, Ol' Dirty Bastard, and The RZA. The vocabulary, posturing, and dress of the early rap scene was deliberately cliquish and excluding, but its influence was so widespread that half-mast jeans and undone laces became quickly assimilated into more mainstream street fashion.

Baseball cap
The Kangol bucket hat was the hip-hop head wear of the 1980s, although a wave of black nationalism inspired African-style cloth hats to be worn with dreadlocks. Baseball caps started to become part of rap culture in the 1990s, often worn backward. A gangsta take was to wear them with a Du Rag head cloth or under a hoodie.

Hip-hop fashion
It was not only language that was part of establishing the hip-hop culture, but also a dress code that had exacting standards that signified membership. The Wu-Tang Clan were central to a collective which spawned different musical offshoots and were the first to produce their own clothing line, which reinforced their consolidated image. Busta Rhymes, Jay-Z, and Puff Daddy later also started labels.

Oversized silhouette
The layered sportswear became more and more baggy throughout the 1990s to create a menacing, large silhouette. Pants were worn low so that underwear waistbands could be seen, but however oversized, jackets only reached to the waist. After the advent of bling, which stretched further than jewelry to designer brands, fashions became more form-fitting.

Sportswear

The Wu-Wear label, based on the sportswear line of rap culture, was produced by Oli "Power" Grant, also executive producer of the Wu-Tang Clan. As the group became more successful, Grant was able to open four stand-alone stores, as well as selling through Macy's. The quality was publicly decried by Method Man, who was unhappy at the way the Clan was being represented in a status-minded environment.

Layering

Sportswear hip-hop fashion separates were casually layered. Brands that shot to prominence were Tommy Hilfiger, Polo Ralph Lauren, FUBU, and Boss Jeans. Karl Kani became the first label specifically aimed at the hip-hop market; started in 1989 by self-taught Carl Williams, it was worn by Tupac and the Notorious B.I.G., and name-checked in Jay-Z's Takeover.

Timberlands

The box-fresh Adidas and Pumas of the b-boys of the 1980s, which culminated in the Adidas obsession of Run DMC, was challenged by the release of Nike Air Jordans, named after basketball player Michael Jordan. An alternative was outdoor-wear Timberland boots, which traded on their popularity to expand into a lifestyle brand. Nike produced a limited edition Wu-Tang dunk hi in 1999.

The Supermodel 1990s

Allure of the Amazons

In the context of the 1990s, when the catwalk show had reached the high-octane, adrenalin-fueled level of a rock concert, fashion had become assimilated into popular culture. A group of models who came to represent glamorous, fantasy-made flesh—the supermodels—were marketed by their agencies as personalities and commanded higher fees than ever previously imagined. The phenomenon was centered around five girls: Linda Evangelista, Christy Turlington, Cindy Crawford, Claudia Schiffer, and Naomi Campbell. Their selling power was such that they were in demand for celebrity endorsement, calendars, pin-ups, movies, TV, books, and fitness videos. After the group was photographed on the cover of *Vogue* together, they were cast in George Michael's video for his hit single "Freedom!"

▶ **Versace jeans couture advertisement, 1990s**
Gianni Versace created advertising that elevated his brand into must-have status with the winning formula of outfits made completely of his recognizable house print, images shot by big-name photographers, and the most photographed models of the time: Linda Evangelista, Helena Christensen, and Christy Turlington. Versace promoted and profited from the creation of a supermodel clique, using them collectively on the catwalk backed by George Michael's track "Freedom!"

> **"We don't wake up for less than $10,000 a day."**
>
> LINDA EVANGELISTA

THE SUPERMODEL 1990S

Karl Lagerfeld with Christensen, Schiffer, and Crawford, 1993
Supermodels were an expected presence at the couture collections, where it was deemed necessary for the most expensive clothes in the world to be shown by the most expensive models. However, a backlash started when the models started to be perceived as overpaid and overexposed, and the money-led elitist fashion system started to appear vulgar, without the restraint that promotes chic.

Naomi Campbell, early 1990s
Naomi Campbell started modeling at the age of 15 and was instantly hired for high-profile advertising campaigns, which gave her exposure in the United States. Unparalleled as a black model in her status, pay, and notoriety, Campbell has spoken out about the difficulties black models face within the fashion industry. The fact that she has transcended her job description to become an idol in the cult of celebrity has sometimes made the public aware of human fallibility behind the projected image.

Cindy Crawford, ca. 1990
Cindy Crawford was the "all-American girl" of the supermodels and her popularity was instrumental in moving fashion's silhouette toward a more curvaceous figure during this time. Crawford's image was famously subverted when she posed for the cover of *Vanity Fair* in a revealing body suit, shaving the face of lesbian singer k.d. lang, and again when she dressed as George Washington for the cover of the political magazine *George*.

ELEMENTS OF FASHION

- *supermodel waxworks at the Grévin wax museum, Paris*
- *supermodel Barbie dolls*
- *high profile boyfriends (Mike Tyson; Richard Gere; Axl Rose)*
- *Fashion Cafe*
- *exclusive designer contracts*
- *drag queen RuPaul*

247

Antifashion 1990s

An end to excess

The last shout of the 20th century was not without its final swings and roundabouts of fashion. The larger-than-life designer consumerism began to see a backlash that had started with stylists mixing vintage, streetwear, and music influences with high fashion. This continued by influencing a younger generation of designers, photographers, and stylists to produce an aesthetic that was less about a manufactured image. The antithesis of glamor, the postmodern waifs in *Vogue* were pictured wearing sneakers, boys' school shirts, and fetish PVC pants mixed with expensive ready-to-wear. Some designers responded to the rejection of glitz with an extension of their own values into a pared-down purism. The Calvin Klein underwear campaign featuring Kate Moss was an amalgamation of the two.

> **"Kate ... had that thing about her that Twiggy had in the 60s, a freshness that matched the times."**
>
> PHIL BICKER, FORMER ART DIRECTOR OF
> *THE FACE* MAGAZINE

Yasmin Le Bon modeling Rifat Ozbek, 1990
Rifat Ozbek's white and silver New Age collection of 1990 heralded a dawn of new possibilities and seemed to aim to wipe the slate of eighties excess. The nonconsumerist message with its allusions to spiritualism and green issues, together with the club-wear hooded sweatshirt look prophesied the antifashion stance that was to infiltrate the industry during the coming decade.

Kate Moss, 1991
Slightly younger than the other supermodels, Kate Moss was aged 14 when she was shot for *The Face* by photographer Corinne Day in 1990. The original draw was the adolescent gawkiness of Moss's looks, which captured the approaching shift in the fashion world. Moss joined the ranks of the superpaid, bringing her fresh realism to the catwalks of the top brands, but was soon to be accused of being an instigator of "heroin chic".

**Grunge collection,
Perry Ellis, S/S collection, 1993**
In 1992, the young gun designer
at Perry Ellis, Marc Jacobs,
showed his Grunge collection,
a homage to the Seattle music
scene that Jacobs was into, and
a landmark show that mixed
street and high fashion on the
American runway. Jacobs layered
print dresses with cashmere
thermals, flannel shirts, and Doc
Marten boots. Soon afterward he
and his business partner Robert
Duffy were fired from Perry Ellis.

Kurt Cobain, 1993
The alt-rock, indie grunge style
from Seattle that pervaded the
Western world in the 1990s defined
the look of the "slacker" generation.
King of the scene was Nirvana's Kurt
Cobain, who rejected the status of
success that he achieved during his
short and problematic life. Cobain's
unkempt fashion sense of unwashed
hair and thrift-store clothing was
as much the product of a lack of
concern as it was of rebellion.

ELEMENTS OF FASHION

• *Anna Sui's 93 grunge look*
• *Model Stella Tennant's nose ring*
• *Paper Magazine in New York*
• *functional clothing*
• *no ironing*
• *photographers Juergen Teller,
David Sims*
• *tattoos*

Helmut Lang, F/W collection, 1994
Key to the nineties redefinition of fashion was layering.
Helmut Lang took the antifashion aesthetic and layered
different fabrics in a simplified silhouette to create an
urbanized purist style that appeared totally modern.
"Utilitarian" and "futuristic" describe the fabric used
at Helmut Lang, which became the cult label of the
modernist school of Jil Sander and Calvin Klein.

Showstoppers 1990s–2000s

Red-carpet runways

When Elizabeth Hurley accompanied her boyfriend Hugh Grant to the premiere of *Four Weddings and a Funeral* in 1994 in a Versace dress, the front page coverage ensured that she became a household name overnight and secured her a lucrative contract with Estée Lauder. Jennifer Lopez similarly received the Versace magic touch when she wore the jungle dress to the 2000 Grammys. The dress was copied so much that underwear companies started to manufacture "tit tape" to buy in the shopping mall. Red-carpet showstoppers are a two-way endorsement agreement between fashion house and star, and have become a way to get media coverage of couture— the ultimate advertisement.

Tilda Swinton with Viktor Horsting and Rolf Snoeren, 2005
Launching their label, Viktor & Rolf, in 1993 in Amsterdam, Viktor Horsting and Rolf Snoeren brought contemporary design to haute couture in 1998. They have worked with Tilda Swinton several times, basing the ready-to-wear fall/winter 2003/4 collection solely on the actress's singular look, with each model made up to resemble her. The conceptual catwalk shows extended to their menswear launch, when the pair modeled the entire collection themselves.

Princess Diana, Versace, 1996
By the mid-1990s Princess Diana, one of the most-photographed women in the world, was a style icon appearing on the covers of *Vogue* and *Vanity Fair*. Diana was a friend and customer of Gianni Versace, who made many dresses for her public appearances. Allegedly she had been offered a substantial fee to appear on the Versace catwalk to celebrate her divorce, but had declined.

> ❝The runway shows are important to us. They're not just about showing the clothes—they're performances.❞
>
> ROLF SNOEREN

ELEMENTS OF FASHION

- *a celebrity stylist*
- *a cleavage*
- *a train*
- *the Oscar change*
- *the 24-hour face-lift*

Charlize Theron, John Galliano for Dior, 2006
John Galliano's debut couture collection for Dior in 1997 received approbation when Nicole Kidman wore one of the dresses on the Oscar red carpet. Red-carpet agreements have been instrumental in keeping haute couture in existence. In couture, tradition is everything and using the best fabrics, such as French-made silk, is still paramount. Galliano has mixed his historicism with his research of the techniques of the grands couturiers throughout his career and has become an expert in the bias cut, after the style of Madeleine Vionnet.

Kate Winslet, Valentino, 2007
Valentino has been at the forefront of Italian couture since the mid-1960s and received a standing ovation from contemporaries Karl Lagerfeld and Giorgio Armani during his 45th-anniversary celebrations in 2007, when he showed his couture collection in Rome instead of Paris, before announcing his retirement. As this red-carpet example demonstrates, Valentino's dresses were the obvious choice for the woman who was looking for style and form over fashion statement, although his signature red always guaranteed impact.

Jean-Paul Gaultier b. 1952

Christened the *enfant terrible* of French fashion, Jean-Paul Gaultier's career has had a longevity that some classicists could only dream about.

Born in 1952 in Arcueil, in the southern suburbs of Paris, Gaultier did not attend fashion school but precociously took matters into his own hands. At the age of 13, he designed a collection for his mother and grandmother and started sending his sketches to couturiers while still a teenager. In 1970, when he was aged 17, Pierre Cardin hired him as his assistant on the strength of the sketches. After two years at Cardin, Gaultier moved first to Jacques Esterel and then to Patou with a break in 1974, managing the Pierre Cardin boutique in Manila, where he designed for Imelda Marcos.

Gaultier launched his own label in 1976 for the French company Mayagor, and also designed a broad range of work freelance, including prêt-à-porter, swimwear, and furs. In 1978, he was approached by the Japanese clothing manufacturer Kashiyama, who offered him an exclusive contract to design menswear and womenswear collections under his own name.

❝It's always the badly dressed people who are the most interesting.❞

JEAN-PAUL GAULTIER

Born
Arcueil, France

Manifesto
To combine humor with couture skills.

Gaultier's distinctive style developed in the 1980s, when he mixed influences from street fashion into an avant-garde, tough but cheeky modernity that set him apart from his contemporaries in Paris and had more in common with London or New York fashion. His 1985 menswear collection was a huge success when he showed skirts for men, which proved to be influential, both at the time—the look became popular for club wear—and as an important landmark in men's fashion history. In 2003, Gaultier's company sponsored an enquiry into the appropriation of women's clothing by men in the exhibition "Bravehearts—Men in Skirts," at the Metropolitan Museum of Art in New York.

Gaultier's menswear is often influenced by gay culture—he camps up the sailor look with his ever-present Breton matelot T-shirt. Ambiguous sexuality was a constant presence on the Gaultier catwalk throughout the 1980s and 90s, with female models wearing pinstripe suits and smoking pipes while the "men-in-skirts" theme progressed to tutus. The womenswear and menswear collections also featured interchangeable androgynous outfits.

Some of Gaultier's most overtly sexual and outrageous creations have been his costumes for movies. In Peter

Greenaway's *The Cook, The Thief, His Wife, and Her Lover,* Helen Mirren's character wears a bondage-inspired dress that changes color as she moves through the sets. For Pedro Almodóvar's *Kika,* Gaultier designed fetishistic breast-revealing outfits for the character Andrea Scarface, and costumes for Luc Besson's *The Fifth Element* include a futuristic bandage bikini. The underwear-as-outerwear phenomenon promoted by Gaultier was a result of a childhood fascination with a pink laced corset shown to him by his grandmother, which he reproduced for the bottle of his perfume, Classique.

In 1988, Gaultier expanded his ready-to-wear to the Junior Gaultier diffusion line, controversially using retirement-age models for the advertising campaign, which then became the "JPG by Gaultier" unisex collection in 1994. A denim line, Gaultier Jeans, was started in 1992. Advertising for the company has constantly satirized the conventional ideals of beauty in fashion and subverts the feminist ideas of objectification.

In 1997, Gaultier first showed a couture collection, becoming the *enfant terrible* of the Chambre Syndicale. He was the first couturier to show clothing for both sexes in his presentation, including corsets for men. Gaultier's humor, known to audiences of his *Eurotrash* TV show in the 1990s, is ever present in his designs, although his background and apprenticeship in haute couture has ensured a respect for the traditions and technical expertise of the industry.

However, designing for couture, which does not have the limitations of a mass-produced ready-to-wear line, meant that Gaultier could have free rein for his imagination and produced fantastical creations that mixed his preoccupations with sex, religion, exoticism, and subcultures. The success of the couture design led to him being appointed Creative Director at Hermès in 2003 and in the same year he was the subject of a retrospective exhibition at the Victoria & Albert Museum in London.

In 1989, Madonna called Jean-Paul Gaultier two days before his prêt-à-porter show to ask him to design the outfits for her forthcoming tour. A mutual appreciation meant that the two were aware of each other's work, so the pinstriped suits, with cutouts for the conical bra of the corset to poke through, were a collaboration featuring the central elements of Madonna's trademark sex and religion, realized by Gaultier's signature style.

The Sneaker 1990s–2000s

Street style

The influence of street culture on high fashion in the 1990s was represented by the ubiquity of the sneaker. The result was that brands that had originally been known for sportswear, while respected among style tribes at certain times in history, such as mods wearing Spring Court tennis shoes, were now imbued with the same kudos that had been previously reserved for designer labels. The widening of the fashion system, from a market that was concerned with elitism to one that was concerned with youth's interpretation of cool, also led to this mix of fashion design and utilitarian design.

Red stripe sneaker, Prada, 1997
Released at the height of nineties sportswear/streetwear mania, when pretty much everything had to look urban, fasten with Velcro, and be made of Teflon, the Prada Red stripe sneaker could have been a step too far. However, the range was a sell out—the subtlety of the branding predating stealth wealth—and rare sneaker experts were consulted in the media regarding the value and collectability.

Actress Kristen Stewart in Converses, 2009
The Converse Rubber Shoe Company was started in 1908 and has become an American institution—its involvement in basketball meant it was a forerunner of the sports-shoe industry. Long before the sportswear and music industries became mutually beneficent, All Stars were recognizably part of the antiappeal of the Ramones. To the youth generation of the 2000s, a pair of Chuck Taylors or Jack Purcells says indie, alternative, and credible.

Adidas Gazelle, 1990s
Retro sneakers such as Puma States and Adidas Gazelles had a resurgence in the 1990s when skater kids started wearing them. The acid jazz movement, which took diverse ingredients and inspirations from other youth and music cultures, then started wearing the classic lo-tops. The trend quickly spread, and when Kate Moss was photographed in her Gazelles they were soon seen on the feet of every fashionista.

ELEMENTS OF FASHION

- *limited-edition Run DMC Jam Master Jay Adidas shelltoes*
- *Vans for skaters*
- *Dunlop Green Flash*
- *The Rock Steady Crew wearing Puma States*
- *the window in the Nike Air Max that revealed the air cushion*
- *Nike Air Rift split toes*
- *Stella McCartney for Adidas*
- *Paul Smith Reeboks*
- *Yohji Yamamoto for Adidas*

"[Sneakers] are so popular ... that, almost like an ancient tool from our ancestors, we forget what they are actually designed for."

NEAL HEARD,
TRAINERS, 2003

Air Max sneaker, Nike, 1990s
Nike launched its Air Max sneaker in 1987 as the first exercise shoe that houses an air-cushioning unit in the heel. Such is its popularity that new models have been introduced to the range periodically. This is not only due to the preference of athletes and to the rise in gym membership by the end of the 20th century, but also to the adoption of the Air Max by the hip-hop movement. The street kudos of the brand then spread to a wider spectrum of dance clubs.

Deconstruction 1990s—2000s

The Antwerp Six

The Fashion School of the Antwerp Royal Academy of Fine Arts came to the attention of the International Fashion Industry when a group of designers who had graduated between 1980 and 1981 began to produce avant-garde collections that chimed with the Japanese school of design that had become prevalent. In 1988, six of these designers loaded a van with their collections and drove to England to present the designs at London Fashion Week. The deconstruction style of the Antwerp Six and their fellow graduates became an influential factor on fashion in the 1990s and widened the European fashion spectrum.

▶ **F/W collection, Ann Demeulemeester, 2001**
One of the original Antwerp Six, Ann Demeulemeester first showed in 1992, with a style that ripped apart consumerism with unrefined and unfinished detailing. In later years, Demeulemeester has refined her style into a dark, gothic rock aesthetic. Obsessed with the style of Patti Smith, she has become friends with the singer and the two collaborated on her 1999 collection.

S/S collection, Martin Margiela, 2001 ◀
A contemporary of Demeulemeester, Martin Margiela was at the apex of the intellectual fashion movement of the 1990s. Concerned with the natural cycles of objects, Margiela was recycling and remaking before such practices had ethical connotations. Margiela was appointed assistant at Jean-Paul Gaultier in 1985 and by 1997 his conceptualism was considered so important that he was hired as head of the design studio at Hermès.

F/W collection, Dries Van Noten, 2007

Another iconoclast of the Antwerp Six, Dries Van Noten layered themes in his work just as he layers actual garments. Often taking Eastern detailing, print or clothing structures and mixing them with Western concepts of dress, it is his menswear that has given Van Noten his reputation for innovative reinterpretation. None of the original Antwerp designers are self-publicists, but Van Noten has consistently sold on a global scale.

ELEMENTS OF FASHION

- *skinny models Stella Tennant and Charley Speed*
- *Raf Simons's menswear frock coats*
- *Visionaire magazine*
- *Margiela numbered collections*
- *photographers Inez van Lamsweerde and Vinoodh Matadin*
- *Boudicca conceptual couture*

Madonna in gothic dress, Olivier Theyskens, 1998

Brussels-born Olivier Theyskens dropped out of his fashion course in his second year to start his own label. His work was clearly influenced by the earlier ideas of the Antwerp graduates. While working as a costume designer at the Théâtre de la Monnaie, one of Theysken's gothic-inspired ball gowns was worn by Madonna to the Oscars and his subsequent success led to him designing first at Rochas and then at Nina Ricci.

"In fashion, there is a freedom of expression which can at times be shocking, alarming, astounding or tempting."

ROYAL ACADEMY OF FINE ARTS, ANTWERP

The Logo 1990s–2000s

Wearing the designer's mark

Toward the end of the 20th century, branding became an all-important exercise in fashion and, helped along by hip-hop gangsta rap style, ostentation gained kudos. Whether the fashion observer saw it as a street-style in-joke or a collectable trend, logomania, as it came to be called, gathered momentum. It was certainly true, however, that endorsement of a brand by rap stars, either by wearing the logo or by mentioning the product in a song, could have an impact on its success and credibility. In 1999, David LaChapelle photographed Lil Kim for *Rolling Stone* magazine with the Louis Vuitton LV logo in a repeat pattern all over her naked body.

Mary J. Blige wearing Gucci hat, 2003 ◀
The logomania trend at the turn of the 21st century coincided with the bling fashion of rap culture. Bling, short for "bling bling," referred originally to flashy gold and diamond jewelry, but was extended to encompass any kind of branded designer piece. Tom Ford had made the Gucci double-G logo synonymous with sex and money, and Mary J. Blige's album, *Love & Life,* had gone straight into the charts at number one.

Sequin and fabric jacket, ▲
Lagerfeld for Chanel, 1991
Karl Lagerfeld repeatedly reinterpreted and modernized the signature styles and details of Chanel throughout the 1990s. Here, the Chanel suit jacket is channeled into sportswear de luxe— the sequins give the jacket a wet-suit appearance and it is intended to be paired with leggings. The zipper pull has the double-C logo, which was trademarked in 1925 and is one of the most counterfeited logos in fashion.

" I was not an artist, I was creating something that was made to be sold, marketed, used, and ultimately discarded. "

TOM FORD

Advertisement for raincoats, Burberry, 2001

Christopher Bailey, Creative Director at Burberry since 2001, had previously been Womenswear Designer at Gucci. The appointment was part of the drive to revive the traditional British label. The 2001 campaign featured top models and celebrities in a series of narratives that poked fun at the fashion industry as a whole.

Logo-printed shorts, Dior, 1999

Using the logo to assert brand status was partly due to a rush of takeovers and mergers in the luxury fashion industry. John Galliano took the rap culture reference in 1999 and created his "ghetto fabulous" denim for Dior in monogram print. The Brazilian model Gisele won Model of the Year in 1999 and went on in the next decade to become the highest-paid model in the world.

ELEMENTS OF FASHION

- *Kristal, Krug, and Dom Pérignon*
- *the Burberry check bikini*
- *Michael Kors for Céline*
- *Vivienne Westwood Anglomania*
- *gold and diamond logo teeth decoration*

CHRONOLOGICAL CATWALK
The Noughties Female

The superfast woman

Patricia Field was the New York stylist behind the phenomenon *Sex and the City*, which made materialism a lifestyle choice for the independent, modern, 30-something, woman, portraying fashion as the unique ingredient that brought together the elements of liberated sexuality and fast city living. Dubbed the most fashionable show in television history, *Sex and the City's* highest-grossing episode attracted 10.6 million viewers.

Shoes
In a 2003 episode, "A Woman's Right to Shoes," Carrie is requested to take off her shoes at a party and feels compromised immediately. Her affinity with Manolo Blahnik and Jimmy Choos came to represent the frivolous nature of the show, but the aim was to equate Carrie's shoe obsession with a single woman's ability to take care of herself.

Shirt
Patricia Field's talent lay in completing a portrayal of a rounded character by creating a signature style of dressing for each. Carrie's quirkiness never reproduced catwalk looks, but mixed vintage, mainstream and designer, an eclectic way of dressing that was very much discussed in the decade when "individuality" was a key word.

Eclectic silhouette
Carrie is a 30-something party girl, and Field dismisses the dangers of "mutton dressed as lamb" criticism in the modern age. Of the four girls, Carrie's style is very individual. The tutu, for example, that she wears in the series was much discussed as a fashion item, but it became an iconic piece from the wardrobe—not simply as a much-copied trend, but also because it negated the outmoded idea of a woman needing to dress appropriately for her age.

Hatbox
As well as the designer must-haves, Field's choice of accessories could have huge influence—her choices could make or break. Cable network HBO was not happy when they saw Carrie sporting a huge fabric flower corsage, thinking that Field had gone too far, but it jump-started a nationwide trend. Viewers learned to expect the unexpected—of course, Carrie would have a box from London hatters James Lock.

Dress
Shopping is a joy and a balm in the series and the viewer is privy to a world where the perfect dress is only a cab ride away. In fact, designer-clothing accessibility moved a little closer at the start of the 21st century. Noughties woman had a different attitude to spending power, which meant that designer shopping was no longer regarded as elitist, and online shopping from sites such as net-a-porter facilitated the desire.

Miranda's gold metallic dress ◄

Miranda was always the dowdy foil for the others' fashion-forward wardrobes. By the second movie, however, Field apparently projected that her out-of-the-office persona had become as interested in conspicuous consumption as the other girls. This dress was one of a series of statement frocks that Miranda was given in the movie as her fashion redemption. Fashion-obsessed *SATC* fans spotted it online as by designer Alberta Ferretti.

Shopping and the City ▲

Sex and the City captivated so many viewers that two spin-off feature movies were made and the girls' outfits received as much press and speculation as the story-lines. Field was also stylist for the 2006 movie *The Devil Wears Prada* which, with fashion taking the central role around which a comedy of manners was played, was dismissed as fantastical—until the movie *The September Issue* came out in 2009.

The It Bag 2000s

Status in a sac

Nothing defined a fashion season more at the turn of the 21st century than the bag of the moment. The It bag, so called because it was the most photographed bag of the moment, seen on the arm of every celebrity, meant not only the status afforded because of the price, but also that the owner was in the know. The success of the Fendi Baguette meant that the company constantly issued new versions, instantly dating them, but ultimately giving them iconic collectability. The desirability of the designer bag as an obsession that consumed fashion for a moment was satirized in *Sex and the City*, and ultimately was dismissed as *nouveau-riche* vulgarity.

Gisele bag, F/W collection, Luella Gisele, 2002

Luella Bartley grew from kooky London designer to luxury player when the Gisele bag, part of the Luella for Mulberry collection, achieved It bag status in 2002, reviving the British brand. The Gisele was designed by Stuart Vevers before his appointment to revamp Spanish luxury brand Loewe. Luella went on to show in New York, opening a store in London, which was targeted for a smash-and-grab bag raid in 2007. Luella ceased trading in 2008.

Victoria Beckham with Birkin bag, 2009

The Birkin bag was created in 1984 after actress Jane Birkin dropped the contents of her bag on a plane while sitting next to Jean-Louis Dumas, President of Hermès. It prompted a conversation that resulted in the famous bag that bears her name. Costing around $9,000, the bag is completely hand-made by craftsmen using traditional skills and the waiting list is around two years, depending on the customer's celebrity status. Victoria Beckham is said to be able to color-coordinate a Birkin with every outfit in her wardrobe.

ELEMENTS OF FASHION

- *the Chanel 2.55*
- *Coach*
- *Longchamp*
- *Bottega Veneta*
- *www.bagsnob.com*

"Fashion is like the id. It makes you desire things you shouldn't."

BOB MORRIS

Agyness Deyn with Speedy bag, Louis Vuitton, 2009

Marc Jacobs collaborated with New York designer Stephen Sprouse for a collection in 2001. Eight years later, he revisited the collaboration to create a further Louis Vuitton collection with the Sprouse print, which coincided with the first retrospective of Sprouse's work in his home town. The pieces, which included the LV Speedy bag, appeared iconic to a younger generation inclined toward 1980s and 90s revivalism due to their age.

Prada bag, S/S collection, 2006

When Miuccia Prada took control of the family firm in 1978, she and her future husband, Patrizio Bertelli, set about modernizing the look. The practical black nylon bag (above), the forerunner to the It bag of the noughties, was made out of the covering fabric that her grandfather had used for steamer trunks. It was placed in high-end department stores and priced expensively. Prada became known for its functional, stylish products and the leather bags that followed used logos just as unobtrusively.

New Futurism 2000s

British innovation

While the Royal College of Art produced so many of London's fashion stars in the 1960s, by the end of the 70s St. Martin's College of Art had became a renowned hub of creativity. The fashion school, which later became part of Central St. Martin's, consistently turned out successful graduates, spotlighting London as the place to which the industry looked for fresh talent. Louise Wilson, a graduate of St. Martin's in the 1980s, became a driving force behind the MA fashion-design course and received an OBE from the queen in 2008. Graduates have included Stella McCartney and Phoebe Philo, who took over at Chloé, Giles Deacon, Matthew Williamson, Jonathan Saunders, and Alber Elbaz.

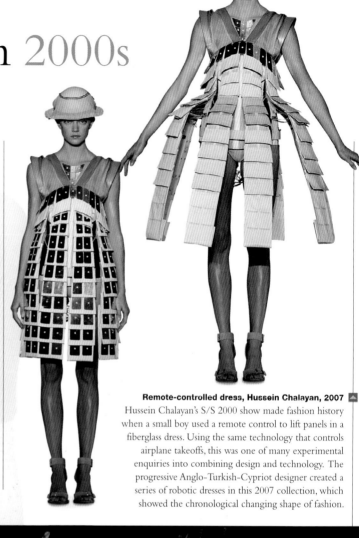

Remote-controlled dress, Hussein Chalayan, 2007
Hussein Chalayan's S/S 2000 show made fashion history when a small boy used a remote control to lift panels in a fiberglass dress. Using the same technology that controls airplane takeoffs, this was one of many experimental enquiries into combining design and technology. The progressive Anglo-Turkish-Cypriot designer created a series of robotic dresses in this 2007 collection, which showed the chronological changing shape of fashion.

▶ **Spray paint dress, S/S collection, Alexander McQueen, 1999**
London Fashion Week was the port of call for avant-garde inspiration, despite its reputation for underfunded disorganization. McQueen was part of a wave of St. Martin's graduates to be employed by prominent fashion companies in the 1990s and 2000s. Consistently employing technology to project the idea of futuristic design, his 1999 show closed with model Shalom Harlow wearing a white dress that was spray painted by two robotic arms.

"British fashion is self-confident and ... refuses to bow to commerce, thus generating a constant flow of new ideas whilst drawing on British heritage."

ALEXANDER MCQUEEN

St. Martin's Graduate Show, Christopher Kane, 2006

Christopher Kane's graduate show at St. Martin's in 2006 won him a position from Donatella Versace to consult on the Versace Atelier line. Kane also designed collections for British chain store Topshop. Fellow successful CSM alumni Danielle Scutt, Jonathan Saunders, Mark Fast, and Richard Nicoll have also worked with Topshop Boutique, an innovation that has promoted a generation of fashion-savvy youth.

Outfit, F/W collection, Gareth Pugh, 2006

Gareth Pugh's work was featured on the cover of *Dazed and Confused* after he graduated from St. Martin's in 2003, and was invited to participate in Lulu Kennedy's Fashion East, which had been started to encourage young design to show during London Fashion Week. Pugh's sculptural designs, which address the perception of body shape and draw reference from London club culture, were initially only showpieces and did not go into production until 2007.

ELEMENTS OF FASHION

- stylist Katy England
- Sarah Harmarnee jewelry
- fashion-show producer Simon Costin
- Scott Wilson headpieces
- Sophia Kokosalaki at Vionnet
- Phoebe Philo at Céline

Vintage 2000s

Retro individuality

The forays that fashion made into secondhand clothing and retromania during the 1960s and 70s freed stylists in the 1980s and 90s to mix secondhand finds with contemporary clothing when shooting editorial fashion spreads. Celebrity stylists began seeking out speciality stores to find pieces that would give their clients an individual look. Dealers became aware of the value of the second life of clothing, and "vintage" as a concept was introduced to the wider fashion system. Newly opened vintage stores had a boutique feel and celebrated the preciousness of their wares.

ELEMENTS OF FASHION

- *vintage fashion fairs*
- *Sotheby's Passion for Fashion auctions*
- *Dita Von Teese*
- *Anita Pallenberg at St. Martin's*
- *vintage as new sustainability*
- *Biba relaunch 2010 at House of Fraser*

Fifties femininity, S/S collection, Prada, 2004
Prada collections throughout the 2000s revisited earlier decades and reinvented styles into the label's aesthetic of quirky femininity, which gave high-end designer goods a geeky chic feel. Marc Jacobs also employed this technique for his label, while Giles Deacon reinterpreted the elegance of seventies and eighties prêt-à-porter for his timeless collections. Vintage had pervaded all levels of the fashion system.

Iconoclasts, hats collection, Prada, 2009
Nostalgia lovers often choose a particular decade to focus on. When fashion is inspired by vintage, as with these hats, a style is again imbued with a fashion-forward status. The recent obsession with the past has created an engagement with fashion history for the shopper who studies this season's trends.

Eyewear, F/W collection, Cutler and Gross, 2010
Established in 1969, Cutler and Gross were responsible for Michael Caine's trademark glasses, and since then have worked their collections around the iconic image of eyewear, revisiting classic styles. Linda Farrow launched their vintage range in 2003 when Farrow's son, Mark, found a cache of designer pieces that had been made for other companies including Pucci. Vintage sunglasses became a craze that affected the design of all the major brands.

"Vintage is not only ... stylish, it's also the way forward in terms of recycling."

THANDIE NEWTON

Dress by Barbara Hulanicki for Topshop, 2009
After two decades designing interiors in Miami, fashion again called on Barbara Hulanicki. The vintage industry had brought Biba to the attention of the next generation, with the originals, which were marketed for affordability, reaching double figures on eBay and in speciality fashion auctions. Hulanicki related to Topshop's fast turnaround and agreed to design a capsule contemporary collection.

Alexander McQueen 1969–2010

Lee Alexander McQueen grew up in Stratford, East London. The youngest of six, and son of a cab driver, he left school at 16 with one grade in art and started an apprenticeship at the Savile Row tailors Anderson & Shepherd, before moving to Gieves & Hawkes. After working for the theatrical costumiers Angels and Bermans, he assisted Koji Tatsuno and Romeo Gigli in Milan. Both designers were concerned with conceptualizing historical design and McQueen was able to utilize his cutting skills and costume experience.

Back in London, McQueen won a place on the MA course at Central St. Martin's. His 1991 graduation collection was spotted by fashion stylist Isabella Blow. She bought the entire collection for £5,000 (about $7,500), and wore it for a feature on McQueen in *Vogue*. Blow became McQueen's patron, insisting that he design under his middle name, and introducing him to influential people.

Alexander McQueen catwalk shows were unsettling creative pieces of showmanship, combining art and

Born
Lewisham, London

Manifesto
To push the boundaries of technical innovation.

technology in dramatic narratives. The press leaped on these outlandish presentations, falling back on that useful phrase, *enfant terrible*, which had been Gaultier's preserve a decade before. McQueen shared Gaultier's predilection for subversion and looking beyond the clothes, but his interpretation was altogether darker. McQueen's shows panned out like psychological thrillers; indeed Hitchcock's movies *Vertigo* and *The Birds* inspired one collection.

A McQueen show was always scheduled at the end of the week, and the jaded press and buyers would leave feeling awed and privileged to have been privy to such spectacles. For the S/S 98 show, the models walked down a catwalk of underlit water tanks under indoor rain from a sprinkler system; the S/S 99 show closed with model Shalom Harlow in a white dress being spray painted by robotic arms. F/W 06 had a glass pyramid that emitted a hologram of Kate Moss in a puff of smoke.

These extravaganzas, while retaining the fashion world's attention, did not belie the fact that McQueen's most bankable value was his technical brilliance. He was an outspoken champion of the skills that went into a designer dress when the price was questioned. Marrying his provocative vision and his cutting prowess, McQueen unveiled the bumster pants in the early

> **"Clothes and jewelry should be startling. When you see a woman in my clothes, you want to know more about them."**
>
> ALEXANDER MCQUEEN, 2010

McQueen's S/S 99 show featured double amputee Aimee Mullins on the catwalk. A paralympian, Mullins wore intricately carved wooden legs commissioned by McQueen for the show, which ended in exquisite boots. Nick Knight photographed her wearing the legs for a story for *Dazed and Confused*, which raised issues about the way people with disabilities were disregarded in the fashion industry.

1990s, which launched the trend for low-rise pants, although most did not stay up like a McQueen. A signature was working with contrasts: romantic gowns, cut to flow with contemporary prints, were harshly belted to constrain the breasts. Such severe corsetry and elevated heels mixed with historical fantasy had fashion theorists scratching their heads over misogyny versus emotional response.

In 1996, at the age of 27, the English young rebel was appointed Head Designer at Givenchy, succeeding John Galliano. The same year saw McQueen awarded the "British Designer of the Year" title, one of the youngest ever to do so. The award was repeated jointly in 1997 and again in 2001 and 2003. Despite, or perhaps because of, the accolades, McQueen's first collection for Givenchy was poorly received, no less because the designer was quoted as calling Hubert de Givenchy "irrelevant." The aesthetic of the two came together later with McQueen continuing at Givenchy until 2001. In 2000, the Gucci Group acquired 51 percent of McQueen's company, leaving him as its Creative Director, extending the collections and products into a superbrand and opening new flagship stores. In 2003, McQueen was awarded the CBE.

Forecasting 2005–2020

Ethical issues and sustainability

Futurism in fashion has, in the last fifty years, existed side by side with a looking back. It is this mix that contributes to creativity—recognizing the value of things past, and a desire to push things forward. The future of the fashion industry, however, is as much of a juggling act. Predicting what will happen in fashion is a necessary part of marketing, and predicting whether the resources will be available to make it happen has rendered sustainability a concern. Ethical issues are a factor in a consumer society with an increased awareness. The velocity of the industry due to blogs, online editorials, and e-commerce does not afford much time and space for reflection.

> **"Prejudice is a social disease. So is fashion. But I will not wear prejudice."**
>
> LADY GAGA

▶ **Plato's Atlantis, S/S collection, Alexander McQueen, 2010**
Always recognized as a visionary, McQueen's fashion experiences encompassed an entire otherworldly dimension where time frame became irrelevant. The silhouette of his Plato's Atlantis collection was true to form in its use of historical clothing structures. McQueen's awareness of the cyclical nature of fashion reinterpreted corsetry, crinolines, and collars to futuristic levels. The shoes in the S/S 2010 collection, clawlike and animalistic, seemed to be a dark prophecy of evolution.

Digital imaging as surface print, 2010

Designers such as Peter Pilotto and Jonathan Saunders have become known for forwarding the use of digital imaging in fashion surface print. This technique has revolutionized 1970s photo-printing to produce surreal manipulated patterns often from unreadable origins. McQueen's use of background for his presentation produced a magic-eye experience suggesting the necessity of camouflage for future survival.

"I'm Not a Plastic Bag," Anya Hindmarch, 2007

London bag designer, Anya Hindmarch, designed the canvas tote which read "I'm Not A Plastic Bag" in 2007 and launched it at London Fashion Week. Sold for £5 (about $7.50) in a main grocery-store chain, the bag was produced in collaboration with the We Are What We Do—a movement that campaigns for global social change. Fake "I'm Not A Plastic Bags" joined the luxury counterfeits on market stalls before long.

THE : FUTURE : LABORATORY
23 : 07 : 2010
15 : 30 : 08

PRODUCTS
EXPLORE
CONTACT

CURRENT ACTIVITY :: 0   FOLLOW LS:N GLOBAL ON TWITTER   FIND OUT WHAT'S GOING TO HAPPEN IN THE TURBULENT TEENS   US DESIGNERS CREATE AVANT-GARDE LIGHTING RANGE

Sound on / off   Photography: Kai Wiechmann : Sound: Pär Grindvik

ELEMENTS OF FASHION

- *Lady Gaga*
- *three-dimension*
- *Ethical Fashion Forum*
- *Sustainable Futures exhibition at London's Design Museum*
- *Exception de Mixmind, Beijing ethical fashion label*
- *fashiontrendsetter.com*

S/S collection, Alexander McQueen, 2010

In 2000 the British fashion photographer Nick Knight launched the SHOWstudio web site as a "multimedia workshop"— an online gallery that invites creatives to showcase their work to an immediate audience. He is interested in collaborations and often worked with Alexander McQueen. The attempt to stream the McQueen S/S 2010 show live crashed the web site due to the concentration of visitors after Lady Gaga tweeted that she would launch her new single during the event.

Future Laboratory homepage, 2010

The future of fashion has become an important insider part of the industry. Speciality forecasting companies, such as Future Laboratory and WGSN, analyze trends, moods, and color palettes and make up mood boards for corporate clients whose marketing departments work seasons in advance. Forecasting organizations look at major shifts in world politics, ecology, population, and consumption to project trends for the fragrance and cosmetics divisions, upon which designer labels are dependent for finance.

Appendices

Time Line

1783

Marie Antoinette scandalizes the French court by wearing the "*gaule*," a simple muslin dress, for a portrait by Elisabeth Vigée-Lebrun.

1785

Machine-printing process patented by Thomas Bell.

1793

Execution of Marie Antoinette in Paris. It becomes unfashionable in France to be seen as patrician.

1795

The "Directoire" neoclassical style is adopted in Paris.

The classical influence page 15

1837

Ascension of Queen Victoria to the British throne, and a period of morality affects fashion.

1846

Isaac Singer patents the sewing machine.

1846

Henry Poole opens the first tailor shop on Savile Row, in central London, beginning the long tradition of custom-made tailoring.

1856

The crinoline cage is patented by W. S. Thomas in the United States.

1858

Charles Frederick Worth opens in Paris, and so launches haute couture.

1860

The English Woman's Domestic Magazine sells paper patterns by mail order.

1870

The crinoline develops into the bustle.

The bustle page 66

The gigot sleeve page 23

1909

Designer Mariano Fortuny patents his pleat-setting technique.

1910

Gaston Worth establishes the Chambre Syndicale de la Couture Parisienne to promote and protect Parisian haute couture.

1912

Madeleine Vionnet opens in Paris.

Vionnet petal dress page 105

1914

Outbreak of World War I sees women in uniform.

1925

The Exposition des Arts Décoratifs is held in Paris.

1927

Elsa Schiaparelli designs her first knitwear collection in Paris.

Early 20th-century haute couture Page 78

1929

The Wall Street Crash.

1937

Wallis Simpson marries the Duke of Windsor wearing Mainbocher, so endorsing the couture designs of her fellow American.

1938

The influence of surrealism is taken up by Elsa Schiaparelli. Many of her witty designs reveal the double meaning introduced by the surrealist artists.

Schiaparelli/Dalí "Tear" dress, page 125

1942

American ready-to-wear industry develops in response to WPB l-85 clothing regulations and creates the American look.

1943

First New York Fashion Week.

1945

Hardy Amies opens his couture house in Savile Row.

Wallis Simpson marries in Mainbocher page 108

Wartime work wear page 130

1796

Beau Brummell meets George, Prince of Wales.

1804

Napoleon is crowned Emperor of the French. Classical style becomes the Empire-line dress.

Josephine Bonaparte page 12

1850

Women's-rights advocate Amelia Bloomer attempts to reform female dress.

The Bloomer page 36

1818

Mary Shelley publishes *Frankenstein*, one of the first "gothic" novels. Gothic romantic fashion in Britain includes medieval and Tudor detailing and a return to the corset.

Return of the corset page 20

1851

The Great Exhibition opens at the Crystal Palace, London.

1854

Henry Creed opens in Paris. His tailoring skills are introduced to both the French and the English aristocracy and royalty.

1884

Liberty of London opens a department for the making of artistic and historical dress.

1892

Vogue launches in New York.

1900

Madame Gaches-Sarraute, a Parisian corsetière, designs the health corset which gives women the distinctive belle époque and Edwardian S-bend.

1904

Paul Poiret opens in Paris and is inspired by arrival of the Ballets Russes under the directorship of Serge Diaghilev five years later.

The S-bend corset page 72

1919

Gabrielle "Coco" Chanel opens in Paris.

1923

"The Charleston," a tune by American composer James P. Johnson, is performed in the Broadway musical *Runnin' Wild*. It becomes the definitive dance number of the decade.

Silk and wool jersey, Chanel page 97

1932

Costume designer Adrian's MGM *Letty Lynton* dress as worn by Joan Crawford sells over 50,000 copies at Macy's.

1933

Elizabeth Hawes designs a ready-to-wear collection in New York.

1937

Charles James designs the quilted jacket that Salvador Dalí calls "the first soft sculpture."

1940

The fall of Paris during World War II. Lucien Lelong resists the Nazi plan to move couture to Berlin.

1942

The Incorporated Society of London Fashion Designers of Great Britain designs the Utility range of clothing. Its early members include Hardy Amies, Norman Hartnell, Digby Morton, Victor Stiebel, Edward Molyneux, and Charles Creed.

Charles James's quilted jacket page 118

1947

Christian Dior's Corolle line becomes the New Look—and makes fashion history.

Hat by Madame Suzy page 136

1952

Cristóbal Balenciaga designs the Sack line.

1955

Mary Quant opens Bazaar in Chelsea, and Bill Green opens Vince in Carnaby Street, London.

1958

First Milan Fashion Week.

Time Line

1961

Woollands opens the 21 Shop, in fashionable Knightsbridge in London, for young design.

Yves Saint Laurent page 193

1962

Yves Saint Laurent opens in Paris.

1964

André Courrèges shows his Space Age collection in Paris.

Ziggy Stardust page 212

1969

Dior presents the gypsy look. Ethnic blending and peasant styles permeate mainstream fashion.

1970

The innovative boutique Mr. Freedom opens in London.

1973

Kansai Yamamoto designs for David Bowie's *Ziggy Stardust* tour.

1973

Malcolm McLaren and Vivienne Westwood reopen their World's End store as SEX.

Westwood and McLaren page 231

1977

New York's nightclub Studio 54 opens.

1977

The Sex Pistols perform "God Save the Queen" on a boat outside the Houses of Parliament wearing Westwood. Malcolm McLaren is arrested.

1980

Launch of *The Face* magazine.

1980

Giorgio Armani designs Richard Gere's wardrobe in *American Gigolo*, establishing the look for successful eighties males.

1990

Peter Lindbergh shoots the *Vogue* supermodel cover.

1990

Paris is Burning—a documentary on the New York drag balls' voguing scene—is released.

1990

Madonna wears Gaultier for her Blonde Ambition tour.

1993

Kate Moss appears in a Calvin Klein underwear campaign.

1998

Nicolas Ghesquière revives Balenciaga.

1998

Sex and the City first screened.

1998

Prada launches Red Stripe urban sports range.

Prada Red Stripe page 254

1998

Vogue launches in Russia.

2000

Fashion photographer Nick Knight launches the online fashion and art web site SHOWstudio.com.

Prada, page 263

1964

Biba opens in London.

1964

The Beatles go to the United States.

Foale & Tuffin mini page 179

1965

Ossie Clark designs for Quorum.

1967

The "summer of love" heralds the start of a counterculture revolution, culminating in the Woodstock Festival.

1973

Prêt-à-porter Paris Fashion Week is established.

Prêt-à-porter page 217

1974

Beverly Johnson is the first black model to feature on the cover of U.S. *Vogue*.

1974

Glam, glitter and rock take center stage as seventies pop stars, such as David Bowie and Elton John, take designer clothing and footwear into the realm of performance art.

1981

The Japanese deconstructionalists show in Paris.

1981

Dynasty is first screened.

power dressing page 239

1984

First London Fashion Week.

1988

A group of Belgian avant-garde fashion designers – Walter Van Beirendonck, Ann Demeulemeester, Dries van Noten, Dirk Van Saene, Dirk Bikkembergs, and Marina Yee—known as the Antwerp Six—bring their collections to London.

Bill Whitten boots page 213

1994

Tom Ford is appointed creative director at Gucci.

1995

American actor and drag queen RuPaul becomes the first face of MAC cosmetics.

1996

John Galliano is appointed designer at Givenchy then moves to Dior; Alexander McQueen takes over at Givenchy.

1997

Marc Jacobs designs for Louis Vuitton.

1997

Stella McCartney is appointed designer at Chloé.

2004

Sienna Miller channels the boho hippy look.

2004

Ethical Fashion Forum, a network focusing on social and environmental sustainability, is founded.

2005

Victoria Beckham is photographed wearing Roland Mouret's galaxy dress: it becomes the most photographed dress of the decade.

2005

Vogue launches in China.

2007

Kate Moss dresses down as the festival look; festivals become cool.

2007

Vogue launches in India.

2009

Balmain under Christophe Decarnin brings in the hard shoulder.

2009

Tom Ford directs a self-financed movie, *A Single Man*, to critical acclaim.

2010

Condé Nast rejects licence for *Vogue* Africa.

2010

Burberry streams its F/W 2010 show live in three-dimension to six cities, allowing viewers to preorder directly from the catwalk.

2010

British Fashion Council launches a future vintage show at the "Vintage at Goodwood" festival in West Sussex, England

2010

Stella McCartney is announced as the choice to design uniforms for the British team going forward to the 2012 Olympics.

2010

Sarah Ratty, designer of Ciel and Conscious Earthwear, sets up a campaign for the fashion industry to be completely sustainable by 2020.

Glossary

AESTHETIC DRESS in the second half of the 19th century a movement formed in Britain that set itself against the conventional tight-fitting clothes for men and women. Its adherents took inspiration from medieval women's dress, and this type of gown was sold by Liberty's of London.

ALTA MODA Italian couture.

ANILINE DYES a group of synthetic fabric dyes that became commercially available in the 1850s.

APPLIQUÉ a method of decorating fabric by applying other fabric shapes or trimmings to the surface.

BALLETS RUSSES Russian ballet company formed in 1909 under the directorship of Serge Diaghilev, which relocated to Paris after the Russian Revolution.

BAYADÈRE a fabric with horizontal banded stripes of color or design.

BIAS the thread line at a 45-degree angle to the lengthwise and crosswise grain of fabric.

BLAZER a jacket, usually double-breasted, and traditionally in navy with metal buttons. It derives from a jacket worn by the British Navy in the 19th century.

BLITZ KIDS habitués of the early 1980s London nightclub, who developed the new romantic look.

BODICE the top half of a dress from shoulder to waist.

BOX-FRESH a term used in hip-hop culture to describe sneakers that look as if they have just been bought.

BRACELET SLEEVE a length of sleeve finishing before the wrist.

BROCADE a weave for a silk fabric with a pattern created in colored yarns that can have the appearance of embroidery.

BUSTLE a structure worn at the back to hold out the skirt. Bustles varied in size from a small cushion to a curved frame extending from waist to calf.

CAFTAN a loose, usually ankle-length robe with long or mid-length sleeves from Eastern Mediterranean countries and North Africa.

CASHMERE a natural fiber made from the fleece of the kashmir goat found in mountainous regions of Asia.

CHEONGSAM a body-hugging one-piece dress, usually ankle-length, that is distinctly Chinese in character.

CHIFFON a weave that produces a sheer soft fabric that is ideal for draping.

COCKTAIL DRESS a dress, short or long, less formal than a full-length evening dress and particularly popular in the 1950s.

CORSET a close-fitting undergarment worn to create a particular top-body shape, usually with the aid of lacing.

CREPE a weave that produces a fabric that is matte with a crinkly texture that drapes well.

CRINOLINE originally a fabric, crin, made from horsehair and cotton or linen, used to stiffen petticoats. In 1856, it was used to describe a bell-shaped structure, usually made of steel, that replaced layers of petticoats to support a skirt.

CSM short for Central Saint Martins, the London-based College of Art and Design.

DA or duck's tail, a fifties quiff hairstyle adopted by Elvis Presley and widely copied.

DART a tapered tuck of material most often used to allow the fabric to fit the curves of the body.

DENIM literally "*de Nîmes*," ("from Nîmes") the town in southwest France known in the 18th century for the production of hard-wearing cotton. Denim has a twill weave and a fine diagonal, ribbed appearance.

DITTO SUIT an early precursor to the lounge suit that featured a jacket, vest, and pants made from the same fabric.

EMPIRE LINE refers to Napoleon I's empire, when the style of a woman's dress was cut with a high waistline, under the bust.

FICHU a square scarf or shawl made of fine linen, lace, or cotton, folded in a triangle and tied loosely around the shoulders to cover a low bodice. Popular in the 18th century.

F/W fall/winter, referring to a designer's twice-yearly showing of an upcoming seasonal collection.

FLANNEL a fabric, usually wool, with a plain or twill weave where the surface is soft and fuzzy. It originated in Wales from the Welsh word for wool, *gwlanen*.

FROCK COAT in the 19th century a formal coat with a fitted body and full skirts.

FUTURISM an artistic movement that originated in Italy in the early 20th century and spanned the creative media with a single manifesto, which celebrated new technology.

GABARDINE a firm, tightly woven fabric of worsted cotton, wool, or other fibers with a twill weave and fine diagonal lines on the right side. It resists creasing and drapes well.

GAITER a protective covering worn over the legs and shoes, originally made of leather.

GARÇONNE first used in the 1920s in France to describe the new type of young women who started dressing in men's clothing, particularly pants, and cutting their hair very short.

GARIBALDI SHIRT a scarlet military-inspired blouse worn by women in the 1860s, named after the Italian soldier Giuseppe Garibaldi, and often worn with a black silk skirt.

GAZAR a weave related to organza, but the fabric is more tightly woven and, therefore, more stable. Silk gazar is an expensive fabric that is sheer and crisp, shiny on one side and dull on the other.

GLAM ROCK a style of music in the 1970s. Performers wore flamboyant glittery and camp costumes.

GODET a piece of material, often triangular, added to a garment to give fullness.

GO-GO BOOT a low-heeled three-quarter-length shiny PVC boot worn in the 1960s.

GROSGRAIN a closely woven fabric with narrow horizontal ribs, often used for trimming such as ribbons.

HAIR WORK jewelry popular in the 19th century woven from human hair.

HAUTE COUTURE literally "high sewing." The highest-quality clothing for women, which has assumed a different meaning since the introduction of prêt-à-porter collections between the 1950s and 70s. Rules governing fashion houses that have the right to show haute couture collections, in Paris, are under the control of the Federation of French Fashion.

HOMBURG a high-crowned felt hat made popular by Edward VII, who brought one back from Bad Homburg in Germany.

HOUNDSTOOTH CHECK a pattern of broken or jagged checks used on jackets or skirts.

JERSEY a knitted fabric of any fiber known for its stretch and draping qualities.

KATE GREENAWAY a popular 19th-century artist who depicted children in her own versions of late 18th-century and Regency fashions: typically smock-frocks for boys too young to wear trousers, and high-waisted pinafores and dresses for her girls, with bonnets or mobcaps. Her drawings were adopted by Liberty's of London as designs for children's clothes.

LAMÉ a woven fabric with metallic threads.

LBD short for "little black dress."

LUREX a type of metallic thread.

MERVEILLEUSE DRESS a diaphanous muslin gown worn in the 1790s in the wake of the Terror in Paris, inspired by the T-shaped shifts worn to the guillotine, and predating the Directoire and Empire styles.

MOIRÉ a finish that gives fabric, often silk, a watered, wavy appearance.

MONO-BOSOM the effect of the Edwardian S-bend corset, which gave the bust the low-slung pouter-pigeon silhouette of the mature woman.

Glossary

MUCHA Alphonse Mucha, artist in the art nouveau style of the turn of the 20th century. Prints of his advertising posters had a resurgence in popularity in the 1960s.

MUSLIN a woven cotton fabric, originally imported to Europe from the Indian subcontinent. Manufactured in England and France by the 18th century.

NAP the pile or surface of a fabric, obvious in weaves, such as velvet where the long threads protrude on the surface.

NEO-CLASSICAL literally "new classical"—the dominant style in architecture, design, and clothing in the late 18th and early 19th centuries.

ORGANZA a weave for silk that produces a light, sheer, and crisp fabric.

PAGODA SHOULDER the padded, concave shoulderline favored by Elsa Schiaparelli and popular in the 1930s, and again in the 1970s and 2000s.

PETTICOAT in the 18th century the name for a skirt, which later became a concealed undergarment.

PLEXIGLASS a shatter-resistant transparent material, often used as an alternative to glass. Popular in the 1950s and 60s for jewelry.

PRÊT-À-PORTER a French term from the American "ready-to-wear," created to give a more positive image to mass-produced clothing in France. A collection of clothing produced twice-yearly in a range of sizes.

PRINCESS LINE a cut for a dress, first used in the 18th century without a waist seam but with panels from shoulder to hem.

POLONAISE a type of 18th-century gown where the skirt was pulled up to form a pouf shape, leaving a curved hem revealing the petticoat underneath.

PUNK a late 1970s movement in British music and fashion that was strongly antiestablishment. In fashion terms, it was associated with Malcolm McLaren and Vivienne Westwood.

PUTTEES bandages wound around the lower leg for protection and support. Part of the military uniform in both world wars.

RAVER'S GUIDE published in the 1960s as a guide to the happening boutiques, clubs, and restaurants of the London scene.

RAYON the first man-made fiber, an artificial silk made from cellulose at the end of the 19th century.

READY STEADY GO a 1960s pop-music program shown on TV in Britain.

RETICULE also known as a ridicule. The name given to small purses in the early 19th century.

RUCHED fabric that is gathered between lines of stitches.

RUSSIA BRAID a narrow, military-style trim used on coats and jackets.

SACK DRESS a waistless style of dress introduced in the 1950s.

SACK-BACK GOWN an 18th-century gown that had a long, loose back, gathered or pleated from neck to hem.

SATIN a weave with a smooth, shiny surface.

SAVILE ROW an area of central London where a concentration of custom-made tailors developed in the early 19th century.

SEERSUCKER a rippled or puckered cloth resulting from the vertical alternation of two layers of yarn, one taut and one slack, which also creates the characteristic stripe.

SHANTUNG a plain-weave silk cloth made from yarns with irregular or uneven texture.

SMOCKING decorative stitching that creates a pattern across gathered fabric.

SMOKING JACKET a soft, unstructured jacket originally worn for smoking at home in the second half of the 19th century.

SPANDEX a man-made stretch fiber introduced by the DuPont US textile company in 1958. Also known as elastane and the brandname Lycra.

SPATS a shoe cover that fits over the ankle and instep, worn in the late 19th and early 20th centuries.

SPINNAKER BACK a cut of dress in the 1950s where the back panel billowed out in the style of the spinnaker sail.

S/S spring/summer, referring to a designer's twice-yearly showing of an upcoming seasonal collection.

STILETTO describes the spiky heel of a shoe and can also refer to a shoe with a variety of upper designs, provided the heel itself ends in a point with a small diameter.

STOCK a made-up neck-cloth fastening at the back, worn from the 18th century.

STYLE ANGLAIS the French interpretation of English style, based on the traditional outfits worn for outdoor pursuits of hunting, shooting, and fishing, and on traditional fabrics, such as tweed.

SURREALISM a cultural movement of the 1920s that developed artistic methods to liberate the consciousness.

SWISS BELT a wide belt worn in the 19th century to separate blouse and skirt. Often widened in front into a diamond shape.

TAFFETA a weave that is used for silk and synthetic fabrics that produces a crisp, smooth fabric with a sheen. It is often produced with warp and weft threads of different colors, called a "shot" effect.

TAILCOAT a man's coat that finishes at the waist at the front but at the knee at the back, worn since the 19th century, particularly for evening wear.

TANGO a dance that originated at the turn of the 20th century, possibly in Buenos Aires, and particularly associated with Argentina and Uruguay.

TEA GOWN a loose gown of rich silk and lace, popular in the late 19th century, particularly for informal gatherings at home.

TOILE DE JOUY may today refer to any cotton printed in a single color with floral or rural motifs, typically on an off-white background, and in the past produced in Jouy near Versailles, France.

TRENCH COAT a rain coat that is named after its use by soldiers in World War I.

TRICKLE-DOWN EFFECT a term used for the progress a style makes from high-fashion origins to mass-marketing for large retail stores.

TROMPE L'OEIL a French expression that literally means "to deceive the eye," and often an effect used in dress inspired by Surrealism.

TULLE a fine machine-made net of silk or synthetic fibers, originally made in Tulle, France, in the early 19th century.

TWEED a coarse wool cloth in various weaves and colors, originally from Scotland. Many tweeds are multicolored and textured.

TWILL WEAVE one of three basic weave structures in which the filling threads (woof threads) are woven over and under two or more warp yarns, producing a characteristic diagonal pattern. Today, refers to any fabric with this appearance.

V&A short for the Victoria & Albert Museum in London.

VELVET a weave where the pile is long, standing up above the surface of the fabric.

VOILE a sheer woven lightweight fabric of cotton, silk, wool or man-made fibers in the 20th century.

WARP threads running lengthwise on a loom.

WEFT threads carried widthwise across the loom in a shuttle by the weaver.

WORSTED a firmly twisted yarn or thread spun from combed, stapled wool fibers of the same length. Cloth produced from this yarn has a hard, smooth surface and no nap.

YOUTHQUAKE the term given to the influence of British youth in the first half of the 1960s and to British fashion design introduced to the United States at that time.

Resources

BOOKS

BLACKMAN, C., *100 Years of Fashion Illustration*, London: Laurence King, 2007

BORKOWSKI, M., *The Fame Formula*, London: Pan, 2009

BORRELLI, L., *Net Mode: Web Fashion Now*, London: Thames & Hudson, 2002

BRACEWELL, M., *Re-make, Re-Model*, London: Faber & Faber, 2007

BRADDOCK CLARK, S. AND O'MAHONY, M., *Techno Textiles: Revolutionary Fabrics for Fashion and Design*, London: Thames & Hudson, 1998

BROMLEY, I. AND WOJCIECHOWSKA, D., *Very Vintage: The Guide to Vintage Patterns and Clothing*, London: Black Dog, 2008

BUCK, A., *Victorian Costume and Costume Accessories*, Bedford: Ruth Bean, 1984

BUXBAUM, G. (ed.), *Icons of Fashion: the 20th Century*, Munich and London: Prestel, 1999

BYRDE, P., *Nineteenth Century Fashion*, London: Batsford, 1992

CARTER, E., *20th Century Fashion: A Scrapbook, 1900 to Today*, London: Eyre Methuen, 1975

CARTER, E., *Changing World of Fashion: 1900 to the Present*, London: Weidenfeld & Nicolson, 1977

CARTER, E., *Magic Names of Fashion*, London: Weidenfeld & Nicolson, 1980

CASTLE, C., *Model Girl*, New Jersey: Chartwell, 1977

CHAMBERLAIN, R., RAYNER, G., AND STAPLETON, A., *Artists' Textiles in Britain 1945–1970*, London: Antique Collector's Club, 2003

CONNOLLY, R. (ed.), *In the Sixties*, London: Pavilion Books, 1995

COSGRAVE, B., *Costume & Fashion: A Complete History*, London: Hamlyn, 2000

CREED, C., *Maid to Measure*, London, Jarrolds, 1961

CUNNINGTON, C. W., *English Women's Clothing in the Nineteenth Century: A Comprehensive Guide*, New York: Dover, 1990

DE LA HAYE, A. (ed.), *Cutting Edge: 50 Years of British Fashion 1947–1997*, London: V&A Publications, 1997

DE MARLY, D., *History of Haute Couture, 1850–1950*, London: Batsford, 1980

DORNER, J., *Fashion in the 20s and 30s*, London (Shepperton): Ian Allan, 1973

DORNER, J., *Fashion in the 40s and 50s*, London (Shepperton): Ian Allan, 1975

DORNER, J., *Fashion: The Changing Shape of Fashion Through the Years*, London: Octopus, 1974

DRAKE, A., *The Beautiful Fall: Fashion, Genius and Glorious Excess in 1970s Paris*, London: Bloomsbury, 2006

DRAKE, N. (ed.), *The Sixties: A Decade in Vogue*, London: Pyramid, 1988

ENGELMEIER, R. AND P. (eds.), *Fashion and Film*, Munich, New York: Prestel, 1990

EWING, E., *Everyday Dress: 1650–1900*, London: Batsford, 1984

FOGG, M., *Boutique: A 60s Cultural Phenomenon*, London: Mitchell Beazley, 2003

FRISA, M. L. AND TONCHI, S. (ed.), *Excess: Fashion and the Underground in the 80s*, Milan: Charta, 2004

FUKAI, A. AND SUOH, T. (eds.), *Fashion: From the 18th to the 20th Century*, Cologne: Taschen, 2004

GAN, S., *Visionaire's Fashion 2001: Designers of the New Avant-Garde*, London: Laurence King, 1999

GARLAND, M., *Fashion 1900–1939: A Scottish Arts Council exhibition with the support of the Victoria and Albert Museum*, Scottish Arts Council/Idea Books International, 1975

GUNDLE, S., *Glamour: A History*, Oxford: Oxford University Press, 2008

HALL-DUNCAN, N., *The History of Fashion Photography*, New York: Chanticleer, 1979

HASTREITER, K. AND HERSHKOVITS, D. (eds.), *20 Years of Style: The World According to Paper*, New York: Harper Design, 2004

HAYWARD, C., *Man About Town: The Changing Image of the Modern Male*, London: Hamlyn, 2001

HEARD, N., *Trainers: over 300 Classics from rare vintage to the latest designs*, London: Carlton 2008

HILLMAN, D. AND PECCINOTTI, H., *Nova: The Style Bible of the 60s and 70s*, London: Pavilion, 1993

HISLOP, K. AND LUTYENS, D., *70s Style and Design*, London: Thames & Hudson, 2009

HOWARD, D., *In Biba*, London: Hazard, 2004

HOWARD, D., *Sinbiba*, London: Hazard, 2006

HUNT, M., *The Way We Wore: Styles of the 30s and 40s*, Fallbrook, CA: Fallbrook, 1993

JONES, T. (ed.), *Smile I-D: Fashion and Style, The Best From 20 Years of I-D*, Cologne: Taschen, 2001

KODA, H. AND MARTIN, R., *Haute Couture*, New York: Metropolitan Museum of Art, 1995

LAVER, J., *Costume and Fashion: A Concise History*, London: Thames & Hudson, 2002

MARTIN, R., *The Fashion Book*, London: Phaidon, 1998

MCDERMOTT, C., *Made in Britain: Traditional Style in Contemporary Fashion*, London: Mitchell Beazley, 2002

MCDOWELL, C., *Forties Fashion and the New Look*, London: Bloomsbury, 1997

MCDOWELL, C., *McDowell's Directory of 20th-Century Fashion*, London: Frederick Muller, 1984

MCDOWELL, C., *The Literary Companion to Fashion*, London: Sinclair Stevenson, 1995

MUIR, R., *Norman Parkinson: Portraits in Fashion*, Bath: Palazzo, 2004

NICKERSON, C. AND WAKEFIELD, N. (eds.), *Fashion Photography of the 90s*, Zurich: Scalo, 1996

O' HARA, G., *The Encyclopedia of Fashion*, London: Thames & Hudson, 1989

O' KEEFFE, L., *Shoes*, New York: Workman, 1996

O' NEILL, A., *London—After a Fashion*, London: Reaktion, 2007

POLHEMUS, T., *Street Style*, London: Thames & Hudson, 1994

POLHEMUS, T., *Style Surfing: What to Wear in the 3rd Millennium*, London: Thames & Hudson, 1996

RAWSTHORN, A., *Yves Saint Laurent: A Biography*, New York: Doubleday, 1996

ROTHSTEIN, N. (ed.), *Four Hundred Years of Fashion*, London: Victoria & Albert Museum in association with Collins, 1984

ROUS, H. (ed.), *The Ossie Clark Diaries*, London: Bloomsbury, 1998

SCHIAPARELLI, E., *Shocking Life: The Autobiography of Elsa Schiaparelli*, London: V&A Publications, 2007

TAPERT, A., *The Power of Glamour*, London: Aurum, 1998

TAYLOR, S., *100 Years of Magazine Covers*, London: Black Dog, 2006

The Lady's Realm: A Selection from the Monthly Issues, London: Arrow, 1972

TOLKEIN, T., *Vintage: The Art of Dressing Up*, London: Pavilion Books, 2002

TOPHAM, S., *Where's My Space Age: The Rise and Fall of Futuristic Design*, London, 2003

TURNER, A. W., *Biba: The Biba Experience*, Suffolk: Antique Collector's Club, 2004

WATSON, L., *Vogue Fashion*, London: Carlton, 2008

WEBB, I. R., *Bill Gibb: Fashion and Fantasy*, London: V&A Publications, 2008

WILSON, E., *Adorned in Dreams: Fashion and Modernity*, London: IB Tauris, 2003

WILSON, E., *Bohemians: The Glamorous Outcasts*, New York: IB Tauris, 2009

WEB SITES

rockpopfashion.com

runway.blogs.nytimes.com

SHOWstudio.com

thesartorialist.blogspot.com

tmagazine.blogs.nytimes.com

www.ashadedviewonfashion.com

www.catwalkqueen.tv

www.fashion-era.com

www.modeaparis.com

www.nowness.com

www.style.com

www.thelovemagazine.co.uk

www.thestylerookie.com

www.whatkatiewore.com

Index

Index

Acknowledgments

Author's Acknowledgments

Thanks to my Mum and Dad, Jill and Ham Stevenson; my husband Will Hodgkinson and my children Otto and Pearl, for their love, support, patience, and help, with all my love.

Also thanks to all at Ivy Press, especially Stephanie Evans, and to Judith Clark, Amy de la Haye, Liz Hodgkinson, Dominic Lutyens, Ben Olins, Teri Olins, Alistair O'Neill, Alison McCann, Tomomi McMaster, Dennis Nothdruft, Michael Salac, Martin Skegg, Charles Stevenson, Michael Tyack, Mo White, and Stacey Williams.

Publisher's Acknowledgments

Special thanks to Elaine Lucas, Meghan Mazella, Christopher Sutherns, and Roxanne Peters at V&A Images, for all of their effort and support.

All images courtesy of and © V&A Images, Victoria and Albert Museum, except for the following:

Advertising Archives: 131BR, 163BR, 214T, 223R, 225T, 238 BL, 246, 259L.

Alamy/Trinity Mirror/Mirrorpix: 175BC, 211TL.

© Cecil Beaton, V&A Images, Victoria and Albert Museum: 105, 108, 119TL, 123.

Bridgeman Art Library/The Advertising Archives: 93TR; N. Bloom & Son, London, UK: 57TL; Giraudon: 52; Private Collection: 27.

Catwalking.com: 249BR, 249TR, 256C, 256R, 257L, 264B, 269, 271L.

Corbis/Mario Anzuoni/Reuters: 251L; Bettmann: 138BL, 141L, 143TR, 156, 174BL, 186BR, 192; B.D.V: 247TR; Stephane Cardinale: 250L, 259R; Geoffery Clements: 142R; Henry Ditz: 189T; Condé Nast Archive: 179R, 187BL, 187BR, 197CR, 219TR, 231T; Condé Nast/WWD: 268, 270; Allen Ginsberg: 169TL; Martyn Goddard: 203, 228; Hulton-Deutsch Collection: 87, 98T, 132, 150, 194BL; Douglas Kirkland: 241R; Genevieve Naylor: 139TL; Andrew Ross: 251R; Smithsonian Institution: 60; Stapleton Collection: 101; Sunset Boulevard: 168R; David Turnley: 248B; Underwood and Underwood: 102; John Van Hasselt/Corbis SYGMA Collection: 242B; Niels Van Iperen/Retna Ltd: 244-245; Pierre Vauthey/Sygma: 207L, 217R, 239T.

Courtesy of Creed: 42, 43.

Cutler and Gross (www.cutlerandgross.com) art direction by Monica Chong, photography by David Byun: 236, 267R.

© John French, V&A Images, Victoria and Albert Museum: 147T, 149L, 155, 163C, 174R, 177.

The Future Laboratory: 271CR.

Getty Images/Richard E. Aaron/Redferns: 233TL; Waring Abbott: 224BL; American Stock Archive: 143TL; Dick Barnatt/Redferns: 210BL; Justin De Villeneuve: 206R James Devaney: 261; Evening Standard: 215L; Pierre Guillaud/AFP: 243L; Hulton Archive: 41L, 59, 112, 133, 159L, 165TR, 169C, 205TR, 232, 220-221, 233B, 230R; Doug Kanter/AFP: 262R; Keystone: 191R; Jon Kopaloff: 254R; Rob Loud: 263TR; William Lovelace/Express: 197TL; George Marks/Retrofile: 153TR; MPI: 41C; Terry O'Neil: 247B, 247TL; Michael Ochs Archives: 128, 143B; Gregory Pace/FilmMagic: 258BL; Popperfoto: 181; Sasha: 121; Science and Society Picture Library: 135; SSPL/Manchester Daily Express: 215R; Time & Life Pictures: 185R, 195BL, 196BR, 253; Trago/FilmMagic: 262B; Ian Tyas/Keystone Features: 208; Pierre Verdy/AFP: 264TR; Roger Viollet: 90, 104.

Barbara Hulanicki for Topshop: 7TR, 267BL.

Kobal Collection/20th Century Fox: 139TR; Paramount: 162R, 207R; Warner Bros: 198R.

Courtesy Levi Strauss & Co. Archives, San Francisco: 214B.

© L&M SERVICES B.V. The Hague 20101005: 97TL.

Library of Congress, Washington, D.C.: 36L, 37BR, 65, 139B, 140.

© Francis Marshall, V&A Images, Victoria and Albert Museum: 147B.

Mary Evans Picture Library: 17, 18R, 50, 82B, 83T, 83R, 83L, 86, 92C, 96R, 103C, 103TL, 103BL, 111C, 111L, 153L; AGIP/Rue des Archives: 176; APL: 172, 188L; Peter & Dawn Cope Collection: 97BR; Grenville Collins Postcard Collection: 41R; Illustrated London News Ltd: 194TR, 92R, 117BL; National Magazines: 91, 111BR, 113T, 113R, 115, 116R, 117BC, 118BL, 119B, 122, 125R, 129, 136L, 137R, 152BL, 161BC; Rue des Archives: 88BR, 146, 161R; Scherl/SZ Photo: 117TR; Adrian Woodhouse: 149BC.

© Curtis Moffat, V&A Images, Victoria and Albert Museum: 97TL.

Pictorial Press: 199R.

Prada: 2, 4-5, 8-9, 237, 254L, 258TL, 262TL, 263B, 263L, 266B, 267TL, 272, 276B, 278-288.

© Mary Quant: 6C, 179.

Rex Features: 227, 250R, 257R; Clive Dixon: 248T; Fotex Medien Agentur GMBH: 252; Clifford Ling/Evening News: 219B; Steve Maisey: 265L; Sonny Meddle: 255T; Bill Orchard: 212BL; Cavan Pawson/Evening Standard: 265R, 271TR; Sipa Press: 241L, 216, 225B; C.A Spelling/Everett: 239BL; Stockroll: 223T; Stephen Sweet: 249TL; Crispian Woodgate/Daily Mail: 195R.

Scala Archives/Cinecitta Luce: 167; The Metropolitan Museum of Art: 119R, 138L.

Schiaparelli France SAS: 109, 123, 124, 125L, 125C

Topfoto: 169BR, 173, 182, 198L, 198L, 222; The Granger Collection: 76, Heritage Images: 136R, 137L, 224BR; PA Photos: 233TR; Ullstein Bild: 40, 189B.

© Stephen Willats. Courtesy the Artist and Victoria Miro Gallery, London: 187T.

Every effort has been made to acknowledge the copyright and source of pictures; however, the publisher apologizes if there are any unintentional omissions.